MW00648874

Planning for Growth

Planning for Growth: Urban and Regional Planning in China provides an overview of the changes in China's planning system, policy, and practices since the mid-20th century using concrete examples and informative details in language that is accessible enough for the undergraduate but thoroughly grounded in a wealth of research and academic experience to support academics. It is the first accessible text on changing urban and regional planning in China under the process of transition from a centrally planned socialist economy to an emerging market in the world.

Fulong Wu, a leading authority on Chinese cities and urban and regional planning, sets up the historical framework of planning in China including its foundation based on the proactive approach to economic growth, the new forms of planning, such as the 'strategic spatial plan' and 'urban cluster plans' that have emerged and stimulated rapid urban expansion, and transformed compact Chinese cities into dispersed metropolises. It goes on to explain the new planning practices that began to pay attention to eco-cities, new towns and new development areas.

Planning for Growth demonstrates that planning is not necessarily an 'enemy of growth' and plays an important role in Chinese urbanization and economic growth. On the other hand, it also shows planning's limitations in achieving a more sustainable and just urban future.

Fulong Wu is Bartlett Professor of Planning at University College London. His research includes China's urban development and planning and its social and sustainable challenges. He is co-editor of *Restructuring the Chinese City* (2005), *Marginalization in China* (2010), *International Perspectives on Suburbanization* (2011), and *Rural Migrants in Urban China* (2013), editor of *Globalization and the Chinese City* (2006), *China's Emerging Cities* (2007), and co-author of *Urban Development in Post-Reform China: State, Market, and Space* (2007), and *China's Urban Poverty* (2010).

THE RTPI Library Series

Editors: Robert Upton, *Infrastructure Planning Commission in England*
Jill Grant, *Dalhousie University, Canada*
Stephen Ward, *Oxford Brookes University, United Kingdom*

Published by Routledge in conjunction with The Royal Town Planning Institute, this series of leading-edge texts looks at all aspects of spatial planning theory and practice from a comparative and international perspective.

Planning in Postmodern Times
Philip Allmendinger

The Making of the European Spatial Development Perspective
Andreas Faludi and Bas Waterhout

Planning for Crime Prevention
Richard Schneider and Ted Kitchen

The Planning Polity
Mark Tewdwr-Jones

Shadows of Power: An Allegory of Prudence in Land-Use Planning
Jean Hillier

Urban Planning and Cultural Identity
William JV Neill

Place Identity, Participation and Planning
Edited by Cliff Hague and Paul Jenkins

Planning for Diversity
Dory Reeves

Planning the Good Community: New Urbanism in Theory and Practice
Jill Grant

Planning for Growth
Urban and Regional Planning in China

Fulong Wu

Routledge
Taylor & Francis Group

NEW YORK AND LONDON

First published 2015
by Routledge
711 Third Avenue, New York, NY 10017

and by Routledge
2 Park Square, Milton Park, Abingdon, Oxon OX14 4RN

Routledge is an imprint of the Taylor & Francis Group, an informa business

Library of Congress Cataloging in Publication Data
Wu, Fulong.
  Planning for growth: urban and regional planning in China/Fulong Wu.
  pages cm. — (The RTPI library series)
  Includes index.
  1. City planning—China. 2. Regional planning—China. 3. Urban
  policy—China. I. Title.
  HT169.C6W8 2015
  307.1'2160951—dc23
  2014026912

ISBN: 9780415814416 (hbk)
ISBN: 9780415814423 (pbk)
ISBN: 9780203067345 (ebk)

Typeset in 10.5 pt on 13 pt Goudy Old Style
by Florence Production Ltd, Stoodleigh, Devon, UK

Printed and bound in the United States of America by Publishers Graphics,
LLC on sustainably sourced paper.

To Ben and Jack

"Fulong Wu explains the paradox that urban planning had marginal importance in China's socialist era but has become a key mechanism for growth promotion in the market reform period. He details how and why Chinese cities compete with one another, and how they combine with the central government to carry out a national development strategy based on urbanization."

—*John R. Logan, Director of the Urban China Research Network, Brown University*

"*Planning for Growth* is essential reading for anyone who wants to understand the complexity of the planning system, policy and practice in contemporary China. Written in an effective and succinct style, with many interesting examples and illustrations, Fulong Wu provides both clarity and a reflective account of the dynamic interaction between the planning system and the economic growth machinery in China over the last two decades."

—*Cecilia Wong, Professor of Spatial Planning, The University of Manchester*

Contents

Figures

Plates

Tables

Preface

Many years ago I read Professor Sir Peter Hall's classic book on urban and regional planning. Although in the Preface he said the book was 'for a British readership (though hopefully Commonwealth readers will find it relevant),' I, as a Chinese student who had never been to Britain, found the book extremely useful, because it struck an artful balance between historical and technical details on the one hand, and overview and interpretation on the other. The book is not a textbook, as is said right at the beginning of the Preface. Interestingly, a textbook about the British planning system would have been more difficult and more 'boring' for me in China at that time. Professor Hall also said the book 'deliberately excludes the developing world; doubtless, another useful book is to be written there.' As a student of Chinese planning, I wished to read such a book, but I did not realize that I would have to wait 30 years—and actually started thinking about writing such a book myself after I had the privilege of becoming a colleague of the esteemed author at the Bartlett School of Planning. Coincidentally, Professor Patsy Healey gave me the chance to write this book as part of the RTPI (Royal Town Planning Institute) Library Series. Near the completion of this book in May 2014, I asked Professor Hall whether he could read and endorse this book. He said he was delighted to see such a book. But sadly he passed away two months later. This book thus now memorizes him as an outstanding planner and truly great urban scholar.

I hope this book, *Planning for Growth: Urban and Regional Planning in China*, will be a small addition to our understanding of different planning systems. Just like Hall's book, which 'is necessarily written from a British standpoint for a British readership,' I also believed the best approach for my book was for it to be written from a Chinese standpoint for a Chinese readership. If a reader in the Western world were to find this book useful, it would be a happy coincidence. This standpoint requires me to synthesize empirical materials without intentionally distorting the big picture. This is a challenging requirement: I strive to make sense of the planning system for those who are familiar with the planning practices in China and indeed may have an everyday job within Chinese planning. In addition to Chinese Twitter, where criticism is ruthless, I had a chance to meet the challenge through a keynote address at the UPSC (Urban Planning Society of China) annual conference. When over 6,000 professional planners gathered in the exhibition hall in the Qingdao International Convention Center for the opening session and keynotes, I was entirely convinced that this book was timely for the Chinese audience as well as for other readers outside China. The book, however, has not forgotten readers outside China, because after all it is written in English. I adopt what Jennifer Robinson called 'a comparative gesture,' thinking of planning outside China as a reference point.

Throughout the book, I tried to answer the question why in Britain the discourse is to streamline planning in order to promote economic growth, while in China the mayor has to do the opposite. I thought it would be quite straightforward: planning in China is for the market. But when I took some photos for this book on a trip to China in April 2014, I suddenly realized that there was a further explanation—planning is for growth. Growth itself has become an imperative for governance. Hence, the third explanation in this book goes beyond neoliberalism or deregulation. On this front of understanding growth, I have been actively involved in the Urban China Research Network, founded by John Logan, who is the co-author of the seminal book, *Urban Fortunes: The Political Economy of Place*. In the U.S. setting, the market dominates machine politics, and planning is an auxiliary player. However, there is not necessarily only one version of the growth machine. In China, the growth machine has its specific political and institutional drivers but also originated from the long-term desire for modernization. In this sense, there is a historical continuity other than transition.

The book is not a comprehensive survey of Chinese planning practices. Cases are included here not because of their significance, rather they are indicative, as the Chinese idiom says: 'one fallen leaf can tell the coming of autumn.' Here I only included the cases that I am familiar with, either directly as an advisor or a member of a jury panel or indirectly through close contacts and informants. Familiarity allows me to qualitatively grasp the hidden message. Beyond the formal semi-structured interview, informal discussions over tea or coffee can lead to the frank exchange of views. They enrich more formal documents and presentations. When possible, information is verified through triangulation. In this book, despite great changes, I trace planning back to the republican and socialist eras. I argue that the current status of planning as a key player in the growth machine is related to its sustained characteristics over time. Growth is regarded as the key pathway to a modern and stronger nation. The growth agenda is so prominently themed in Chinese planning that I decided to add 'planning for growth' to the main title of this book, and hence this is the message I would wish readers to challenge. Indeed, for the future of Chinese planning, legitimacy derived from 'planning for growth' will not be sufficient to justify its existence.

Acknowledgments

My foremost debt of gratitude is to my alma mater, Nanjing University, for granting me the honorary Siyuan Chair Professorship and to Professor Guofang Zhai, the Head of Department of Urban Planning and Design, for his support. I would like to thank Professors Gonghao Cui, Anthony Gar-On Yeh, Chris Webster, and Alan Penn for helping me research in China at various career stages. I also thank Professor Yuemin Ning for pleasant collaboration under a key project of the Ministry of Education of the People's Republic of China (PRC) on 'migrants' integration in the Chinese society' (11JJD840015). The award of the UK ESRC Outstanding International Impact prize facilitated my fieldwork; and funding support from the Social Sciences and Humanities Research Council of Canada (the Major Collaborative Research Initiative 'Global Suburbanism: Governance, Land, and Infrastructure in the 21st Century (2010–2017)') has been particularly helpful in my research on new town and eco-cities planning. I thank Nan Shi for inviting me to give a keynote at the Urban Planning Society of China annual conference, Professor Patsy Healey for offering me the book contract, and the editors of the Royal Town Planning Institute (RTPI) library, Professors Robert Upton, Jill Grant, and Stephen Ward, for their support. I would like to thank Judith Newlin at Routledge for her efficient editorial support. Many people helped me throughout the process of book preparation. I wish to thank Hongyang Wang, Desheng Xue, Zhigang Li, Shenjing He, Jie Shen, Yi Li, Yang Xiao, Xiang Luo, Jingxiang Zhang, Mingfeng Wang, Yuan Yuan, Shiwen Sun, Song Shi, Xiangming Ma, Yixing Zhou, Chaolin Gu, Jian Feng, Yanwei Cai, Xiaodong Shi, Pengyan Ju, Tiejun Zhang, Le Zhou, Li Hou, Mengli Lü, Lan Zhou, Yanjing Zhao, Xiaohui Chen, Changhong Qu, Lan Wang, Yuxiang Zeng, Han Cui, Nicholas Phelps, Yaping Wang, Nicholas Jewell, David Cobb, Nick Gallent, Matthew Carmona, Tingting Lu, Xuan Li, Sandra Mather, Bruce Hunt, Chuanting Lü, Dongfeng Zhu, Xigang Zhu, and Jiang Xu. Finally I wish to thank my wife for her love and support.

In addition, I would like to thank the following for granting permission to reproduce the following illustrations as listed: Elsevier for Figures 2.1, 3.2, 3.3, 3.5, 4.5, 4.6, 4.7, 5.5, 5.6; Victoria University of Wellington/John Wiley and Sons for Figures 4.1, 5.3; ISOCARP for Figure 4.3; Pion for Figure 6.2; Taylor & Francis for Figure 6.3; Liverpool University Press for Figure 6.4; Xiangming Ma for Plates 6.6, 7.2; Holcim Foundation/Arup UK for Plates 6.9(a) and (b); and Nicholas Jewell for Plate 6.8.

1

China's Planning Origin and Tradition

China's city planning origin

China has a long-standing culture which has shaped its distinctive urban form. The traditional urban form was the 'walled city.' The planning of the walled city followed certain norms and standards. The earliest planning norm can be dated back to the Zhou Dynasty of 1000 BC, when the *Zhou-Li: Kao-Gong-Ji* officially recorded the rules of city planning (Figure 1.1).[1] But such rules were less rigid and had to be applied with consideration of the 'local context.' This local context for city building is referred to as Chinese geomancy, or *fengshui,* literally 'wind and water.' Chinese geomancy strongly stresses the relationship between humans and the natural environment and pays particular attention to orientation with cardinal directions, shape and symmetry, and relative locations (Wu and Gaubatz, 2013, p. 51). Orientation and relative location, for example, determine the location of a site for a city as well as for homes. The ideal location for a city should be selected through considering *yin* and *yang*. The so-called *fu yin bao yang* means 'back away from the shadow and embrace the sunny orientation' (Figure 1.2). This principle is translated into site selection, as a preferable site will be located in an area backed by mountains to the north, facing a river or water to the south. This consideration is practical: orienting to the south for direct sunlight and to block cold wind from the north (Zhang, 2015).

The meaning of 'city' in the Chinese language is literally 'wall and market,' suggesting that city walls and gates are basic elements for the making of a city. The city wall is for defense purposes. The city walls of Beijing comprised four massive layers: the palace known as the Forbidden City, the imperial city, the capital city (the main northern walled area), and the outer city (the walled southern extension).[2] Besides the magnificent walls in Nanjing (Plate 1.1), the capital of the Ming Dynasty, and Beijing, the capital of the Ming and Qing Dynasties, Shanghai, as a county during the Ming Dynasty, built its city wall with six gates in 1553 to defend it against pirates in the Southeast China Sea. The scale of the city wall of Shanghai (Figure 1.3) was quite modest

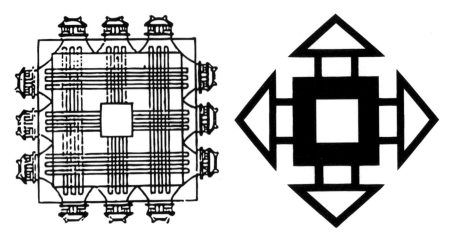

Figure 1.1 **(a)** The *Kao-Gong-Ji* representing the formal rules for the prototype of the
Chinese planned city; **(b)** the logo of the Urban Planning Society of China
(UPSC) to show the origin of Chinese planning in its modern practice.

Source: Dong, 2004; courtesy of UPSC

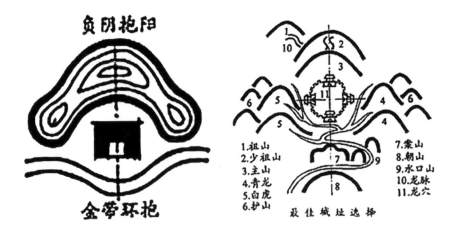

Figure 1.2 Chinese geomancy, or *fengshui* as the principle of planning to adapt in the
physical context: **(a)** the ideal location of a house; **(b)** the ideal location of a
city. The figure shows the ideal location of a city as located with the mountain
to the north to block the cold winter wind (backed away from the *ying*) and
facing a river or water body to the south (embracing the *yang*).

Source: Dong, 2004

compared with the walls of Nanjing and Beijing. In the subsequent 300 years, the city wall deteriorated and it was eventually demolished in 1914, three years after the establishment of the Republic of China.

Besides city walls, other spatial elements of the Chinese traditional urban form comprise monumental structures such as administrative compounds, called *yamen* (Plate 1.2), the Confucian temple or other temples of Chinese folk religions, and bell and drum towers (Wu and Gaubatz, 2013, pp. 57–64). Administrative compounds were built into courtyards surrounded by four rectangular buildings—which is basically scaled-up courtyard housing used for government offices. Beside *yamen* there was usually a temple, which was used as a semi-public space, for the area outside the temple was often used as a marketplace during periodic temple fairs, and later even evolved into permanent marketplaces. The Confucian temple was used as a school and also an examination hall for selecting civil servants. Bell and drum towers were for transmitting reminders of the time, and were often major structures in the city.

Between the monumental constructions were the ordinary neighborhoods that were built upon courtyard housing. There are limited accounts of these neighborhoods. But from the Tang Dynasty onwards, gated wards were set up as a governance mechanism to distinguish residential areas for different social classes. Noble and high-status officials occupied larger wards, while ordinary residents including merchants were located in smaller wards and less central

Plate 1.1 The city wall of Nanjing, showing the layout of Nanjing as the capital of the Ming Dynasty. The city wall has recently been refurbished and become a tourist attraction.

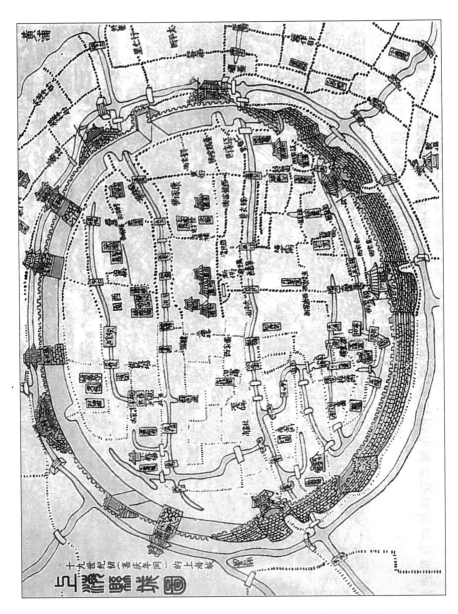

Figure 1.3 The city wall of Shanghai from the Ming Dynasty; after its demolition, a road
was built along the course of the city wall, leaving an imprint on the road
system. The area within the boundary of the walled city was under the control
of the Chinese government during the colonial period.

Source: SPHO, 1999

Plate 1.2 The main hall of the Chinese *yamen* (government compound), showing the dominance of magisterial power. The compound together with the Confucian temple represents governance and ideology.

places. But this ward system collapsed during the Song Dynasty when there was booming commercial activity and the beginnings of urban culture. Residential and commercial uses were mixed, and an initial form of 'urbanism' emerged. Except for road grids dividing residential areas into blocks, social differentiation began to present at the macro scale. For example, during the Qing Dynasty, Beijing showed a concentration of nobles in the west while merchants were in the east. However, there were no planning measures to define this pattern of social space. Differentiation emerged along with the locations of palaces and markets. Clans and places of native origin may be organizing factors, because migrants in certain occupations and trades such as tailoring and metalwork tended to cluster in specific places through their network of origin. In other words, planning in the imperial period concerned only monumental structures and road grids, while vast residential areas were left unplanned or were self-built by residents.

European influence in the later imperial era

After the Treaty of Nanking was signed in 1842, five Chinese coastal cities were opened up to foreign trade. These five cities, Guangzhou (Canton),

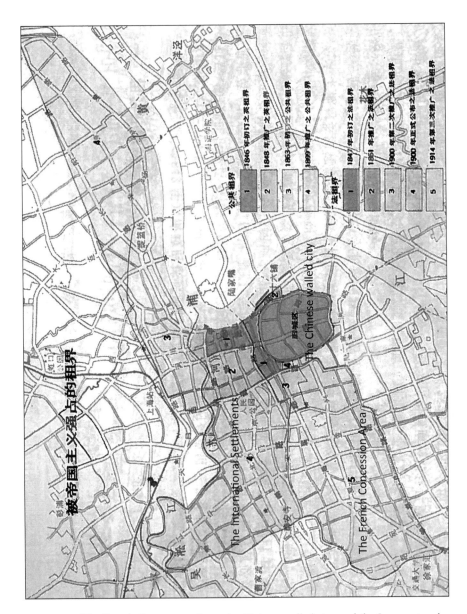

Figure 1.4 The French Concession Area, the Chinese walled city, and the International Settlements in Shanghai. The Chinese city began to show a fragmented spatial pattern, as each component was subject to different building regulations in the late imperial period.

Source: SPHO, 1999

Xiamen (Amoy), Fuzhou, Ningbo, and Shanghai thus became known as treaty port cities. Subsequently, more coastal cities were forced to give concessions to Western powers and their trading companies. As a result of domestic turmoil and the Boxer Rebellion (1900), migrants and refugees flocked into the treaty port cities, leading to their rapid expansion. In addition, these cities accommodated major industrial capacities. Foreign merchants and entrepreneurs arrived and formed their own spaces outside the Chinese walled cities—in the case of Shanghai, there was the French Concession Area and the British and American settlements (which later became so-called 'international settlements') (SPHO, 1999) (see Figure 1.4). Not too dissimilar from other South and Southeast Asian cities in the colonial period, Chinese treaty port cities showed a contrast between the under-serviced Chinese part and a European quarter built and controlled with building codes. The quality of services, for example, road pavements, electricity, and water supply, was much higher in the foreign quarters. By this time, the modern meaning of city planning had emerged as an engineering profession for infrastructure provision but also as land use zoning and building codes to control the form and use of land. For example, in Tianjin the zoning ordinance in 1908 required that residential buildings along major roads had to be in the European style.[3] The residents had to be either European or local Chinese with higher status and a good

Plate 1.3 The cityscape of Qingdao at its city center. It had a distinctive German influence during the colonial period.

reputation, or officials in the Customs offices. The subsequent ordinance specified different classes of residential areas. In Shanghai, the influx of rural migrants and a growing working class led to an increase in population in the 1920s and 1930s. Terraced houses built in the 'stone portal gate' style became a popular residential form. Initially, to separate Chinese and foreigners, areas were designated for foreigners. But because rich Chinese began to seek the protection of the safe haven of Western 'extraterritorial power,' the population in these foreign areas increased significantly. To accommodate the population increase, a boom in real estate business began in the French Concession Area. During the late imperial period, Western building management as well as planning was introduced. For the first time, Chinese cities began to systematically regulate building construction. The quality of the living environment inside the European quarter was generally better than in the indigenous Chinese walled city (Strand, 2000). In the French Concession Area of Shanghai, cultural entertainment and amenities were developed, leading to a flourishing culture of the 'new middle class' (Yeh, 2008). For cities that were completely under the control of Western powers, the influence of the colonial master was dominant. Architects from the nation of occupiers prepared the city plan and created the distinctive layout of a Western metropolis. For example, Harbin and Dalian reflect Russian influence and have the style of boulevard and plaza. The city of Qingdao in Shandong Peninsular resembled a German cityscape (see Plate 1.3).

Modernist planning in the Republic of China

Greater Shanghai Plan

The Greater Shanghai Plan, initially prepared in 1927, became a major development plan for Shanghai during the years of the Republic of China. The plan was to build a new administration area in a designated area of 460 hectares in Jiangwan in northern Shanghai. The plan also proposed the redevelopment of the port. Although the plan included the foreign settlement as a special region, its main objective was to go beyond the foreign settlement to form a Chinese municipality that would parallel the achievements of the foreign settlement (MacPherson, 1990). Because the new civic center was to be built in an undeveloped area, the road system was distinctively designed in a circular radial pattern, with green space, parks, stadiums, and a racecourse. The center of this civic area was a cross-shaped square; public buildings such as the library, museum, and government buildings were adjacent to the square (Plate 1.4). The plan was designed by an architect who had graduated in the U.S. and was coordinated by the city planning commission with the assistance of foreign technical consultants. It foresaw comprehensive infrastructure development in Shanghai. The achievement of this plan was its effort to 'unite the areas comprising Shanghai into one unified administrative whole, encompassing and eventually absorbing the foreign settlements' (MacPherson, 1990, p. 39). The plan is significant, because it developed a vision to overcome the longstanding spatial fragmentation between the European quarter and the indigenous areas in a colonial city. The civic center in the plan was clearly monumental, symbolizing Shanghai as a major metropolis in the world, with municipal capacity in governance and planning. The road system of the plan consisted of main north-south arterials as well as boulevards. Housing blocks were allocated along an east–west axis and thus would have a north–south face, suitable for the local weather (Figure 1.5). The plan deployed impressive engineering skills as well as advanced zoning provisions.[4] The Japanese occupation of Shanghai (1937–45) interrupted and destroyed the plan for the development of a civic center, while the basic road system has left an imprint in the region that would have been a grand civic center. The achievement of the Greater Shanghai Plan as planning is that it was an urban master plan, aiming at a comprehensive redefinition of the urban spatial structure to overcome fragmentation by the International Settlement, the French Concession Area, and the Chinese walled city, and to materialize eventual political unification under the Shanghai Special Municipality designated by its provision regulation in 1927—the first permanent Chinese special administrative municipality. In this sense, the plan, although it did not materialize, is visionary. Another major achievement was its vision for a civic center to serve the public. These public facilities included a library, a stadium, a museum, and a hospital to enhance the quality of life, which would have been open to the public. The center was therefore a public space. This vision has still not been fully achieved over a century later in China (see Chapter 7 for the 'privatization of public space' near the Shanghai Jiangwan Stadium).

The Capital Plan (Nanjing)

In the era of the Republic of China, one of the most profound urban plans made was perhaps the Capital Plan[5] (1929). After the Nationalist government selected Nanjing as its capital, the population of Nanjing increased to almost half a million in 1928 and was expected to increase significantly more. Henry Murphy, an American architect, was invited in that year to prepare a new capital plan. His idea of 'adaptive Chinese architecture' was to apply Western technology to current Chinese styles. The aim of the new capital plan was to create a capital with a Chinese style and a model city that could be applied to other Chinese cities. For Nanjing, as the capital of six imperial dynasties, Murphy urged that the demolition of the old city walls be halted. The city walls of Nanjing avoided demolition and were preserved, while previously when

Plate 1.4 **(a)** The city hall, and **(b)** the library in the proposed new Jiangwan civic center according to the Greater Shanghai Plan (1929). See Plate 7.5 for the Shanghai Jiangwan Stadium built in the period as part of the civic center public facilities. The new civic center was planned to combine Chinese architectural style with a Western planning concept. This would be a new monumental civic center, not like a traditional Chinese government compound—*yamen*, which symbolizes imperial or magisterial power. The central square was to be surrounded by 'public buildings' such as the library and stadium and open to the public, which aimed to enhance the quality of everyday life.

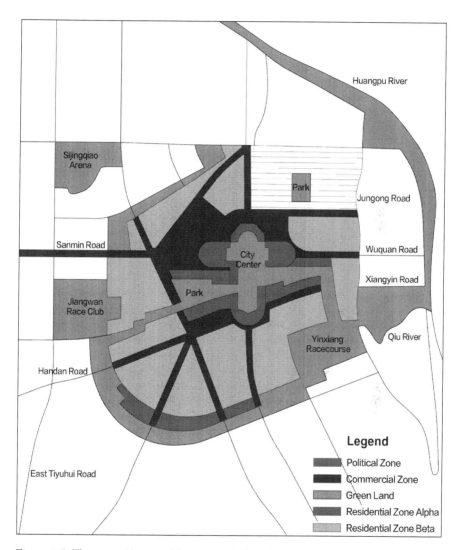

Figure 1.5 The general layout of the proposed Shanghai civic center at Jiangwan. The
plan was abandoned but some key buildings have been built, leaving an
imprint on the built environment.

Source: SPHO, 1999

a new dynasty replaced an old one, large-scale demolition had been common. Before the preparation of the Capital Plan, Nanjing built a new 12-kilometer-long boulevard connecting the wharf and the Sun Yat-Sen Memorial at Zijin Mountain in the east. The road became the main transport route of Nanjing. The most ambitious proposal of the plan was to create a new central administration zone outside the city wall of Nanjing on the southern slope of Zijin Mountain (Figure 1.6). Before that, it was planned to locate the central government in the remains of the Ming Dynasty Palace. The proposal to change the planned location of the central administration area was also practical from the point of view of land development. The new site at Zijin Mountain was spacious, with a natural landscape—the gentle slope would have allowed the creation of a magnificent view. The Ming Dynasty Palace area, however, is a flat area close to the central station. The area was under government control, but it was argued that this site could be better used for commercial development as the government could gain significant income from the increase in land value. However, if the site were to be planned as the central administration area, the government would lose potential income from commercial uses.

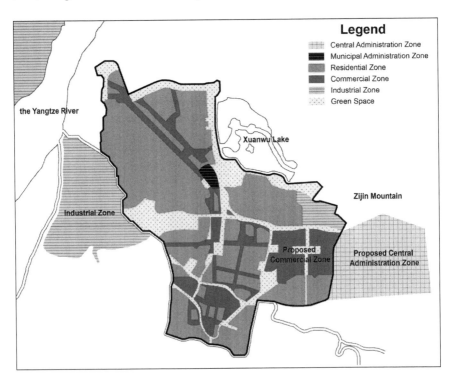

Figure 1.6 The spatial structure of the Capital Plan in Nanjing. The new administration zone was planned outside the city wall of Nanjing.

Source: Redrawn from Tusi (2012), originally from the Capital Plan, 1929

The choice of two alternative sites became a contest originating from political friction between the Nationalist Party and the government. The choice of a new site close to the Sun Yat-Sen Memorial perhaps reflects political symbolism to stress the continuity of the founder of the Party. Murphy was invited by Sun Ke, the son of Sun Yat-Sen, who led the Nationalist Party machine. The Capital Plan placed the headquarters of the Nationalist Party at the top of the north–south axis, indicating the dominance of the Party's power, in the Chinese version of Capitol Hill. However, Jiang Jieshi (Chiang Kai-shek), who led the government–military machine, preferred a more central location inside the city wall. His German advisors argued that the location of the central administration area was too remote, that the main direction of urban development should be toward the western waterfront of the Yangtze River rather than toward the mountainous area in the east, and that the administration area and the rest of the urban area should not be separated. The crucial disagreement between the two was about whether the capital would need large-scale expansion in order to gain additional development space. At that time there was still much vacant land within the walled city, because old Nanjing was much larger than other walled cities in China. But the Capital Plan estimated that in a century the population of the capital would grow to 2 million—looking back now, that forecast was quite conservative.[6] According to this estimate and density control under zoning, the plan suggested that there should be no more than 724,000 people living inside the city wall. The remaining 1.27 million would have to be accommodated elsewhere, outside the city. This estimate, however, was quite different from what actually happened in the history of Nanjing. Until 1992, when Nanjing revised its master plan, the city remained essentially compact within its city walls except for some development in the northern area (see discussion later in Chapter 4 about the strategic plan of Nanjing in 2001). Drastic development outside the city did not happen until the 2000s.

In 1930, Jiang Jieshi (Chiang Kai-Shek) abruptly made a decision that the central administration area should be located at the remains of the Ming Dynasty Palace and ended the controversy about the location of the central government. The preference of the government for the central location arose perhaps from a wish to demonstrate its power. The 'failure' of the Capital Plan may be due to political friction and power struggles between key politicians, which weakened the 'state capacity'.[7] But a review of the fate of all grand new plans proposed in that period or shortly afterwards suggests that the proposal to set up an entirely new center perhaps could not have worked within the condition of development until very recently.

Weak economic capacity is a possible explanation. In a sense, development conditions at that time did not support the large-scale development of a new center. The Greater Shanghai Plan, the Capital Plan, and the Shanghai

Metropolitan Plan as well as the Liang-Cheng proposal for the Beijing Master Plan all attempted to create magnificent civic centers. However, what was adopted in reality was more 'practical' than the grand plans made by architects and planners trained in the Western world. If the Capital Plan had been implemented, Nanjing would have become a multi-centered metropolis. But none of the theories, for example, 'organic decentralization,' imported from the West seemed to work well, because the aim was to apply spatial structures from more industrialized and developed economies to an underdeveloped or developing and pre-industrializing world. The new development conditions that made it possible to initiate large-scale urban expansion are examined in this book. We ask what was the major shift in the dynamics of development that made great expansion possible, and what was the role of planning in this process.

Shanghai Metropolitan Plan

After the victory of the anti-Japanese-invasion war in 1945, architects trained in Western Europe and North America formed a planning team to prepare the Shanghai Metropolitan Plan. Started in 1946 and published in 1949, the team produced three consecutive versions. The plan absorbed some cutting-edge Western planning theories, such as 'organic dispersal,' fast urban corridors, and 'regional planning' (SPHO, 1999). At that time, the central urban area was about 80 square kilometers, accounting for 10 percent of the total jurisdiction area but lived in by 3 million people, equivalent to three-quarters of the urban population. The plan believed that this level of concentration was excessive and proposed a decentralization strategy. Centered on the metropolitan core, the plan proposed the development of 'new urban areas,' forming cities with a population of half to one million each. Below the city were the towns with populations of 160,000 to 180,000 (SPHO, 1999) (Figure 1.7). The plan was that each should have both industrial and residential areas with a 500-meter green belt to separate industrial and residential uses. The plan also used the idea of 'neighborhood units' and proposed that the smaller unit would center on the primary school, with a population of 4,000. The third version of the plan was published just a week after the People's Liberation Army took control of Shanghai. The main principle was still to reduce the population density. This dramatic population decentralization was not implemented. Nevertheless, the idea of building new towns outside the central urban area was maintained and transformed into the development of industrial satellite towns. In 1958, the master plan of Shanghai designated five new industrial areas (see Chapter 2). It is interesting to note that the development of industrial satellite towns was not entirely imported from the former Soviet Union or as a socialist invention but has precedent proposals. These originated from the 'West'—

Figure 1.7 The proposal for new towns in the peripheral areas in the Shanghai Metropolitan Plan, initial draft.

Source: SPHO, 1999

outside the Chinese planning tradition. In this sense, the modernist approach to remaking the metropolitan spatial structure remarkably continued, despite the regime change in 1949.

From the Greater Shanghai Plan to the Capital Plan, or even to the Liang-Cheng proposal for the capital Beijing in the 1950s, there has been continuity in dealing with urban development through creating new urban centers and adjusting the urban spatial structure. But these plans encountered difficulties, because Chinese cities at that time had a much lower density; the old city still had ample empty space and was quite dilapidated. Practically, densification seemed to be the most cost-effective approach at that time. The leading politicians who had the power to make decisions were also reluctant to move from the existing city center to a new civic center. They preferred to build their power at the central location, symbolizing their legitimacy and dominance. The proposal for the new civic center was largely detached from the political and economic conditions of the nation at that time. Organic decentralization, green belts, and modern new civic centers on the basis of administration efficiency were appealing in terms of the improvement of the built environment, but were difficult to realize in the political economic context.

The Western influence

Modern and contemporary Chinese planning has been influenced by Western theories. In the era of the Republic of China, prominent first-generation architects and planners were trained in the Western world, in particular the U.S. (Wong, 2013). Theories of urban decentralization and new towns, neighborhood units, zoning, regional planning and metropolitan structure, boulevards and green belts were imported from the West. For example, the connection between an American planner, Clarence Stein, and a Chinese prominent architect, Liang Sicheng, indicates the great influence of American planning over the Capital Plan, the Greater Shanghai Plan, and many other plans even in the early years of the People's Republic of China. For example, in the early 1950s, architects Liang Sicheng and Cheng Zhanxiang proposed a new structure for Beijing, an alternative to the proposal of former Soviet experts. Besides Liang Sicheng's study at the University of Pennsylvania and Harvard, Cheng Zhanxiang was a graduate of Patrick Abercrombie at the civic design program at the University of Liverpool. In the late 1920s, the influence of Western planning practices was advanced by the publication of the *Complete Book of Urban Administration*, which was the most advanced planning publication at that time (Wong, 2013). The book consists of six volumes covering municipal governance, public finance and projects, and planning systems. These publications 'served an important role in introducing western planning practices to Chinese readers, and paved the ground-work for the impending plan-preparation movement,' and 'helped diffuse municipal expertise to small cities and to technicians who had not gone abroad' (*ibid*, p. 422). Planning was part of a modernization process, which led to the adoption of building codes. Both the Capital Plan and the Greater Shanghai Plan even considered sourcing funding from land development. For example, for the Capital Plan, the development of a new government district would allow more profitable commercial use of the land under government control.[8] The building codes enforced in the International Settlement and French Concession areas in Shanghai as well as other zoning reinforced residential segregation. The influx of rural refugees into Shanghai led to the spread of slums encircling Shanghai, while the richer rural landlords moved into the French Concession Area for better services and greater property security, leading to a boom in the property market. For older urban areas such as the southern part of Nanjing (known as *chengnani*)[9], because the area was outside the planning area and there were fewer government and educational establishments, the area remained poor and dilapidated. The trend even continued after 1949. The influence of the former Soviet Union was significant in the development of industrial–residential complexes and industrial satellite towns. The old areas remained dilapidated or even experienced deterioration. Western influence over Chinese planning practice in Republican China is perhaps the earliest example of 'policy mobility'[10]. The external influence continued in the socialist period, although attention shifted away from the building of new civic centers or government administrative areas to industrial districts.

China's planning tradition

Regarding the origin of planning in China, we can see that there are at least two different traditions. The first is the Chinese tradition from its cosmology that guides the layout of houses and cities. For building a walled city, the traditional norms set the road grids and the location of administrative compounds, the temple, the marketplace, and other major structures. The general principle of the layout was then adapted at a local scale with 'practical' consideration given to natural conditions (wind and water—*fengshui*). Remarkably, this tradition of urban forms shows an enduring stability. Wu and Gaubatz (2013, p. 67) suggest that

> the traditional Chinese cities were remarkable artifacts which reflected the ideals of Chinese culture and society. Their sites and layout were carefully chosen and preconceived to align with beliefs in cosmology, to serve as formidable defensive structure, and to maintain the ordered social structures of Confucian society. Despite centuries of political upheaval, cultural and

social development, and natural disasters, these cities were built and rebuilt much along the same lines from ancient times to the nineteenth century. Change was accommodated through accretion. (*Ibid*, p. 67)

The nineteenth-century treaty ports brought a more open European approach. However, "the vast majority of Chinese cities retained their distinctive urban form" (*ibid*).

The second tradition is the modernist planning approach brought in by Western powers and their extraterritorial space of governance. Architects and planners trained in the West transferred the knowledge of planning. At that time, the concepts of 'neighborhood units,' land use zoning, population decentralization, and the development of new civic centers were quite new to China. Besides the ideological consideration (as the Chinese tradition), the latter was new because it emphasized 'scientific' analysis and administrative efficiency.

However, this early modernization attempt essentially applied the theories developed in the industrialized and metropolitan countries to an under-developed and pre-industrial context. Weak governance and economic conditions gave rise to enormous difficulties in implementing the grand vision. The development conditions were quite different from those for the redevelopment of Paris by Haussmann.[11] When the Western city planning approach was introduced, China was in its late imperial era. The eclipse of imperial power, the rise of warlords, and weak state governance meant spatial fragmentation, with the co-existence of European quarters and the walled city. Planning for the city as a whole was never achieved.

In the traditional Chinese city, the norm or cosmology only provided a framework for city building, while actual construction, except for the palace and other monumental structures, was quite discretionary and left to a society with strong traditional characteristics. There was no 'municipality' government that carried out public infrastructure development or provided facilities and services. These emerged in the colonial city or European quarters in the late imperial era. For example, uniformed policemen, paved streets, and electricity and water supply modernized the Chinese city, which required the planning profession.[12] In Shanghai, the first municipal council was set up to build roads (MacPherson, 1990). Until that time, the modern profession of city planning was absent. As far as urban development was concerned, the emperor was rather symbolic and far away from everyday urban lives.

What is the implication of Chinese planning traditions for socialist and current planning practices? The socialist system built after 1949 was quite different from the feudal system, because unlike a symbolic imperial power, the socialist state became powerful and organized collective consumption.[13] This new way of consumption transformed the city of individual households into an organic society. This led to the penetration of the state into individual lives, or the politicization of everyday urbanism.[14] Before 1949, modernist planning was limited to only a few major coastal cities such as Shanghai, Nanjing, and Tianjin. A large number of smaller cities were unplanned. The modernist planning tradition was essentially an experiment within a traditional society[15]—which determined that modernism was quite ephemeral. Without modernizing society, it was difficult to fully implement a modern city plan. Socialism could be regarded as a continuing effort to modernize society. In this regard, the change was quite profound. On the other hand, the modernist tradition meant that in the course of modernization, China became used to looking to the West for inspiration. Borrowing modern and 'more advanced' concepts and practices from developed countries is not entirely new, whether the civic center and zoning from America or industrial satellite towns from Russia. In fact, many concepts such as *mikrorayons*[16] (micro-districts) in the former Soviet Union were related to its modernist origin, for example, 'neighborhood units': when the concept was imported into China, it became essentially the Chinese *xiaoqu* (micro district). Nowadays, other Western concepts such as 'smart growth,' 'new urbanism,' and 'transit-oriented development' (TOD) have been imported into China. But when these concepts are applied in China, they are transformed into specific local phenomena, and the deviation of the name and substance means that these phenomena would have to be understood holistically and totally, rather than by their labels and discourses.[17] At the present time in China, city planning is essentially a modern practice, which means that Chinese planners believe the West to be more advanced in planning theory and practice, and that China should learn from the development experience of the West. This mentality sometimes even requires the involvement of foreign consultants in Chinese planning so as to justify the claim that the most advanced technology has been applied.

Imported Western planning practices represent the tradition of planning by civil engineering and architecture, which emphasizes spatial structure and form. It was easier to import spatial forms from one country to another than to transfer the political and institutional set-ups and governance of planning. For example, the legitimacy of planning in China does not come from legislation or the power of civil society. For a long time during the socialist period,[18] China did not have a mechanism of development control, which is different from the planning system in the U.K. where the nationalization of development rights and consequently the establishment of development control mechanisms laid down the British post-war planning machine (Hall and Tewdwr-Jones, 2011). During the socialist period and the planned economy, coordination was built upon a different set of mechanisms outside the system of land use regulation. The tradition of the engineering-based planning approach imported from the West may help explain why city planning in China was more about construction than regulation. The approach of socioeconomic planning imported from the former Soviet Union was more dominant in resource allocation than city planning. The framework of modernist city planning had not really been set up in the industrializing socialist city. Despite the advocacy of various modernist concepts of metropolitan structure and urban forms, Chinese society retained some of the essential characteristics of traditional rural society.

Conclusion

China has a long tradition of cosmology and geomancy in city building, but the modern meaning of city planning as civic design and building regulation only appeared in the late imperial era. Western influence on city planning began not only with the physical presence of extraterritorial space in treaty port cities but also through the professional exchange of architects and planners. However, planning as a process of modernization has been extremely difficult, because following the Opium War, China experienced endless warfare, which seriously interrupted urban development. The Capital Plan and the Greater Shanghai Plan in the era of Republican China were either abandoned because of political strife, or interrupted by warfare and unrest. Besides political instability, weak economic capacity constrained the government from building an entirely new administrative center outside the city proper. The modernist grand vision proposed by planners was not realized, although some intervention has left an imprint on the built environment. Compared with what we see a century later, there is a significant difference—planners are now pressured by politicians to produce more ambitious plans;[19] and politicians tend to prefer a grand vision as never before.

Notes

1   See Zhang (2015) for a brief history of Chinese planning. For historical urban morphology, see Whitehand and Gu (2006). William Skinner (1977) provides the most comprehensive study. Gaubatz (1996) provides a good summary and an elaboration on the conventional urban form. See also Wu and Gaubatz (2013) for an account of the development of Chinese cities, particularly Chapter 3 about traditional urban form. Friedmann (2005) gives an accessible account of social development in history and its transition in the contemporary period.
2   See Wu and Gaubatz, 2013, pp. 58–60; Sit, 1995.
3   Li and Gu (2011, p. 57) describe the social areas of Chinese cities. For more social area analysis in Chinese cities, see Li and Wu (2006; 2008).
4   MacPherson (1990) provides a comprehensive account of the Greater Shanghai Plan.
5   For the Chinese literature on the history of city building, see Dong (2004). Jun Wang, a Chinese journalist, provides an accessible account of the history of Nanjing (Wang, 2011b). See Tsui (2012) for a description of city planning in the period and Cody

(1996) for the involvement of American planners; Cody (2001) gives the most comprehensive and detailed discussion of Henry Murphy's career in China.

6   In 2010, the population census shows that in six districts (Xuanwu, Baixia, Qinghuai, Jianye, Gulou, and Xiaguan), the total population reached 3.35 million. The new district Jiangning, to which Nanjing has relocated urban residents, had a population of 1.15 million. This, to some extent, suggests that population decentralization and suburbanization is inevitable, and urban expansion has its foundation in population growth.

7   Tsui (2012) puts the failure down to the weak capacity of the state, in contrast to the 'developmental state' in East Asia after the Second World War.

8   This has now been widely used in China, for example, the relocation of the municipal government of Qingdao and Hangzhou as a way of stimulating the development of a new area as well as gaining income from redeveloped land.

9   See Liu and Wu (2006) for a description of the pattern of urban poverty in Nanjing. The older area of *chengnan* remains poor.

10   Policy mobility has recently received attention, which is believed to be associated with globalization (McCann and Ward, 2011). In China, the borrowing of concepts has become widespread since the 2000s. For example, new concepts such as 'new urbanism' are utilized by the developers or government to justify the development of large suburban estates and new towns.

11   See Harvey (2003) for the redevelopment and modernity of Paris.

12   See Lu (1999) for details of everyday life in Shanghai.

13   Collective consumption is a concept developed by Castells (1977), referring to consumption in a collective form organized by the capitalist welfare state at the scale of the city. For the role of the Chinese state, see Wu (1997, 2003b).

14   See Yan (2010) on the return of private life in the post-reform era.

15   For the nature of society, see Fei (1992) which describes the essence of rural society, and Wu (2011) for the implication of traditional rural China for urbanism in present times.

16   See Grava (1993) and Hirt (2012) for more explanation of the concept of micro-district.

17   See Fei (1992) for a description of the process of modernization of the rural area, sticking to the old labels but injecting new content to suit the changing conditions. It seems that the Chinese particularly love to see 'imported concepts.'

18   More specifically, development control had not been established until the 1984 Planning Preparation Ordinance.

19   See Chapter 6 for new towns in contemporary China, which can be more ambitious than the proposal of a new civic center.

2
Planning During the Socialist Period and its Legacies

A brief history of planning during socialism

This chapter gives a brief review of Chinese planning history during the socialist period. Although excellent reviews are available (see Leaf and Hou, 2006),[1] the intention here is to summarize the development of planning practices without giving excessive historical detail. The period covered here is from 1949, when new China was founded, to 1984, when urban reform started[2] and the city planning ordinance was promulgated. In terms of planning practices, the brief period from the start of economic reform in 1979 to 1983 was seen as the time of the restoration of planning institutions and planning practices similar to those in use in the socialist period.

In the early 1950s, city planning in China experienced a period of rapid development. The key task for city planning was to support the development of industrial cities, especially the 156 key industrial projects aided by the former Soviet Union. In a sense, Chinese city planning originated from industrial site planning in the 1950s. Developments were organized around key state projects, which were often under the control of various ministries of the central government and their local departments. In some industrial towns, larger state-owned enterprises dominated economic development and were even more powerful than the local government because the former had the resources to build their own infrastructure and services. However, the need to coordinate these industrial projects began to require city planning. In the beginning, factories were built without giving much consideration to each other. Soon, the problem of a lack of coordination began to emerge, as the central government reported in 1953, "[F]actories are constructed according to our plans, but cities are not; factories are managed well but cities are not."[3] Consequently, the urban master plan was proposed to support industrial development at the city level.

In 1953, China started its first five-year economic plan. In major cities that had received more than three key state projects, urban master plans were prepared under the charge of the Urban Construction Committee. Because China lacked experience of planning, Soviet experts trained Chinese planners and advised on plan making in major cities that received industrial projects. Planning was heavily influenced by the principles of socialist city planning (Fisher, 1962; French and Hamilton, 1979). In the peripheral area, workers' villages were planned to improve the living conditions of the working class. The practice of city planning during this period was also influenced by the discipline of civil design, for example, the application of symmetrical layout, radial roads, grand boulevards and avenues, and magnificent street landscapes. But in contrast to the previous application in the Republic of China, industrial development was much more emphasized.

For the first time, Chinese cities began to experience large-scale industrial development. The Soviet model of industrial-driven economic development was adopted. Chinese cities began to transform from consumption-oriented and government administrative functions in the past to new economic growth poles. For example, the city of Baotou in Inner Mongolia was only a small town in 1948, but with large iron and steel industries set up in the first five-year economic planning period, the city evolved and expanded, creating three new industrial districts together with the central area.

Soviet land use and housing standards, however, were not suitable for Chinese conditions at that time, because the former assumed low building density in a sparsely populated environment and cold weather. The building density was too low for a more densely populated and mixed-use Chinese city. Some industrial buildings only occupied 20 percent of the land within the compound of state development projects, which caused inefficient land use and even urban sprawl.[4] From 1958, the Soviet housing standard of 9 square meters of floor space per person was reduced to 4 square meters after criticism of this being an excessive standard.[5] In the city proper, under the influence of 'socialist monumentalism' (Forest and Johnson, 2002), large squares and grand avenues were designed. These grand plans were criticized later after China broke off its relationship with the former Soviet Union. The problems of using an unrealistically high design standard that occupied too much land led to subsequent attacks on the planning system. 'Land hoarding,' that is, occupying more land than is actually needed, was a unique phenomenon in the shortage economy in which there was no land market. Because of the absence of the land market, land users tended to use as much land as possible. In the shortage economy, the input rather than the market was the constraint on development.[6] But city planning, as the government's internal control mechanism, did not manage to effectively regulate land use. This absence of control had its political economic causes. At this stage, the initial planning system with two-tier plans, namely the master plan and detailed layout plan, was set up. The master plan was generally prepared to coordinate newly built factories and existing urban areas, while the detailed layout plan was used for the construction of industrial projects and 'workers' villages.' As urban plans were made to support industrial projects that were managed by the state, the local control of development in the planning system was minimal.

Grand plans were prepared during the Great Leap Forward (1958–1959). In 1958, the first National City Planning Meeting was held in Qingdao, which called for speeding up 'urban modernization' and plan preparation.[7] The meeting also invented the fast approach to plan making, that is, to prepare the outline first and then fill in the details later in order to save time. Later, this fast planning approach incorporated a utopian concept of 'Peoples' Commune' to modernize cities but at the same time maintain some of the characteristics of rural communities. During the Great Leap Forward, industrial development became the priority. At that time, every city tried to create industrial projects and planning was conducted through a simplified approach.

The failure of the Great Leap Forward and the withdrawal of Soviet assistance to China changed the emphasis from promoting heavy industry and large cities to the development of agriculture and small- and medium-sized cities. From 1960 to 1965, China experienced economic difficulties and entered a period of recovery and consolidation. Urban planning was blamed for the promotion of unrealistic plans. In 1960, the National Economic Planning Meeting announced that city planning would be suspended for three years.[8] Further, the Cultural Revolution started in 1966. City planning was totally abandoned. In 1967, the Beijing Master Plan was suspended. Developments were carried out on any available sites irrespective of urban plans. The planning authorities were dismissed. Planning and design institutes were dismantled, and planners were sent to the countryside or forced to transfer to other jobs. Plans and documents were discarded or destroyed.[9]

In the 1960s and 1970s, only two cities prepared city plans: Panzhihua, an iron and steel city in southwest China, and Tangshan, a city that experienced a severe earthquake in 1976. Panzhihua was an entirely new city built in the region of the so-called 'Third Frontier'—the most interior area—to maintain the Chinese defense industry capacity, as it was thought that coastal regions would be bombed if there were a war with the West. Tangshan was severely damaged by an earthquake and needed reconstruction. The restoration of Tangshan actually marked the prelude of the recovery of city planning in China, because the year 1977 saw the end of the Cultural Revolution. For the restoration of Tangshan, city planning principles were stated as being to facilitate industrial production, to make living more convenient, to propose a realistic and reasonable layout, and to protect the environment (Zhang and Luo, 2013). This is the best summary of planning principles during the socialist period and also reflects the shift towards a pragmatic approach, which is less ideologically bounded and more realistic regarding socioeconomic conditions.

From 1978, China entered a period of economic reform. City planning began to be restored. In 1978, the State Council emphasized the role of city planning and proposed to control the size of large cities and to actively construct small cities and towns. In 1980, a draft of a city planning ordinance was prepared, leading to the promulgation of the 'city planning ordinance' by the State Council in 1984; in December 1989, ten years after the preparation of the draft act, the Peoples' Congress enacted the 1990 City Planning Act. On the administrative front, in 1979, the National Bureau of Urban Construction was set up, which was upgraded to the Ministry of Urban and Rural Construction and Environmental Protection in 1982. Within the Ministry was a city planning bureau. From then on, departments of construction were set up at the provincial level and planning bureaus opened in major cities, while smaller cities might have had planning and construction combined into a planning and construction bureau which was in charge of city planning at the local level. The number of planners increased from about 700 in 1973 to 15,000 in 1980.[10] The city planning ordinance of 1984 formalized the practice of the two-tier planning system. At the top was the urban master plan that designates the major function and size of the city and overall land uses; and at the lower tier was the detailed construction plan to specify the layout and design of buildings. A planning index was applied to ensure standards of provision. The development of planning in the 1980s was in essence a process that strengthened the role of the local government in planning, coinciding with the decentralization of economic decision-making in post-reform China. Governance in the post-reform period was transformed from a hierarchical to a horizontal model.[11]

Planning rationale: state-led industrialization and enforced accumulation

Industrial development was an overwhelming priority during the socialist period. This was due to the imperative to strengthen the capacity of the defense industry during the Cold War. The development of heavy industries was believed to be the way to maintain the sovereignty of new China. Transformation from a 'consumptive' to a 'productive' city was proposed as a major planning goal. This production-centered national revitalization movement could in fact be dated to the late imperial era, when the government hoped to learn from Western technologies. But the Chinese city had remained an administrative center until the establishment of socialism. In 1949, industrial workers accounted for less than 4 percent of the total population, a fact that was severely criticized by Soviet experts (Zhang and Luo, 2013, p. 39). The dominant planning rationale at that time was to prioritize industrial production, as reflected in the slogan 'production first, consumption second,' which marked the prelude to state-led industrialization and enforced capital accumulation.

This was achieved through 'compressed urbanization' (namely to compress the cost of urban development, because investment in consumption was believed to be wasteful and unproductive).[12] Through compulsory purchase of agricultural products in rural areas and the establishment of household registration (*hukou*), the state effectively extracted surplus capital from rural areas to support industrialization. The need to compress 'urbanization' was to avoid the 'wasteful use' of this precious accumulated capital for industrial development. In the planning sphere, investment projects were divided into 'productive' and 'non-productive' categories.[13] In 1955, the central government ordered the reduction of 'non-productive investment,' because 'non-productive investment did not generate value; adopting a lower standard would not affect productivity'[14]—non-productive projects in this case included workers' clubs, theaters, and stadiums. The standard used in the early 1950s under Soviet influence was regarded as too high and inappropriate for China. For example, wasteful housing investment was constrained, and the housing standard was lowered from an average of 9 square meters per person to 4.[15] Consequently, planning was centered on state industrial projects. During the socialist period, planning was thus more project-oriented. This urbanization policy helped avoid 'pseudo-urbanization' in developing countries, especially Latin America, through restricting rural to urban migration. The urbanization level, namely the ratio of urban population to total population, lagged behind the level of industrialization in China. In other words, the socialist city was 'under-urbanized' (Szelenyi, 1996), and industrialization in China was achieved without urbanization.

Besides the political economic rationale, the actual planning process followed a technical rationale about industrial location. For example, industrial areas should be located at the lower reaches of water flow and in a downwind area so as to reduce pollution in residential areas. Industrial and residential areas should be located in proximity to reduce commuting distance but be separated by a green belt. These are referred to as 'planning principles.'

Planning policies across spatial scales

Spatial policies at the national scale

Immediately after the establishment of socialist new China, the national spatial policy was to change the concentration of cities in the coastal region. This spatial concentration was believed to exist as a result of Western imperialism, which had turned the coastal cities in China into treaty port cities and used them to amass natural and agricultural resources from the inner regions and rural areas to export to the West for industrial production. The new policy

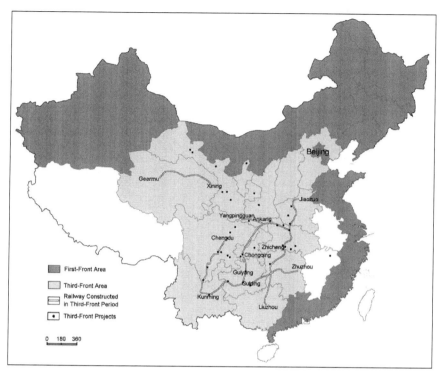

Figure 2.1 The designation of the 'third frontier' in China in the 1960s. This is the spatial policy that treats the coastal areas as the first frontier if war were to break out, and the western region as the second frontier under the intensified relationship with the former Soviet Union. The area of the third frontier was used to preserve the strategic defense capacity of China.

Source: Adapted from Li and Wu (2012b, p. 64)

required the redistribution of cities according to the distribution of natural resources and energy and the development of industries in underdeveloped areas. Thus the first five-year plan allocated 472 out of 624 industrial projects to the inner regions. This policy evolved into an extreme version of spatial decentralization during the heyday of the Cold War. In 1964, the national spatial policy required industrial projects to be dispersed in the mountains or even hidden in caves. The 'third frontier' was designated at that time in the central mountainous areas for industrial development (Figure 2.1). Because of the dispersal of industrial projects, urban development in the period was severely constrained and dismantled along with the projects in the mountainous areas.

This national spatial policy has changed since China opened its doors to the world in 1978. In the 1980s, a policy of differentiated regional development, or the so-called 'ladder theory' of coastal, central, and western regions, was proposed.[16] Instead of pursuing regional balance, the policy recognized the advantages of the coastal region. In addition, rather than concentrating development in the central mountainous areas, the policy proposed a T-shaped spatial framework, consisting of the coastal region and the Yangtze River area as two spatial corridors. Led by the newly established National Bureau of Land Resources (which later became the Ministry of Land and Resources) under the National Planning Commission (later the NDRC), 'comprehensive territorial planning' was introduced as an experimental type of planning. The National Comprehensive Territorial Plan Outline was prepared in 1985. At the same time, the Ministry of Construction began to prepare the national urban system plan outline. The so-called urban system plan became an important component of 'territorial plans.' National spatial policy in this period recognized the key development areas of the Pearl River Delta, the Yangtze River Delta, and Beijing–Tianjin–Tangshan region (capital area), Liaoning peninsular, and Shandong peninsular. In particular, the policy attempted to foster cross-regional development and break out of jurisdictional constraints. For example, the so-called Shanghai Economic Zone was proposed (Li and Wu, 2012b), consisting of Jiangsu and Zhejiang provinces, and it was asked to prepare an urban system plan (see later discussion on the 'urban system plan' and Chapter 5 for national and regional planning). But the new national and regional policies were formulated during the time of economic devolution, and thus these policies have not been effectively implemented. The National Comprehensive Territorial Plan was distributed as an internal document rather than being adopted. The Shanghai Economic Zone did not function, and the attempt to control the growth of heavy industries in the capital of Beijing was not adopted by the municipal government of Beijing; Capital Steels significantly expanded its capacity in the 1980s, contrary to the territorial plan.

National policy for the 'control of city size'

The control of city size was a sustained planning policy during the socialist period. The rationale was 'anti-urbanism'[17] to help the state concentrate its capital in industrial development. In 1955, the central government explicitly required that

> the principle of urban construction should focus on the development of small cities and workers' towns. When it is possible, we can build a few medium cities. Without special justification, we should not develop large cities, . . . we should not blindly develop large cities. In addition to Shanghai, Tianjin, Qingdao, Guangzhou, Dalian in the coastal regions, which should be strictly restricted for their growth, we should not allocate large

industrial projects in the cities that received industrial projects in the first
and second five-year plan periods. The scale of population development
should be strictly controlled. (Zhao, 1984, cited in Zhang and Luo,
2013, p. 53)

City size control was restated in 1980, when the State Council approved the
policy to 'strictly control the large cities, reasonably develop medium cities,
and actively develop small cities.' This policy has been implemented for about
two decades.

During the socialist period, the mechanism to implement this policy was
project approval by the state, because the central government could decide
whether a specific project should be approved to be located in a city.
Consequently, a project might indirectly affect city size. The policy also
encouraged the development of small cities and towns to intercept the influx
of rural migrants to the large cities. However, in the post-reform period,
economic decentralization has made this policy of city size control ineffective.
The population tends to flow into large cities where better social services,
educational resources, and public facilities are concentrated. Planning targets
were constantly exceeded by actual population growth.

Planning for 'satellite towns' at the municipal scale

At the municipal scale, planning policy was influenced by the Soviet approach
of the industrial complex built at the periphery of the city. The policy pursued
the development of industrial suburbs and satellite towns. In 1958, Shanghai
planned five satellite towns in its master plan: to build Minhang, Wujin,
Anting, Songjiang and Jiading at the periphery of Shanghai municipality
(Figure 2.2). This plan in fact reflects the continuity of planning objectives
for dispersal initially proposed by the Shanghai Metropolitan Plan (prepared
1946–1949, see Chapter 1). It also reflects the influence of the idea of 'organic
decentralization' in the 1944 Greater London Plan by Abercrombie. Similarly,
Beijing first proposed the development of 'decentralized clusters' (*fengshan
jituan*) at the urban periphery in 1958 and further formalized this in the 1982
urban master plan (Figure 2.3). Despite the policy to build satellite towns,
these towns failed to attract population before large-scale suburbanization in
the 1990s and 2000s, because these places generally lacked social services and
facilities and were inconvenient for living.[18] The planning standard, known
as the 'the service provision standard per 1,000 people,' was adopted to provide
relevant services and facilities, which were quite modest and insufficient under
the shortage economy. Because of the constraint of 'non-productive investment'
in infrastructure and facilities, satellite towns were inadequately serviced.

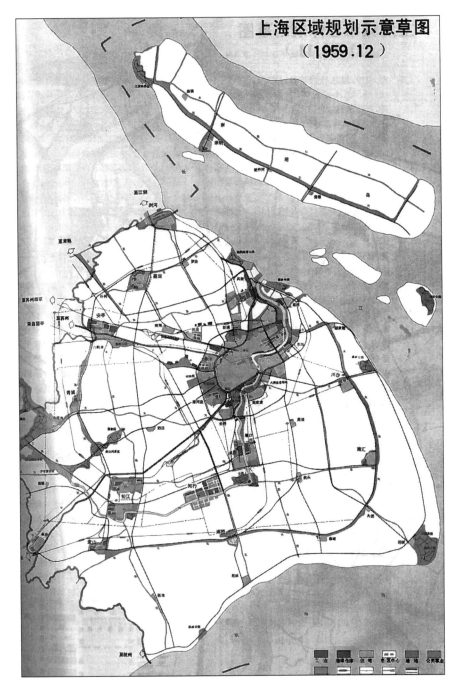

Figure 2.2 The 1958 Shanghai Master Plan proposal for the development of satellite towns in Shanghai.

Source: SPHO, 1999

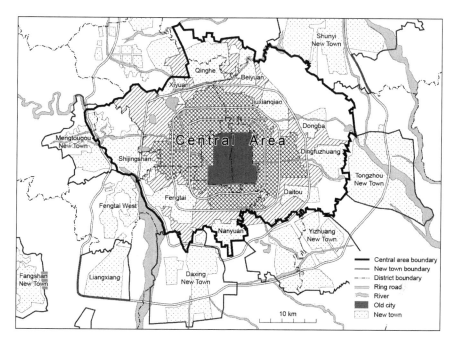

Figure 2.3 The ten 'decentralized clusters' at the periphery of Beijing. These clusters helped to concentrate industrial development and were separated by green belts from the urban area proper.

Source: Beijing Planning Exhibition Hall

Socialist residential planning: the workers' village

Planned residential development is perhaps the salient feature of socialist planning. Caoyang new village in Shanghai is an exemplar of the planned 'micro-district' during the socialist period, lasting for nearly three decades (Figure 2.4). It was the first large-scale residential development in China for industrial workers. The first phase started in 1951 and was completed in 1952, with 48 two-floor buildings, amounting to 1,002 housing units. The first phase then became No. 1 Caoyang new village (Plate 2.1). The housing was allocated to 'model workers' in the textile and metallurgy industries in the western area of Shanghai. Interestingly, when its planning history is carefully examined, it is found that the design of this new village followed more closely the American concept of the 'neighborhood unit' rather than any imported practice from the former Soviet Union. Its chief planner, Wang Dingzeng, was a graduate from the U.S. and well before the socialist period he had suggested the adoption of the neighborhood unit to promote the large-scale redevelopment that could solve the post-war housing shortage in Shanghai

Figure 2.4 The layout of Caoyang new village in Shanghai, designed in 1951; the final phase was finished in 1977, just before the start of economic reform. The village is an exemplar of the workers' village and was the first such village built in Shanghai during the socialist period.

Source: SPHO, 1999

Plate 2.1 **(a)** No. 1 Caoyang new village in Shanghai. The new village was built for industrial workers. **(b)** The relief at the workers' village. On the thermos it was engraved 'for model workers.'

(Lu, 2006, p. 29). The construction of the village took more than 25 years, with completion just before the start of the era of economic reform.

The total area of Caoyang occupied 94.63 hectares, and the first phase was 13.3 hectares. As with other residential micro-district plans, the structure was divided into three levels: neighborhood, cluster, and micro-district (*xiaoqu*). Each cluster had its own nurseries and primary schools within walking distance of the housing units in the cluster, and the *xiaoqu* level had community facilities such as co-op shops, banks, a post-office, and cultural clubs, which were located in the center of the new village (Lu, 2006). Later the area was extended, and the buildings were upgraded or had more floors added. Up to the end of 1990s, the whole area occupied 180 hectares, with 718 buildings with from 2 to 6 floors, amounting to a floor space of 1.7 million square meters. The population reached 107,000 people.[19] The department store at Caoyang was one of the largest shops in Shanghai at that time.

The standard of housing was quite modest but a significant improvement for industrial workers. The average living space was 5 square meters per person.

Plate 2.2 Baiwanzhuang residential district in Beijing. It was designed on the principle of the Soviet 'superblock,' which located large extended buildings along the streets; there is an internal space encircled by the residential buildings at the edge. Owing to its convenient location and solid building structure, Baiwanzhuang was developed as one of the staff living quarters of the central government. In 2014, the district was demolished.

Three families shared a kitchen, but each household had its own simple flushing toilet (this was indeed quite a luxury in Shanghai, because even in the 1990s a large proportion of families in old Shanghai still used 'night stoves').[20] Six to eight household units shared a courtyard. The bus line was extended into the village center for workers to conveniently commute to their workplaces. The plan used the river for landscaping and designed a park in the center. Between blocks, small green spaces were reserved. Trees were planted in the front and back areas of houses. Public green space occupied 29 percent of the total area, much higher than the city average. Compared with the widespread shacks for workers before 1949 (Lu, 1995), this was indeed a significant achievement. But the supply of this kind of municipal housing was very limited. Caoyang new village is unique in the sense that it was one of a few municipally supplied housing estates for workers who did not have housing allocated from their workplaces. The latter, or so-called 'work-unit housing,' was common.[21]

In the 1950s, when the link with the West was cut off, the superblock schema was introduced from Russia as a new orthodoxy for residential planning

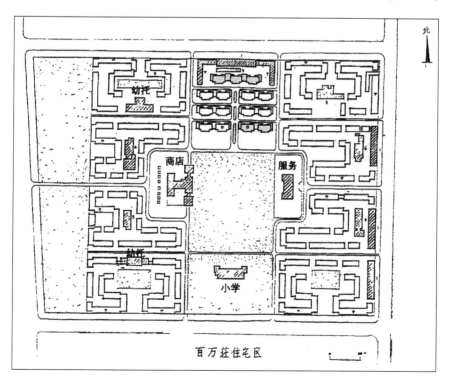

Figure 2.5 The layout of Baiwanzhuang residential district in Beijing, which followed the Soviet residential model of 'superblock' in the early 1950s.

Source: Wu S., 2008a

(Lu, 2006). In Beijing, the famous example was Baiwanzhuang residential district near MOHURD (the Ministry of Housing and Urban-Rural Development) (Plate 2.2). The buildings were built along the four sides of the street block, which was enlarged to accommodate more residential buildings (Figure 2.5). The inner area is an open space encircled by the buildings. The stern layout created a problem for west-facing windows, which suffered from the cold wind in the winter. The preferred housing orientation for the local weather is to the south, which gives direct north–south wind ventilation in hot summers.

In 1984, Beijing planned a major residential district—Fangzhuang in the southeast area of the second ring road. Initially the government hoped to finish the project in two years, but the actual construction took ten years. Because of the requirement for speedy development, many residential development projects in the district started at the same time. The district consists of 280 residential buildings, occupying 147.6 hectares, with a total floor space of 2.66 million square meters.[22] In the 1980s, high-rise residential buildings began to appear in Fangzhuang, with a population density higher than the superblocks built in the 1950s (Plate 2.3). The residential district is divided into four major

Plate 2.3 The planned residential district of Fangzhuang in Beijing. The residential area was the largest planned development in the 1980s. Although it was built after the economic reform, its building principles followed those of the socialist period.

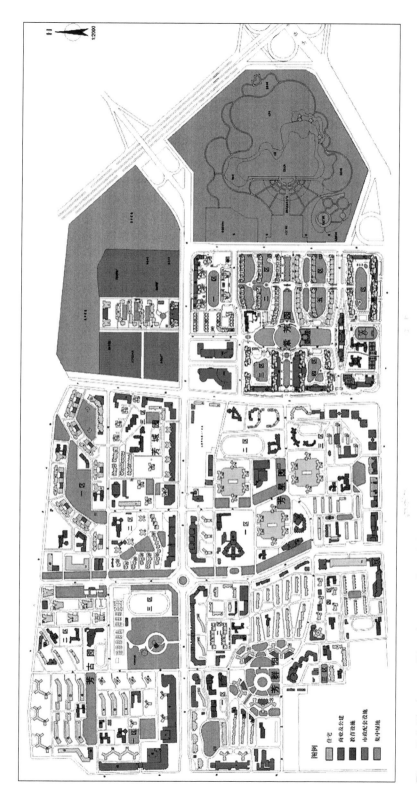

Figure 2.6 The layout of Fangzhuang residential district; it was one of the largest planned residential districts in the 1980s in Beijing.
Source: Wu S., 2008b

areas (Figure 2.6). The district represented the promotion of 'comprehensive development' organized by the local government rather than individual work-units to achieve large-scale development and full provision of services.

Can the socialist state plan its city?

While state socialism upheld the doctrine of 'central planning' and regarded 'comprehensive planning' as the mechanism to achieve socialist superiority to 'unplanned' market-driven capitalism, the actual planning process was extensively distributed to different government departments. Physical planning was separated from economic planning, and in fact the former was subordinate to the latter, just as with planning in Eastern Europe.[23] The approach of central planning is 'comprehensive balance,' which collects various lower level plans of administrative units including, for example, public institutions and factories, and then aggregates these plans into a top level plan. During the aggregation, the final figure may not reach the required overall target or may exceed the desired figure. This then requires the adjustment of individual targets so as to meet the overall target. So planning involves both upward and downward processes, through which 'efficiency' and 'balance' can be achieved. In this process, physical planners actually occupy a rather weak position.

While the discourse of socialist city planning was to create a new built environment—the socialist city—to shape a 'new socialist man,'[24] in reality, the weak economy and the stress on 'productive' industrial investment meant that large-scale new town development was difficult in China. After Beijing became the capital of new China in 1949, Liang Sicheng and Cheng Zhan-xiang, two well-known architects, proposed the development of a new adminis-trative center to the west of Beijing so as to relieve the pressure on old Beijing and enhance administrative efficiency by co-locating government depart-ments. The plan was in contrast to the proposal made by the planning experts from the former Soviet Union, which suggested the development of the central administration along Chang'an Street around Tiananmen Square. It was said that the latter proposal could utilize the existing infrastructure and facilities inside Beijing. In the Liang–Cheng proposal, a business district would be built to the south of the new administrative district, thus forming three major districts in the metropolis—the cultural area in central Beijing, a new adminis-tration district, and a business district. However, the government did not adopt the plan. Besides the high cost of developing new districts, it was politic-ally problematic to let the new and old centers co-exist, and the preference of the central government was to rebuild Beijing, which symbolized the new regime replacing the old. In the end, the government decided to use existing space inside Beijing for administrative purposes and prioritize industrial development in Beijing. Since then, the city of Beijing has taken on more industrial functions.

Because of the lack of a funding mechanism, it was impossible to redevelop old urban areas. Moreover, due to the priority to invest in 'productive' infrastructure, namely industrial rather than housing projects, the state geared investment towards industrial areas and compressed the cost of urban development. Large-scale urban redevelopment projects were absent. For inner urban areas, self-refurbishment and extension were the norm rather than the exception. The socialist city thus contained a significant degree of informality. The belief that the socialist city had to conform to a particular set of socialist planning principles was not entirely accurate—it says more about the ideology or principle of planning than the reality of the actual Chinese city during the socialist period.

Despite the difficulty of coordinating development due to the fragmentation of government departments, Chinese city planning during the socialist period adopted a futuristic and forward-looking style. The ideology of 'planned development' justified the superiority of socialism over capitalism because the latter experienced periodic economic crises without government intervention. It was believed that public ownership guaranteed more balanced development. However, in reality, Chinese urban development was far from organized, because public ownership did not lead to a unified system of land management, and actual land uses were fragmented by 'compartmentalization' between different land users, that is, the departments and their subordinate enterprises.

The more profound constraint on city planning during the socialist period was that physical planning was not at the center of development politics. City planning was subservient to economic planning, because the latter set the objectives of economic development. The former did not raise development initiatives or propose projects of 'state capital investment,' which were the duties of various government departments. The purpose of city planning was mainly to design a physical layout to accommodate and arrange production and related residential development in order to achieve the goals set by economic planning. Planners were thus used to meet development targets outside their field—in this case the five-year socioeconomic plans, and perhaps also the 'guidance' from their political leaders and relevant agencies. The process of city planning was outside the politics of resource allocation, which was the function of the economic planning commission and their agencies. The objective of planning was not to 'reduce negative externalities' of land uses in a market economy or to balance conflicting interests. The politics were settled in five-year planning and the government budgetary process. When the economic plan was revised, the plan would be modified accordingly.

The implementation of city plans relied on the mechanism of economic planning, specifically the registration of state projects, because only after a project was registered with the economic planning commission could it be allocated the necessary investment and resources. Land allocation was part of this process of resource allocation. Because planners were outside this process, they did not undertake a regulatory function or mediate different interests.

The output of city planning during the socialist period was the 'blueprint' of future development. As will be seen in the next chapter, this consisted of a master plan and a construction plan. The master plan is a more generalized blueprint. Its implementation relied on it being translated into a process of resource allocation. It was also dependent upon the 'understanding' of government officials of such a master layout. In particular, a list of key projects was required to be prepared with a proper understanding of the intention of master plans. This proved to be difficult, because the master plan was quite general about the future urban structure and less specific about the development projects needed to realize the plan. In terms of the relationship between these two types of plan, the economic plan was perhaps closer to the reality of decision-making and development. The plan-making process carried out by the planners was separate from the politics of the real decision-making process in land development, and it was not surprising that very often the master plan could not be implemented (Yeh and Wu, 1999, p. 234).

A master plan alone is inadequate for 'development control' without supplementary 'detailed construction plans.' This problem became more serious after the introduction of market mechanisms and economic decentralization, as investment came from outside the government plan and was unpredictable. The initiatives of the private sector meant that it was impossible for the government to prepare a 'detailed construction plan.' The design of these projects was no longer undertaken by the same planning department that had prepared or was familiar with the master plan. Bottom-up initiatives seriously challenged the master plan approach after economic reform, because the master plan did not provide adequate guidance for evaluating the planning application.

The process of plan-making was top-down, and lacked public participation. The general public was not consulted during plan-making, because no channel for participation existed and there was virtually no need for it to do so. People's interests were represented by their respective work-units. The legitimacy of planning was not conferred by public participation but by the state administrative system. The work-units that represented their employees and sectoral interests might have participated in the planning process, but this level of participation was still quite modest. It was difficult to implement urban plans because the stakeholders were not fully involved in the planning process. The role of coordination was limited in city planning. In the city, land users belonged to different government departments, and the city government might not have been able to coordinate the various development projects in the city because these projects might have belonged to different government departments. The conflict of interests was mainly resolved within the administrative system. Planning was a process dominated by government administration. The process of economic planning used a so-called 'comprehensive balancing,' which required different sectors and units to submit their targets so that the planning commission could aggregate them into city level targets, which were adjusted to meet the requirements of the upper tier of government. Further, this might have required some adjustment of the targets of the sector or unit plan. This process involved complicated 'negotiation' between different departments. In contrast, city planning did not require such lengthy deal making. Moreover, there was little resistance because society was not self-organized and had very limited demands regarding planning. For many years, until the enactment of city planning act, the urban plan did not have any legal status.

The meaning of the 'socialist city' and its implication for planning

Work-unit collectivism and spatial fragmentation

Under the capitalist welfare state, the city became the basic unit for organizing 'collective consumption' (Castells, 1977). What then is the meaning of the 'socialist city'? In the history of Chinese socialism, state work-units were the basic unit for housing provision and organizing consumption.[25] The city, in contrast to the countryside, represented the domain of the state, and the city was a container for state work-units (Figure 2.7). The notion of the 'public domain' (Friedmann, 1987) implies the sphere outside the private realm but with the influence of the public sector as well as civil society. In China, the absence of civil society, and the influence of the state over everyday lives through its state work-units, meant that the state had strong control over urban development. State work-units played an important role in urban development through their discretionary decision-making over land uses. The role of the local government was to fill the gap between the work-units for infrastructure provision at the citywide scale. A comprehensive development approach through the micro-district was rare.

The implication for planning is that planning deals with the sphere within the boundary of the city but outside the territory of state work-units. The space in between work-units is where city planning played its part. The pre-socialist old urban areas had not been planned and were largely left untouched. But there were also places where the concept of the micro-district was applied through residential planning, although this was not extensive and quite limited.

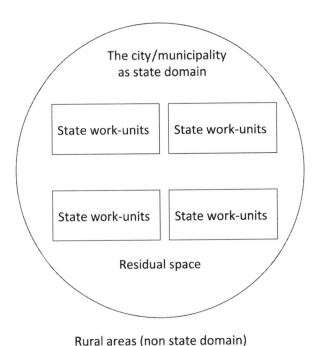

Rural areas (non state domain)

Figure 2.7 The sphere of planning in the socialist period. Planning was conducted in the 'state domain' in contrast to the 'public domain.'

Land use subdivision within the space assigned to an enterprise or institute was at the discretion of the local user, although the local government tried to regulate without success.[26] This is because the work-units were responsible for providing infrastructure and housing rather than the state. Resource flow and allocation which achieved through a hierarchy rather than horizontally in the locality. To repeat, physical (city) planning did not undertake the function of 'resource allocation,' which was done by the tool of economic planning. Following Castells' perspective, the state assumes responsibility for social provision, and hence the city under collective consumption becomes politicized. In contrast, planning in the socialist city was outside the political process. We may call this 'pre-political'.[27] The mechanism of development control was not established until 1990, and the regulatory power of planning ended at the boundary between the city and state work-units.

The absence of the 'growth machine': 'productive and non-productive investment'

Because the city lacked a mechanism to capture the benefit of infrastructure investment, investment in infrastructure development became a real burden for the investor during state socialism. The municipal government was reluctant to invest in infrastructure because it could not get a return from investment. More importantly, because of the multiple departmental ownership of enterprises in the city, the economy was organized based on industrial sectors. The profits made by individual enterprises were levied by their 'owners,' which were different government departments. While the state owned the means of production and land in name, in terms of actual operation there was severe fragmentation of ownership. Because of the lack of a mechanism for the city government to capture the benefits of urban development, and there was no way to exclude 'free riders' of infrastructure improvement, the city tended to classify investment into productive and non-productive types—the former as investment in enterprises that could bring direct profit from its investment.[28] The distinction between productive and non-productive is more than a technical categorization but rather has substantial meaning in terms of the operation and governance of the economy. As a result, the socialist city was not a 'growth machine.'[29]

In short, city planning during the socialist period played a complementary role to economic development and was not regarded as an obstacle to economic growth, because planning was outside the political and regulatory processes. In the post-reform period, the role of economic planning was significantly reduced but not entirely abandoned.[30] In the initial stage of reform, China took a gradual approach, which relaxed state control and created the co-existence of administrative allocation of resources and the market mechanism. Consequently, this system of 'dual prices' created corruption and speculation, which led to a political crisis and the outbreak of the Tiananmen Square event in 1989. Since then, a more market-oriented approach has been adopted in response to the crisis, as the state believed that only through a more radical market-friendly approach could the Chinese state survive the period of crisis.[31] On the other hand, the Chinese reform was not a shock therapy as in the former Soviet Union and Central and Eastern European (CEE) countries, and did not lead to a legitimacy crisis. In this context, planning has been strengthened rather than abandoned, in contrast to what has been seen in CEE countries (Nedovic-Budic, 2001; Hirt, 2005), because city planning was not identical to 'economic planning,' and the former took a blueprint physical design approach, which actually fits in with the practical need for managing construction in the post-reform period.

Socialist monumentalism: non-commercial use of the central area

In terms of the built environment, the socialist city lacked diversity and had a high level of uniformity (Szelenyi, 1996; Hirt, 2012). Industrial and public

Plate 2.4 The Beijing Exhibition Hall, built in the Soviet style. Local workers made a
great effort to put the heavy 'red star' on the top of the building, demonstrating
the great victory of socialism.

land uses were oversupplied, and commercial uses were constrained. The city
center saw less intensive commercial uses but was often dominated by grand
public buildings, referred to as 'socialist splendor' (Hirt, 2012) or 'monumentalism' (Forest and Johnson, 2002). In the 1950s, under the influence of
the former Soviet Union, the 'Stalinist style' building (with a magnificent base
and pointed roof) appeared in Chinese cities. The Beijing Exhibition Hall
(Plate 2.4) and the Shanghai Sino-Soviet Friendship Building (now the
Shanghai Exhibition Center) are typical such buildings of the time, intended
to present socialist superiority, magnificence, and a strong moral order.

In the socialist period, the city center was used for political gatherings rather
than commercial activities. In the 1950s, the central government decided to
adopt the recommendation of Soviet experts to redevelop central Beijing, and
reconfigured Tiananmen Square, expanded Chang'an Boulevard, and allocated
major government buildings along Chang'an Boulevard (Plate 2.5).

With the absence of land and housing markets, the private realm was
diminished. The socialist city forged a new form of 'collectivism' based on
state-organized collective consumption. The basic form was the compound of
state work-units. The provision of public housing and services was achieved
through technical standards, for example, the space of built-up land per

Plate 2.5 Chang'an Boulevard and the cluster of government buildings along the boulevard.

thousand people. This was based on the understanding that there was a baseline requirement for a standard household unit. Close proximity between staff living quarters and workplaces helped achieve greater job and living balance (Wu, 2005), which was also a by-product of public transport because it was difficult to commute over a long distance. As a consequence, Chinese cities were quite compact during the socialist period. For example, the built-up area of Nanjing remained almost the same over the 30 years of socialism, mostly within the city wall. Although the state attempted to develop peripheral industrial estates and even industrial satellite towns, except for some large state projects infrastructure at the peripheral areas was underdeveloped, compared with the central areas. It was inconvenient to live in these peripheral places. The 'suburb' had never been an ideal living environment, and the notion of 'suburbia' was entirely missing in China.[32] Compared with socialist cities in CEE countries, Chinese cities were even more compact, because they were at an initial stage of industrialization and lacked the capacity for large-scale urban development for a long period of time during the socialist period. The constraint on public investment in old areas, plus the abolition of private property rights, led to housing deterioration. Courtyard housing in Beijing had survived for several hundred years and was constantly refurbished by residents

Plate 2.6 Courtyard housing at Nanchizi near Tiananmen Square in Beijing. Courtyard housing in Beijing fell into disrepair. In the post-reform period, the relocation of original residents to 'commodity housing' estates plus the influx of rural migrants have changed the social composition. The courtyard was extended to accommodate rural migrants and became a junk yard. This place has been renovated but the approach of replication became controversial because redevelopment may actually have altered the history of courtyard housing.

themselves to maintain a livable standard. But during the socialist period courtyard housing began to deteriorate (Plate 2.6), which is attributable to the confiscation of private ownership and the lack of interest in maintenance by residents, according to the Chinese journalist, Jun Wang.[33]

Legacies of socialist planning

What are the legacies of socialist city planning? First, the most profound legacy of socialist city planning is that planning was outside the political process. It was rather a technical activity that aimed to convert the targets set by socioeconomic planning into the built environment. The latter was under the political process of economic planning. Because of its technical nature, city planning is very 'adaptable' in the process of marketization. City planning was developed to fulfill economic development targets rather than for development control. It remains as an instrument in the post-reform era but just to serve different 'masters'—local government officials such as the party leader and mayor and their development agenda. Because of its blueprint approach and detachment from the actual politics of resource allocation in the planned economy, city planning was not powerful enough to coordinate different development interests. During the socialist period, land management was rather fragmented—self-organized work-units, especially those large land owners, or so-called socialist 'land masters' (Hsing, 2010) were powerful enough to decide their own land uses.

Second, the spatial coverage of socialist planning was rather limited. City planning did not cover the whole national territory. Rural areas were left out and were not subject to a universal system of development control until the 2008 City and Countryside Planning Act. In rural areas, development control was rather ad hoc, leaving great scope for informality (Wu, Zhang, and Webster, 2013). In essence, city planning was confined within state land ownership. For rural land outside the state domain, the regulation mechanism was different. Management was concerned with different agricultural uses rather than with building activities. Agricultural land use plans were prepared to give guidance on what to cultivate, not what to build. This spatial limitation created scope for a new mechanism of development control outside the conventional planning system. It was deemed at that time that the most effective way was to give the administrative task to a survey and land management authority (which later became MLR). But land management was achieved through 'quotas,' linked with land certificates or deeds rather than planning permits. The strength of using quotas was that they could be aggregated for the overall control of development quantity, while they could be disaggregated and allocated to specific administrative bodies for implementation. This was particularly important when the central government wished to carry out macroeconomic control. As a by-product of land management, the quota system artificially created a fixed amount of land supply, in a way similar to land lease control in Hong Kong or land supply within the green belt of London. Another side effect of quota management was that it ignored location, which created a loophole for manipulation by local governments. They could convert village sites (as built-up areas), back agricultural uses in order to release development quotas, or swap quotas with different administrative units.[34] In theory, city planning could effectively deal with this location issue of agricultural land loss, just like the designation of the green belt in London. But in reality, the administrative power of the planning system was in local hands. In a sense, just as in the socialist period, city planning was never really made to be hierarchical. Although MOHURD has the power to approve the plans of large cities, it is extremely difficult to examine these plans in full spatial detail.

Finally, socialist planning created a compact urban morphology. The inner areas were very congested; land uses were mixed, and the quality of the living environment was poor. The redevelopment of inner areas required dealing with complex and fragmented land ownership, and it was easier to occupy farmland in the suburbs. This legacy means that suburban development became a practical solution for improving living conditions in the post-reform era when incomes rose and there was strong demand for improving the living environment.

Conclusion

The most surprising finding from reviewing the history of city planning during the socialist period is that 'planning' was not quite as dominant as we thought. It occupied only a rather 'peripheral' position in the process of economic decision-making. The role of city planning was just as an instrument to 'materialize' the development targets set by a separate political process via economic planning. As an extension of national economic planning, city planning was largely successful in supporting state-led industrialization. However, its role of guiding urban development was not fully developed. Another function of planning was to promote an image of the socialist city—so-called 'socialist monumentalism' to reflect the 'superiority and achievement of socialism' as seen in CEE countries (Forest and Johnson, 2002; Hirt, 2012) as well as in China (Smith, 2008). However, when this function was applied to China in the 1950s, it was quite problematic, and even led to the abandonment of city planning during political turmoil. This was because the Chinese economy was less industrialized and much weaker than the 'second world' of CEE socialist countries. The breaking of the Sino-Soviet alliance in the late 1950s led to criticism of the adoption of high standards of urban construction (in particular the impractical design approach under Soviet influence), which were not suitable for the Chinese situation. In terms of residential development, large-scale residential estates like Caoyang new village in Shanghai were rare. The living quarters of state employees were built as auxiliary components of state industrial projects. Public housing development and land use management contained a greater degree of self-sufficiency at the discretion of state-owned enterprises. It is important to understand this 'marginal' role of city planning, because city planning continued to serve as an instrument in the process of market transition rather than representing a substantial regulatory power of control over development, although political and city leaders now pay much attention to city planning and are keen to fund 'plan-making' activities.

Notes

1   Chinese references are plentiful: see Hou (2010) and Zhang and Luo (2013), for example.

2   Although the economic reform officially started in 1978, it was limited until 1984, when the Third Plenum of the 12th Chinese Communist Party (CCP) Congress decided to extend the reform from rural areas to the cities.

3   This is a report mentioned in an urban construction book.

4   This is discussed in Ma and Hanten (1981). Also see Ma (1979).

5   Hou and Zhang (2013).

6   See Tang (2000) for the history of socialist planning.

7   Hou and Zhang (2013) specifically discuss the implications of the Qingdao conference.

8   See Li (2012, p. 75).

9   There are various descriptions of this period, see Xie and Costa (1993), Tang (1994), Wu (1997), and Yeh and Wu (1999).

10 These figures are cited in Zhang and Luo (2013, p. 85).

11 See Yeh and Wu (1999) for a description of the change. There are extensive studies on urban and regional governance. Wu (2002) elaborates on the governance of the cities.

12 See Wu (1997) for the dynamics and rationale under socialism, Wu (2011) for an overview of the social characteristics of Chinese socialism and its transformation in the post-reform period, and Wu (2012c) for an overview of the particular urbanization processes.

13 Wu (1997) discusses this division and its implication, which was the dominant rationale for planning.

14 This was cited in Zhang and Luo (2013, p. 39).

15 *Ibid*, p. 40.

16 See Fan (1997) and Wei (2000).

17 See Szelenyi (1996); in the Chinese literature, see Ma (2009), Chan (1994), and Wu (1997) about the bias towards industrial development and urbanism.

18 See Zhou and Ma (2000) and Feng, Zhou, and Wu (2008) for China's suburbanization.

19 This is from SPHO (1999, p. 528), which provides a comprehensive documentation of the history of planning in Shanghai.

20 When the author visited his grandmother in an old alleyway house in Shanghai in the late 1990s, the family still used the night stove.

21 See Wu (1996) and Zhou and Logan (1996) for a discussion of the Chinese housing system, and Wu (2012b) for an updated description of it.

22 This was documented in Wu (2008b).

23 See Hirt (2005, 2012).

24 Fisher (1962) discusses socialist planning principles. The ideal 'cities of socialist man' have the following characteristics: uniformity, standardization, the use of neighborhood units, and a limit to the city size.

25 See Whyte and Parish (1984) and Walder (1986) for a discussion of the comprehensive role of the work-units.

26 Lu (2006, pp. 85–88) described construction outside the plan in Beijing as quite 'chaotic'.

27 The notion here is raised deliberately, with reference to a 'post-political,' i.e. after the Keynesian state, rather than a neoliberal shift; the decision was made outside the democratic political process, see Swyngedouw (2009).

28 See Wu (1997) for a more detailed operational mechanism under socialism.

29 See Logan and Molotch (1987) for the growth machine in capitalism.

30 See Chapter 5; economic planning has been transformed into a kind of 'spatial planning' in the form of national and regional plans.

31   See Wu (2010b) for the adoption of a market approach in response to the crisis.

32   See Zhou and Ma (2000) and Feng et al. (2008) for a description of suburbanization in China; and Shen and Wu (2013) for a demand side explanation for moving to the suburb as a 'residential preference', despite widely noted supply factors (e.g. the supply of suburban land by local government), Zhang (2000).

33   Wang (2011a) describes the demolition and preservation of old Beijing. The original Chinese version was published in 2003. See also, Shao (2013) for housing demolition in Shanghai.

34   For complex land management and planning, see Lin (2009) for the land use system, Yang and Wang (2008) for land conversion in development zones, Po (2008) for rural collectives and their roles in land conversion, and more recently Rithmire (2013) for land management.

3

The Chinese Planning System

For those who are not familiar with planning in China, understanding its system is like the story of 'the blind men and the elephant.' There are actually three parallel types of planning, all related to the conventional functions of urban planning—the urban plan series under the Ministry of Housing and Urban-Rural Development (MOHURD), the land use plan under the Ministry of Land and Resources (MLR), and the five-year socioeconomic development plan under the National Development and Reform Commission (NDRC).[1] The last has evolved from a non-spatial plan into a particular type of 'spatial plan'—the so-called 'main functional area plan'—which will be discussed in Chapter 5, as it is more at the regional level.

To take an example from Beijing, in 2005 the State Council (of the central government) approved the Beijing Urban Master Plan (2004–2020); but soon after, in 2009, the State Council again approved the Beijing Municipal Land Use Master Plan (2006–2020). The two plans both bear statutory status[2] and in effect co-exist. As its name suggests, the land use master plan focuses more on the protection of agricultural land. But the approach used is very similar to urban planning in the West. It divides the municipal region into four zones: the core functional area, the extension of central urban areas, the coordination area of new town development, and mountainous and ecological preservation areas. The Beijing Planning Exhibition Hall[3] is named as a 'planning' exhibition hall rather than specifically for urban planning, like the Shanghai Urban Planning Exhibition Hall. The second floor of the Beijing Planning Exhibition Hall exhibits the land use master plan, while the third floor displays a gigantic model of the master plan and the fourth floor describes what the model is about—the urban master plan. However, not all visitors understand that in China, these are actually two different types of plan. For the next round of urban master planning in Beijing, the planners recognize that the two plans have to merge or be reconciled into one.[4] Since the planning system under MOHURD has the longest tradition and is the closest to the conventional meaning of planning, while land use planning is more for specific agricultural land planning and planning under NDRC is an economic program, this chapter provides an overview of this planning system and its evolution during market transition.

Over the last three decades, China's planning profession has experienced significant growth. The number of registered planners under the professional accreditation system adopted in 2001 increased to 12,000 in 2011. The total number of planners increased from about 3,000 in the late 1970s to 100,000 in 2011 (China Society for Urban Studies, 2013, p. 299). The educational programs for planning undergraduates have significantly increased (Figure 3.1). The degree program of Urban Planning became a first tier discipline, like the disciplines of Architecture and Geography, while before that period Planning had been a second tier discipline under Architecture. The practice of planning received great attention from both central and local governments. Every city now has an urban planning exhibition hall like the impressive planning hall in Shanghai (Plate 3.1a), and many are equipped with modern lighting and multimedia technologies. In 2014, the new Chinese leader, Xi Jinping, started his inspection visit at the Beijing Planning Exhibition Hall (Plate 3.1c). For various local governments, city planning provides a practical handle for government officials to promote economic growth and thus demonstrates the achievement of government officials. In this chapter, the development of the statutory planning system is examined.

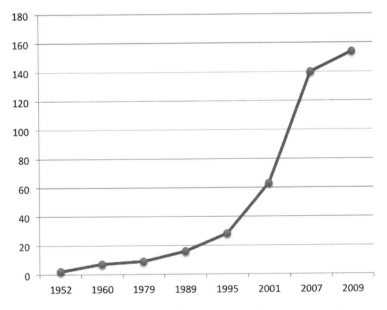

Figure 3.1 The increasing number of undergraduate planning programs in China.
Source: China Society for Urban Studies, 2013

Plate 3.1 (a) Shanghai Urban Planning Exhibition Hall, with a distinctive building style, located near the municipal government. (b) The gigantic urban model of Shanghai occupying the whole floor of the exhibition hall. (c) The model of Beijing Bay at Beijing Planning Exhibition Hall, where the new leader, Xi Jinping, started his inspection visit in 2014.

The 1990 City Planning Act

The statutory planning system officially started with the Planning Act, although before the Act planning practices did exist under government regulation. In 1989, the People's Congress passed the City Planning Act, which came into effect in 1990. The Act set up the statutory status of city planning for the first time and granted the local planning authority power to enforce development control over its territory, that is, regulation of land uses directly at the land parcel level. Before the adoption of development control, city planning existed largely to assist economic planning in assigning space for development projects. There was no mechanism for directly implementing a city plan except that officials could propose development projects according to their understanding of planning intentions. The planning authority had no power to stop a project that was supervised by other government departments, especially those under the central government. The master plan was only a guideline without the power of legal enforcement. Individual state work-units and enterprises managed their own land. They could only be persuaded to follow the master plan. In short, the power was in the hands of those who were in charge of economic planning, because they could determine whether a project could be registered or not, and allocate resources to it. Since 1990, the Planning Act has required all development projects to conform to the master plan.

The development control mechanism consists of 'one report and two permits.' Decisions are made through discretionary judgment of the development in relation to the urban plan. First, the planning department is responsible for preparing a site selection report for each development proposal. Second, a land use planning permit and building permit are required for all projects before they are allowed to be built. The site selection report provides the general judgment of the location and its layout in relation to the plan. The procedure asks the planning authority to provide comments on the sites of development projects. Before 1990, these projects were mostly proposed by the government. Since economic reform, the role of localities has been strengthened. For state projects, the local department was asked to organize site selection, and hence started the cooperation of city planning and economic planning. The land use permit was a formal document to prove that planning permission had been granted. However, since the enactment of the Land Administration Act in 1986, the land authority has been responsible for issuing land certificates (of ownership). For new acquisitions, the developer has to seek planning permission. Building permits are needed for all construction, including the building of roads and other engineering works.

The Planning Act strengthened the role of city planning in economic development. Development projects need to submit a site selection report to the relevant government department when they seek approval for project registration. This requirement relates city planning and economic planning. The report provides the link between development control in land development and project approval in the process of economic planning. This is particularly important for large state 'capital construction projects,' and in theory has strengthened the role of city planning in economic development, because the sector government department needs to consider the recommendation of the local planning authority in terms of planning requirements for a state project (for example, an enterprise belonging to the central government department).

The Planning Act was enacted before the land market was fully established, because the first piece of land put up for auction was in 1988, and land sales were very limited at that time in China. The use of land needed for development was still negotiated between the potential user and the current possessor of the land,[5] and was administratively allocated. The Planning Act strengthened the position of 'development control,' because only after receiving a planning permit could the development organization or developer apply for land allocation from the local land department. In theory, the developer had to obtain a planning permit before a land certificate could be issued. The coordination between these two procedures proved to be more complicated following the development of the land market and the strengthened protection of 'basic agricultural land.' The function of basic agricultural land protection was given to the land authority rather than the planning department, because the land authority has a much stronger role in surveying rural land uses. Underlying the problem of fragmented governance are the divergent interests of two related but separate government departments in the central government —the Ministry of Construction (now MOHURD) and the Ministry of Land and Resources (MLR) (which was set up in 1998, eight years after the enactment of the Planning Act). In reality, despite the double-check mechanism, development control has proved to be difficult and not entirely effective (see Chapter 4 for further explanation).

The 1990 Planning Act is a milestone in Chinese planning history. A decade after the economic reform was launched the planning system was formalized, giving comprehensive planning power to local governments to manage their cities. This was achieved in the middle of a market transition. Planning mechanisms had been in place before the large-scale reform towards the market economy. But the challenge of market development (after Deng's southern China tour in 1992) and the transformation of governance (after the tax-sharing system in 1994) profoundly changed the landscape of city planning.

Although the planning authority has been granted the power to execute development control, in reality the planning system is not fully equipped to deal with the pressure of development and inter-government politics. There are several reasons why development control has been difficult. First, the growth mentality of local government means that it is very difficult for a planning authority to refuse a development proposal, especially when it originated from the municipal government (e.g. the mayor or Party leaders). The intervention of government officials in planning decisions is common. Not all interventions are out of self-interest. For example, the planning authority has to give concessions to major development projects that are regarded as vital to the local economy. Second, the development of the land market has created additional complications. In essence, the Chinese land market is a lease market, that is, the development rights of state land are leased to the developer, and land leasing inevitably leads to conflict with development control, because the lease condition is regarded as an agreement between the government and the user; after the signing of the lease agreement, it would be difficult for a planning authority to refuse its use. In theory, the lease or the land sale should follow the planning requirement. But in reality the city plan has not been able to provide guidance for land sales, because land sales may proceed before the preparation of urban plans.[6] The result is that the plan has to be revised to incorporate the reality—or the government has to negotiate with developers to reach a compromise. The latter is extremely difficult. So, in order to sell land, the usual practice is to prepare the plan first, as seen in the emergence of the so-called 'detailed development control plan' (see later in the discussion of the statutory planning system).

Third, the Chinese city has been experiencing rapid development. The process of plan-making often lags behind the reality. In fact, planners are asked to prepare plans to promote growth rather than to contain development. Fourth, informal development has been widespread as a historical legacy. The capacity for monitoring actual development is not fully developed. As mentioned earlier, in the socialist period development was actually regulated by state work-units themselves rather than through the system of planning permission. The tradition of self-regulation has persisted—planning has not been powerful enough to monitor subdivisions. Spontaneous land use conversions happened in built-up areas to capture new opportunities brought about by market development. To some extent, this reflects the need for land use adjustment in the process of market transition. However, a significant degree of informality exists, because development control under the 1990 Planning Act only covers urban areas, excluding the vast rural areas where planning and land management capacity is severely limited. However, in reality, Chinese cities have experienced rapid expansion into rural areas. In the peri-urban area, therefore, informal land development is rampant (Wu, Zhang, and Webster, 2013). Fifth, the impact of the land market on development control is especially profound, because for a long time (before 2004) even formal development had been obtaining land through negotiation with the government. The negotiation, however, did not include the planning authority. The mayor or senior politicians may have seen development control as a process to formalize a deal rather than a condition to be taken into account during negotiation. Strong inter-city competition means that it is difficult to resist development opportunities. In short, while development control involves complicated politics, the execution of development control by the planning authority is largely a technical process, divorced from a political decision-making process.[7] The planning department can hardly resist the pressure of development.[8] Limited coverage of planning has been expanded into rural areas since the City and Countryside Planning Act of 2008.

The 2008 City and Countryside Planning Act

In 2003, the new generation of Chinese leaders (Hu Jintao and Wen Jiabao) came into office and started to react to the negative impacts of market transformation. The CCP under Hu Jintao raised the concept of a 'scientific approach to development.' The focus of central government policies was placed on the 'five types of coordination,' namely coordination between the urban and rural areas, coordination between regions, coordination between social and economic developments, coordination between the human and natural environments, and coordination between domestic markets and exports under the 'open door' policy. The change marked an overall shift towards state control and the up-scaling of governance (see Chapter 5 for the re-emergence of national and regional planning). However, the change of governance was incremental. The political economic conditions remained the same, and the integration of the Chinese economy with the world was speeded up through joining the World Trade Organization (WTO) in 2001. So the thrust of local entrepreneurialism has become even stronger. Incidentally rather than intentionally, the strengthening of state governance, especially in land regulation, finally completed the last step towards the foundation upon which the Chinese local land-driven growth machine is built. Against this background, in the 2000s planning and governance were strengthened. Ten years after the establishment of the Ministry of Land and Resources (MLR) that is in charge of land protection, the City and Countryside Planning Act was enacted in 2008. But by this time, the landscape of land regulation had changed, and MOHURD could no longer claim a dominant role in land management, especially in the regulation of rural to urban land conversions. MLR had begun to enforce a system of land development quotas from 2004. The enactment of the Planning Act did not reverse the trend.

The 2008 City and Countryside Planning Act finally extended the power of planning to rural areas. It formalized efforts to unify urban and rural planning in the early and mid-2000s. Before the Act, planning in rural areas was limited and separated from the system of urban planning. Rural areas were planned under the 'regulation of rural village and town planning.' In 2006, the regulation of the 'preparation method of urban planning' required the extension of the scope of urban system plans to include the 'strategic development of urban and rural areas.' That is, the conventional approach of urban system planning only covered 'designated towns'[9] at the lowest level, but the coverage was very limited, because it was only concerned with the overall size and functions of towns. Towns were treated as points rather than as built-up areas in the urban system plan. The regulation of planning preparation in 2006 required a comprehensive plan for the whole jurisdiction area. The Planning Act of 2008 formalized planning practices that included rural areas, and therefore the basic system of the 'master plan–detail plan' was expanded into five types: the urban system plan, the urban plan (including master and detailed plans), the town plan, the township plan, and the village plan. In terms of development control, the 'rural construction and planning permit' was added to form the system that consists of 'one report and three permits.' In 2010, MOHURD announced new regulation of urban and rural plan preparation.

Following the 2008 Planning Act, local governments in China began to apply the method of city planning to the whole jurisdiction area (known as planning for the whole territory, *quanyu guihua*). But the technique of planning did not change. Rather, it simply used the existing method of the 'detailed development control plan' in rural areas. This dramatically increased the workload, as in the countryside there might not be such a need for an essentially urban spatial plan. However, the effort to increase the coverage of planning did help to give more consideration to infrastructure development and public services in rural areas, which had been ignored and inadequate. The implementation of the policy has been uneven. Rural planning has been more developed in coastal regions such as Jiangsu and Zhejiang provinces, and Chongqing in Sichuan province, which piloted the program of urban and rural coordination. Some cities even specifically prepared a so-called 'urban and rural coordination plan.' However, with the tightening of rural land management through MLR-directed land protection, the emergence of the urban–rural integration plan was not purely a result of top-down regulation, it was also a countermeasure of urban entrepreneurialism towards state policy (see the example of Nanjing in Chapter 4). It reflects the interest of local government in the 'new' land resource in the countryside. Faced with land constraint, the local government is keen to reduce the built-up area in the countryside in order to gain development quotas for the development of urban areas, because land control from MLR is based on quotas. The policy was invented to maintain the nationwide stock of agricultural land at 1.8 billion mu (15 mu = 1 hectare). As a result, the spatial plan, or so-called urban–rural integration plan, tends to encourage the 'merging' of rural settlements and the demolition of smaller villages so as to free up land quotas. This has been described as the 'socialist new countryside.' Urban–rural coordination plans are prepared by local governments under the thrust of the 'entrepreneurial city,' but are disguised and justified by the discourse of 'scientific development.'

The statutory planning system

The statutory planning system has been established since the 1990 Planning Act, and is in essence a two-tier system. The upper tier is the urban master plan, and the lower tier is the detailed plan. These tiers of plan can in fact be dated back to the 1950s. However, the Planning Act formalized the practice with statutory power. The master plan outlines the general land uses of the city, while the detailed plan is prepared for the area that faces immediate construction or is specified in the master plan. The master plan, according to the statutory planning system, should define the function of the city, the development goals, population size, general land uses, and major infrastructure distribution and structure. The master plan has a planning horizon of 20 years and should consider long-term development strategy. The master plan should also have a map of intermediate construction, which should decide the layout of developments in the near future, usually the next five years. The preparation of the master plan and its content are specified by a clearly defined planning standard.[10] While the contents of master plans may vary slightly, there are some compulsory components such as city function, population size, industrial specialization, and spatial structure of the city. Before the mid-1980s, spatial form was strongly emphasized, because the purpose of planning was to organize urban space for state capital projects. Figure 3.2 shows the urban master plan of Lanzhou, an industrial city along the upper reaches of the Yellow River. In the first five-year plan period, petrochemical, chemical, and machinery projects were allocated to the city. The master plan then accordingly organized the above projects into several clusters on the river terrain. The structure consisted of several self-contained clusters that formed a 40-kilometer belt of industrial complexes.

At the lower tier is the detailed plan (*xiangxi guihua*). The detailed plan should be based on the urban master plan (*zongti guihua*) or district plan (*fenqu guihua*)—a master plan at the district level—to stipulate the detailed layout of construction to be carried out in the near future. In other words, detailed plans are prepared for areas that are facing immediate construction. The detailed plan should specify the boundaries of each construction project within the planned plot, the type of buildings, building height and density, transport lines, entrance and setback from the street, cross-sections and the coordinates of their control points, the layout of pipelines and service radius, and the boundary of engineering facilities. A three-dimensional map may be provided to illustrate the scene of development. The detailed plan is therefore

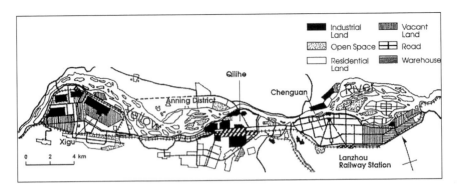

Figure 3.2 The master plan of Lanzhou, an industrial city, prepared in the early 1950s, indicating the general spatial structure, which consists of a belt of industrial clusters. The plan indicates the importance of industrial development and also the style of the 'master plan.'

Source: Yeh and Wu (1999)

quite specific about construction and includes different types ranging from residential plans to plans of large industrial complexes. The latter are often prepared by design institutes that specialize in the sector of the relevant industry.

For city planning, one important category of the detailed plan is the residential district plan, known as the 'residential micro-district plan' (*juzhu xiaoqu guihua*). As discussed in Chapter 2, the origin of this type of detailed plan came from the Soviet concept of 'mikrorayon' (Grava, 1993; Hirt, 2012), which emphasizes the 'neighborhood unit'.[11] In the 1980s, the state began to emphasize 'comprehensive residential development' through planned micro-districts, because there were several foreseeable advantages to this method of development: residential areas could be planned in advance; development could be organized by a major development company (rather than by individual work-units); and services could be provided through the municipal government to achieve economy of scale. Figure 3.3 shows the detailed plan for a typical residential district in the city of Changzhou.

The statutory planning system also includes some supplementary components of the master plan (Figure 3.4). For example, before the preparation of the master plan, an urban system plan for the municipal area is prepared. The urban system plan decides the development of cities and towns within the municipal area, because under the 1990 Planning Act, the master plan only covers the central city proper, not the vast rural areas in the municipality. The urban system plan could be regarded as a city–region plan (*shiyu guihua*) with the focus on built-up areas. The plan covers designated cities and towns that are the seats of county government. The discipline of Urban Geography in the 1980s contributed to the formation of the urban system plan. Planners

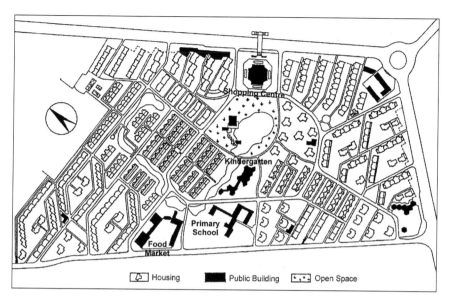

Figure 3.3 The detailed plan for a residential micro-district in the city of Changzhou. The plan was prepared in the early 1980s, showing the features of the detailed plan as a layout of construction and services, for example, the location and layout of green space and parks, the food market, kindergarten, primary school, and community center as well as apartment buildings.

Source: Yeh and Wu, 1999

from a geographical training background advocated that the urban system plan should focus on 'three structures and one network,' that is, function, size structure and spatial structure, and the transport network. Function refers to the specialization of cities and towns in terms of their dominant industries and specialization; size structure refers to the distribution of size of cities and towns; spatial structure refers to the geographical distribution of cities and towns; and finally, transport network refers to infrastructure and transport links. The statutory planning system requires that the urban system plan should be prepared at the national, provincial, and municipal scales. The last is part of the urban master plan of the municipality. The strength of the urban system plan is that it expanded the scope of city planning to city–region. However, its limitation is that there is actually no implementation mechanism for the urban system plan that is prepared for the urban master plan. That is, implementation requires that these 'structures and network' should be absorbed into the preparation of the master plans of individual cities. In reality, this is not often the case.

In practice, before the preparation of the urban master plan, a strategic planning outline (*guihua gangyao*) is usually prepared as an intermediate step. The outline sets down the principles and major issues of the master plan,

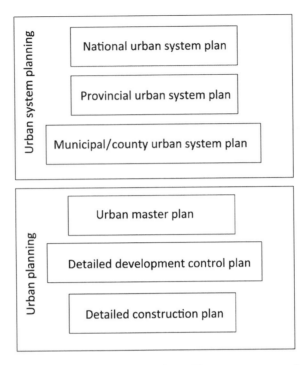

Figure 3.4 The statutory planning system in China. This system consists of two tiers: the urban master plan and the detailed plan. But there are supplementary plans to support these tiers, for example, the urban system plan before the preparation of the urban master plan. For large cities, a district plan may be prepared to make the overall master plan more concrete. And at the lower tier, the detailed development control plan appeared as a zoning type of development framework for land sales and development.

analyzes the technical and economic conditions, opportunities, and constraints of development, and sets goals for socioeconomic development. But later in the 2000s, when the non-statutory plan—'conceptual plan' or 'urban strategic plan'—emerged, these non-statutory plans began to influence the strategic outline, which can be regarded as a prelude to the preparation of the strategic outline.

The urban district plan is not compulsory and is an independent tier. It supplements the master plan in large cities, because a single urban master plan often cannot provide sufficient detail for the lower tier of the detailed plan. The district plan is very similar to the style of the master plan. But sometimes it may be more detailed in land uses, becoming similar to 'zoning.' This zoning-style plan is perhaps the most outstanding variation of the detailed plan, and is called the 'detailed development control plan' (*kongzhixing xiangxi guihua*). Since market reform, the government has no longer controlled resources and development projects. Many projects have been initiated by the market. The role of state-owned enterprises in the economy has declined. To cope with the change, the detailed development control plan was invented to suit the situation of land market development, because in the land market developers need to know the planning conditions before they can calculate the bidding price for the land. For a development area, land plots are divided and assigned with codes or a control index that usually include the land use type, building height and density, plot ratio, and other design requirements. However, the preparation of such a plan is quite difficult, because of the uncertainty and the lack of justification for planners to assign land uses.

This new type of plan, instead of specifying detailed layout, provides only the framework of development. The origin of this type of plan was influenced by 'zoning' practice in the U.S. For projects of foreign or private investment outside state control, the government cannot prepare a detailed construction plan. There is also great uncertainty in the market when the plan is being prepared. So instead of designing the layout, the plan delineates the boundaries of the plots and specified land uses, and the required control indexes, such as building height and plot ratio. This control plan was experimented with in the 1980s, and finally evolved into the current style—which is unique to China.

In the 1980s, Shanghai tested a type of zoning plan (Figure 3.5). The plan consisted of many land parcels, which were all indexed with their land uses. The zoning map gave a set of control indexes such as plot ratio, setback of buildings, building density, the direction of major entrance, height limits, and the number of car parking spaces for each land parcel. Later, the experiment was also carried out in the planning of Shanghai's Hongqiao Economic and Technological Development Zone (ETDZ). In the late 1980s, the city of Wenzhou in southeast China conducted an experiment in land use zoning in its urban renewal plan.[12] Although the 1990 City Planning Act did not recognize the status of the control plan, in the subsequent planning preparation ordinance the status of the detailed development control plan was established, and became a major planning control measure throughout China. The emergence of this plan reflected a major change in planning under market transition to cope with the situation of development uncertainty. It aimed to specify conditions for the land leasing market. Faced with the land market and the diversification of investors and developers, the preparers of plans and management began to adapt their practices to the new environment. They began to go beyond morphological design and introduced regulatory control. Later, the preparation of detailed development control plans together with the non-statutory 'strategic plan' (see Chapter 4) became a tactic for selling state land: the strategic plan is to sell a 'concept' such as a financial district, a central business district (CBD), or an eco-town, while the detailed plan describes the specifications of the spatial product. Interestingly, the purpose of the so-called

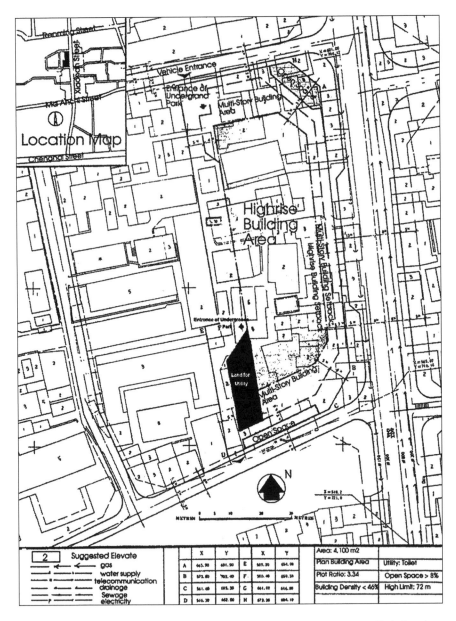

Figure 3.5 The zoning experiment in Shanghai in the 1980s which eventually led to the development of the so-called detailed development control plan in China as part of the development control mechanism.

Source: Yeh and Wu, 1999

'development control' plan in this context is not control, but rather to promote product specification.

The detailed development control plan mostly remained a technical document. The only exception was Shenzhen. As a special economic zone with its own legislative power, Shenzhen was the first Chinese city to transform the control plan into a zoning ordinance. Following the model of Hong Kong, zoning ordinances are required to go through a special board—the Shenzhen Urban Planning Board, an authority comprising government officials, experts, and members of the public. The plan stipulates land use types, development intensity, and the planning requirements of plots. For each land use type, there are three classes: the first stipulates land uses that are automatically allowed; the second consists of land uses that may be approved by applying for planning permission from the planning bureau; and the third lists possible uses that can only be approved by the board (Wu, Xu, and Yeh, 2007, p. 170). The preparation of zoning ordinances in Shenzhen attempted to involve public participation and tried to make the plan more transparent.

However, nationwide zoning ordinances are rare—the control plan lacks substantial public participation and power of monitoring. The major drawback of the control plan is that the approach relies too much on technical rationality, which is divorced from the politics of development. Although the stated purpose of the control plan is to reduce administrative discretion during the process of planning permission, in reality arbitrary modification of the plan happens. There are reported corruption cases in Shenzhen as well other cities, where the control plan was modified for developers. The existence of corruption means that the plan does impose some constraints on development, since the developer tries to influence the plan through illegal means. On the other hand, the lack of political process in the preparation and implementation of the control plan means that the plan cannot resist pressure to alter it. The control plan is usually prepared over a short period and is required to cover the whole territory of the city. It is difficult to forecast future development, and thus there is no proper foundation for development intensity control. Sometimes planners find it difficult to face challenges from developers. It is common for the government to manipulate the control plan to generate land revenue and boost economic development. It is observed that

> Most cities could not properly implement the detailed development control plan; on the contrary, the practice remains as a merely technical activity, trying to regulate development intensity in the land market and cannot be regarded as real zoning. The plan could be arbitrarily modified without going through proper legislation processes, and even sometimes the plan was modified for a single project. (Zhang and Luo, 2013, p. 167)

Sun (2006) argued that the development control plan has become a means for the developer to achieve higher development intensity. For the planning institute, it may mean a chance to make extra profits. For the planning authority, the implementation of the plan is far from an easy task. However, the plan is still a major method for the planning authority to maintain some control over development. Recently, the city of Wuxi attempted to add some indexes of carbon emission control in the planning of its new low-carbon eco-town (see Chapter 6). This is an interesting combination of the detailed development control plan and the low-carbon plan.

Planning and design contests

The process of plan-making in the pre-reform period was an internal government task assigned to a planning institute. As there was a tradition of close association between universities and the government, some planning schools might have been involved in advisory support but this involvement was not a large-scale commercial activity. There were virtually no international planning contests in pre-reform China. The process of plan-making reflected the fact that city planning was purely a government activity. Once the task assigned by the government had been received, the planning institute began to organize meetings with various 'stakeholders,' for example, various government departments and their subordinate enterprises or work-units. This sort of meeting was not treated as consultation or negotiation. Rather, the process of economic planning set the objective of growth. In planning-related meetings, the requirement and preference for location was listened to and incorporated in the city plan. In short, there was no need to organize consultation activities, because the centralized process of economic decision-making gave much certainty to city planning. Consequently, the planning process did not involve external consultancy outside the city in the planned economy.

In the 1990s, external consultancies were still sporadic, instructed only for major developments in large cities such as the Lujiazui Financial and Trade Zone of Pudong new district in Shanghai in 1990[13] and the Pearl River new town (CBD) in Guangzhou in 1993. Since the late 1990s, however, external consultancy has become the fashion. In major cities, planning and design contests began to involve international consultancy companies. For prominent and strategic projects, the involvement of international consultancy is now regarded as a necessary approach, and increasingly the participation of international firms in planning and design competitions has become a common practice. For example, the municipal government of Beijing invited eight international firms to participate in a planning competition for Beijing's new CBD in Chaoyang District.[14] The planning and design of mega urban projects such as the Beijing Olympic Area and the National Theater involved foreign consultancy companies. Planning consultancy tends to involve foreign companies, and has become popular in second and third tier cities too.

A planning and design competition attracts publicity. The local government is keen to use the design contest as a sensational approach to place promotion. In essence, the use of foreign consultancy reflects some important changes in the Chinese planning system. First, planning is no longer a purely technical activity—a blueprint to 'materialize' national economic plans. Contracting the plan to a prestigious consultancy firm or 'signature architects' is itself an indication that the government is active in the promotion of local development. The simplest approach is to organize a design contest, because it is at this scale that foreign consultancy has a clear advantage, as it does not require an understanding of the complicated institutional process. An assignment of the design of a mega urban project (equivalent to a key urban area) is easier for the government and foreign consultancy firms to manage. 'Master planning as design' thus becomes a popular means to enhance publicity and economic 'competitiveness'—although it has not been proved that this is effective. The major planning journal in China—the *City Planning Review*—published an editorial in 2001 criticizing how local government spent millions asking foreign firms to prepare urban plans, under the discourse of 'conforming to the international standard of good practice.'[15] However, since then the use of both foreign and domestic planning consultancies has escalated—and indeed forms a large consultancy market. So, instead of discouraging the use of foreign consultancies, the Urban Planning Society of China (UPSC) provides a professional service to organize events or help find a proper foreign firm. For example, UPSC organized the international consultancy in 2013 for the new Jiangbei District of Nanjing, in which experts associated with the International Society of City and Regional Planners (ISOCARP) participated. After more than 20 years' practice, major multinational consultancy firms have now become well established in China and have even localized their employees while being very active in the planning market.

Second, the wide spread of external consultancy is due to the limitation of training in the planning profession inside China. Domestic planners have been mainly trained in physical design, and planning practice has followed a much narrower mandate for the design profession compared with that in the West (Abramson, Leaf, and Tan, 2002). But recently, many Geography and Planning graduates have joined the profession. Some younger planners have studied at overseas planning schools and returned to China. Nevertheless, in the process of rapid economic development, the capacity of the domestic planning profession still faces some constraints, because developments may take a new form or use a new concept that is unfamiliar to local planners. With China's opening to the world, foreign investors now participate in the development of mega urban projects. The mayor or local leaders may negotiate directly with investors outside the planning sphere. This all requires a broadening of the scope of planning. Moreover, the planning profession itself is experiencing commodification, and the government planning institute has been converted to the status of an enterprise which has to consider profits rather than government funding (see the discussion about the case of the Nanjing Urban Planning and Design Institute). This has further stimulated the planning market.

Third, since planning has become a consultancy service, foreign firms have acquired good experience in the consultancy market. In the beginning, they may not have been familiar with the Chinese politics of governance and development. But learning has been very fast. Many foreign firms now understand very well the motivation of planning consultancy as place promotion, and quickly adapt their style to suit the aspirations of local political leaders.[16] In a way, their unfamiliarity with the local context may help them develop an even grander vision. In the same way Olds (2001) refers to global architectural firms as 'global intelligence corps' who introduce foreign concepts without paying full attention to local socioeconomic conditions, these consultancy firms are distant from local politics, and when facing competition in the consultancy market are very efficient in providing the service that will achieve the assigned task. Large foreign firms have a competitive edge, because they have an international reputation and deliver the product on time, in a professional way, which means that contracting to them is less risky for a government under a tight time framework. The local planning bureau in charge of these tasks is inclined to find a suitable and well experienced service provider. If a large consultancy firm were to fail, it would be beyond the control of the government official in charge, and hence the responsible official would have an excuse. One major contribution made by foreign consultancy firms is that they "help shape an appropriate commercial market for planning con- sultancies," as proudly boasted by a firm's general manager in China, because domestic firms face payment delay, while foreign firms insist on payment on schedule before the work can be conducted.

The practice of using external consultants and organizing design com- petitions has had an impact on the process of plan-making. First, the planning process has become more open than it was in the past. The participation of consultancy firms and design institutes introduces a source of non-local input, which may broaden the perspective of planning and development. Multiple scenarios are prepared and compared, which at least suggest some different possibilities, although the government maintains a strong directive towards the selection of development scenarios. The practice of using external consultants has led to the establishment of a planning market. Making the city plan a technical service has turned the government into the 'client' of planning firms and institutes. But the 'client' is not entirely rational in its development impetus[17]—influenced by its political economic context (land development as a driver for growth and revenue source) as well as the politics of urban governance (e.g. the short-term appointment of the mayor and Party leaders). When the influence of the external 'expert' is introduced, the simultaneous commodification of plan-making constrains its role, because there is competition among consultancy firms for planning services. Similarly, an expert member of the planning jury may not be re-appointed in future if their advice contradicts the government's preference, because serving as a jury member is also a type of paid consultancy service. The request for planning consultancy from the government has the effect of stratifying planners based on their reputation outside the administrative system. Consultancy work is assigned not only to major planning institutes but also to key planners who are known in the field. The individual key planner plays a critical role in securing consultancy work. The local government wants to use known consultants to add to the credibility of the planning program. Control over the appointment of experts gives the government leverage to obtain the desired outcome. The government may include experts nominated by their professional organizations in their planning advisory groups. Their presence adds credibility to urban policy or to proposed mega urban projects. Further, in the actual process of organizing consultancy, expert opinion is often used selectively. In short, the so-called 'expert advisory board' is now widely used in Chinese cities.[18]

Second, using external consultancy in planning has diversified the presentational form of plans and broadened the scope of planning services. The final product of planning is thus not limited to the blueprint of development. The government may require consultants to provide policy recommendations, implementation measures, and even development tactics. In fact, these actions might be required when the planning task is outsourced. The demand pushes the planning consultant to go beyond the role of 'physical planner' and become an advisor to the government. As a matter of fact, the renowned planning consultant often provides value-added services, which creates a reputation for good service. The demand for value-added services is very high. Zhao (2013) argued that planners should rethink their role and pay more attention to serving a self-interested government. For example, for the strategic plan of Guangzhou, the successful consultant provided various development strategies to outbid its competitors. For the development of Guangzhou university town, the advice included the use of public–private partnership and urged that the government only needed to consider planning the infrastructure, while the development committee (in charge of the development corporation) should manage the sharing of facilities among the universities that relocated into the town, and other services such as student halls should be contracted to companies. The consultant suggested that the development approach should be 'market-oriented, state-facilitated and university-managed.' It was also suggested that the government should acquire land nearby as soon as possible to capture the increase in land value so as to fund the project.[19] For the purpose of maximizing land income, it was recommended that the development should start from the area around the planned metro-station. The spatial strategic plan report of Hangzhou even advised the government of the need to transform the traditional 'laid back civic culture' into a new 'competitive city spirit' (Wu and Zhang, 2007). So the scope of planning has been significantly broadened to include governance, development strategies, and the operational mechanisms of planning projects.

Commodification of planning

The development of a planning market has stimulated the growth of planning consultancy firms in China. Near the campus of Tongji University, a cluster of architecture and planning firms as well as many printing and model-making companies has formed to serve these design and planning firms (Plate 3.2). The urban planning and design institute affiliated with Tongji University, as well as other planning institutes, became profitable businesses.[20]

Along with the development of planning consultancy market, some state planning institutes have been privatized. For example, the Nanjing Urban Planning and Design Institute was required to change its ownership from a state-owned institute to a private firm. However, the privatization of state planning institutes created an awkward situation for the government, because planning is closely associated with the government. When the planning institute was state owned, the operation used to be based on government budget allocation. The institute usually took the assigned work and there was no contract for individual planning work. This allowed planning work to be done swiftly without negotiating a contract or commercial considerations. The government feels this is more convenient for some types of work, especially when some work is less 'profitable' than others. Eventually, the government had to set up a separate institute, Nanjing Urban Planning and Research Center, a state-owned institute, in 2003,[21] to assist the government in planning procurement and completing the assigned task. Because of this complication, some cities stopped the privatization of their urban planning institutes. For those cities that have already privatized their planning institutes, a parallel new planning center has usually been set up to take over some functions of the planning institute. For example, in Guangzhou, the center is part of the planning bureau, which is responsible for public procurement.

The procedure of public procurement has also been formalized to avoid corruption. For projects over a certain threshold, a public tender is required.

Plate 3.2 The cluster of architectural design and planning firms and auxiliary printing shops near the campus of Tongji University. The commodification of planning has led to the proliferation of planning consultancy firms. Planning is now 'big' business through the procurement of local government.

However, the 'client'—the local government—can set some special requirements that limit the participation of other competitors, as it may prefer some firms that either have a close relationship or have worked with it in the past and have sometimes already conducted preliminary work. Universities have a long tradition of involvement in enterprise activities. These projects, known as 'horizontal projects', in contrast to the 'hierarchical projects' that are funded by research councils or foundations, serve to supplement the formal salary income of teaching staff. In the system of the Chinese Academy of Sciences, there is a deliberate policy to require researchers to take on consultancy work to fund part of their salaries, after the reduction of funding to these institutes. In fact, the operation of some institutes has become quite 'commercial' as staff are required to contribute to office rental, electricity bills, and other estate costs through their projects. The development of consultant functions in university-affiliated planning institutes provides a good opportunity for students to learn from live projects. On the other hand, sometimes students become part-time cheap labor and are distracted from their formal learning. This happens to such an extent that some students may call their supervisors the 'boss,' as they literally receive stipend from their supervisors, because formal scholarships are quite modest and sometimes insufficient to live on.

Because of severe competition to secure consultancy work, larger institutes with a track record have a competitive advantage. This is not only due to their credibility but also because of their ability to help the plan get approved by the relevant government. For example, the Chinese Academy of Urban Planning and Design (CAUPD) has a close relationship with MOHURD and thus may understand policy better and have a wider informal network with the government. Similarly, provincial planning institutes have an advantage through association with provincial governments. Interestingly, MOHURD operates a qualification list of planning institutes for statutory planning. Only qualified and graded institutes can prepare statutory plans. The procurement procedure sometimes specifies the minimum requirement for qualification, in addition to the accreditation system for individual planners. However, there have been some complaints that the qualification system is an administrative interference in the planning market and prevents other non-accredited institutes or organizations from participating in planning.[22] Because of this qualification control, there is a common practice of 'borrowing' qualifications, either through joining with those who have qualifications or paying a fee for a plan to be stamped with the official seal. Sometimes even an academic department outside the field of planning may use the name of the university to practice consultancy, because the university may be known for planning practice. Occasionally, two professors leading different studios in the same university may submit for the same tender without knowing there is another submission from the same university, creating rather an awkward situation.

Public participation and planning governance

Public participation in planning in China is different from other market economies. In the Western democratic political system, public participation is a method of ensuring planning legitimacy. An important development in the theory of public participation in planning is the advocacy of 'collaborative planning' by Healey (2006). This treats participation as more than just providing legitimacy for planning decisions, but rather as building a consensus for local planning. Inspired by 'communicative rationality,' public participation is used to achieve 'communicative democracy.' Public participation thus is not just a means but also an end for stakeholders to shape places. The shift from government to governance in the Western political system has brought about new spaces for public participation. But the dominance of the market in governance at the same time imposes a 'democratic deficit.'[23]

Regarding public participation in China, there are two misconceptions that need to be corrected. The first concerns the argument that there was no consultation under the 'authoritarian state.' Such a claim denies the complex politics or political processes in China, although the politics were manifest more within the government or as inter-governmental politics (e.g. central versus local) as consultation took place within the state regulatory system rather than between the state and society. This is because under the formal state system, work-units, as representatives of their employees, were involved through a more sector-based administrative hierarchy in the process of economic planning. So-called 'comprehensive coordination and balance' of economic planning was actually achieved through intensive negotiations between the central and local governments, and between different local governments. Increasingly, however, politics has moved out of the government, involving a wider range of actors.

The second claim is that more market-driven politics (marketization) counter the enclosed political process, opening an avenue for greater participation and eventually, democratic politics. This is only partially true and is too economically deterministic. Resource mobility does introduce diverse interests and greater inter-city competition but, on the other hand, competition leads to a shift towards emphasis on the business interest and treating participation as a cost towards 'competitiveness.' This may result in a coalition between the government and developers. Participation may become more procedural rather than substantial, because the planning process is constrained by resources and the stakeholders (interest groups) become dominant. As interests become diversified, the state cannot simply represent *the* interest of the people. Instead, a more procedural and formal process of public involvement is required to check and balance various conflicting interests in planning. In this respect there are many experiences in Western countries, in particular in the development control process, to be learned from.

Recent practices in China's urban planning have shown two trends. First, at the plan-making level, the planning system has been greatly opened up. In the past, city planning was merely a kind of internal government task assigned to local planning bureaus or planning and design institutes. However, with the increasing popularity of using star consultants and design competitions, plan-making processes have come to involve external expertise. The practice of 'expert consultation' has opened the planning process to professional organizations. Although the presence of experts is often used to add credibility to the proposed urban policy, such a quasi-participatory decision-making structure introduces greater scope for planning participation (Zhang 2002a). This is especially evident in non-statutory plans such as strategic development plans (also known as 'concept plans,' see Chapter 4). It is now almost the norm for the large strategic plan to involve at least two planning teams and a comparison of multiple planning scenarios.

At the development level, the tension in redevelopment decisions continues. Property-based interests such as homeowners' associations are under formation. Because of the absence of participation and opaque development control processes, the public is not informed about development decisions, and often blames the state for allowing developers to carry out such developments. The boundaries between the state and the market are blurred (as many development companies have government backing); some developers tactically pursue profits in the name of the public interest and often claim to act as state representatives. Therefore, if the redevelopment goes wrong, the public tends to blame the state for causing the problem. This is particularly evident in housing demolition and relocation. Conflict in the process of redevelopment has evolved to such an extent that the state has had to step in to control the pace of redevelopment so as to pacify social contests. But if there had been greater checks and balances in development control, forced demolition could have been avoided.

In short, in the socialist period, the general public did not directly participate in the process of planning. Their 'communities'—the state work-units and workplaces—represented their interests. After economic reform, the system of planning was reoriented towards pragmatism for economic growth rather than ideological correctness (Yeh and Wu, 1999). But public participation in planning has been weak. The Chinese planning system is still heavily dominated by the administrative system. However, local governments have begun to use various opportunities, such as expert meetings and plan exhibitions, to enhance the publicity of plans. Sometimes, specialized public relation companies are employed to organize various events and exhibitions. Public participation is treated as a method of place promotion (Wu, 2007). In this context, local governments' enthusiasm for pursuing planning awards, in particular from overseas organizations, is understandable. While the power of the public is still weak, there is an increasing awareness of environmental risk and growing 'not in my backyard' (nimbyism). In 2007, the city of Xiamen had to suspend the petrochemical PX project, which was planned to be near the urban area, because of public protest. The event had almost evolved into social unrest, which forced the local government to change its decision out of consideration for social stability. This event reflects the emerging civil society in China and its influence over urban planning.

In terms of planning governance, besides administration dominance, there have been some limited experiments with so-called 'urban planning boards.' Most cities use such boards as an expert consultation arrangement or publicity mechanism.[24] At most, some limited information dissemination and coordination effect may be achieved. The city of Shenzhen, however, experimented with a more executive role for the urban planning board, learning from the approach of Hong Kong. According to the Shenzhen Urban Planning Ordinance, a local piece of legislation, its urban planning board has the power to approve 'zoning' plans and urban designs of key areas. The practice of Shenzhen is an exception in China but even so, the municipal government still plays a critical role in plan implementation.

Conclusion

The profession of city planning, in the sense of the modernist and regulatory function of the state, was restored after China adopted economic reform. The enactment of the 1990 City Planning Act symbolizes the establishment of a comprehensive planning system. However, this system was set up before the arrival of the market economy. The mechanism of development control at that time gave city governments the power to coordinate development. This was essentially a planning permission system, similar to the administrative-based planning in the U.K. Despite some similarity, development control was not really designed to cope with market demand. The system did not stand up to the impact of marketization, initially from the establishment of the land market (the land boom in 1992) and the housing market ('commodification' in 1998), and later from global economic integration (joining the WTO in 2001). First, the urban system plan had virtually no influence over resource allocation during the period of economic devolution. Second, the detailed development control plan sounds plausible, because it tries to define the details of development indexes at the plot level. Fundamentally, the 'failure' of planning is not due to the design of the planning system but rather the problem of governance. Development control is centered on the politics of governance, but the system of planning has been maintained as 'scientific' and technical work. Planning, as part of government functions, simply could not resist the thrust of the entrepreneurial city. To become more entrepreneurial, non-statutory plans have been invented and funded by local governments. Non-functional development control, especially the failure to contain urban expansion, led to the establishment of 'agricultural land protection' by the land authority—a separate government department from planning—because conventional urban planning had been underdeveloped in rural areas and did not provide effective development control. In fact, in the peri-urban area where the powerful state confronts weak farmers, planning has never been a mechanism to balance the demand for growth and growth containment. When the central government tried to strengthen land administration, the function of development control of basic agricultural land was not placed under the city planning system but rather in the MLR established in 1998, with the enactment of the Land Administration Act in the same year. While MOHURD lost an essential component of development control, the new 'land development control' established under MLR is *not* spatial. That is, the state is concerned with the quantity rather than the actual location of arable land. Moreover, in 2003 and 2004, MLR under the central government strived to restrict informal land sales (e.g. through negotiation between the municipality and developer) and enhance the 'transparency' of the land market. Strangely, this effort actually formed the land-driven growth machine, because land development and the sale of development rights now became a major business for local governments. Not until 2008, ten years after the establishment of a separate line of land management (in a more vertically controlled way), was the Planning Act amended to cover rural areas. However, planning has now become more localized and growth-oriented. Driven by the local growth machine, planning plays a greater role in place promotion. As an instrument of entrepreneurial governance, the extension of planning coverage into rural areas does not lead to more stringent development control. Rather, the inclusion of rural areas gives an opportunity to a city government to manipulate the overall spatial pattern in its jurisdiction area, for example to carry out 'land swaps' between preserved arable land and the built-up land of villages. With planning, this is done in a more 'strategic way' to free up space for urban development. The locally funded 'spatial plan' (as a non-statutory plan) is generally growth-oriented.[25] After losing its strategic growth management function, the city planning system has reinvented itself, intentionally or inevitably, as a development instrument.

In short, the Chinese city planning system is essentially a permission-based, administrative-led system. At this point, it is interesting to compare it with the system in the U.K. In the U.K, the 1947 Town and Country Planning Act nationalized development rights and established the postwar planning machine (Hall and Tewdwr-Jones, 2011). The planning system could therefore require the developer to contribute 'planning gain.' The system has been criticized for its non-transparency and administrative discretion. The essential feature of planning processes is to use planning gain for the public good. The question is: where is the 'planning gain' in China? The answer is that the planning gain in China is deposited in the premium of land that is sold in the land market by the government. The profit from land sales contributes to local government revenue. The system of tax-sharing highly incentivizes local governments. They are very entrepreneurial, but they are not 'trustable' from the perspective of the central government. The central government wanted to make land sales more regulated. Before the mid-2000s, 'planning gain' through direct negotiation between the city government and developers had been quite opaque. MLR strived to set up a more transparent land market. With the establishment of the land market through competitive auction, the growth machine developed. With the absence of the local community as a stakeholder in the development process, the planning process, driven by the growth machine, aims to maximize land revenue. But this form of 'planning gain' exists in monetary form and often constitutes part of the capital circuit in land development. Revenue is often re-invested in new development projects for land appreciation, fuelling the growth machine. Planning gain, therefore, is used for profitable purposes. The 'community' is less interested in planning gain, because the gain is unseen by them. This being the case, Chinese planning does not set obstacles for development and thus is not the 'enemy of growth,' as it has been criticized for being in the neoliberal discourse of the West.

Notes

1 See Song (2012) for a brief introduction to the institutional aspect of planning.
2 The former is defined by the Planning Act and the latter is defined by the Land Administration Act.
3 The Chinese name is: Beijing *shi guihua zhanlanguan*. The meaning of *shi* is 'city' or 'urban.' But the meaning here is not Beijing *Urban* Planning Exhibition Hall, but, rather, the planning exhibition hall of the city of Beijing.
4 Personal communication on a field visit to the Beijing Urban Planning and Design Institute, April 2014.
5 In the city, the land is owned by the state; and in the rural areas, farmers collectively own the land. So the change of users in the developed state land was difficult because of the absence of a land market; in the case of land acquisition of rural land, usually the project negotiated with famers to reach a deal and got approval from the government as if the land were 'administratively allocated.' There was land compensation but it was quite modest. This is the so-called 'project-based' development approach; see Yeh and Wu (1996). This approach, before the enactment of the Planning Act, sidelined the planning process. In other words, land development in a planned economy was in fact quite 'spontaneous' and discretionary.
6 But increasingly the government has to prepare a detailed regulatory plan (or 'detailed development control plan') in order to provide information about the condition of the land and specify the type and intensity of development allowed so that the developer can calculate the land value of tender.
7 The decision-making process has been improved; for example, the invention of so-called 'detailed development control plan' requires the formal process of its approval and adjustment in cities such as Shenzhen and Guangzhou.
8 See Wu, Xu, and Yeh (2007) for further details and Ng and Xu (2000) for an example of the failure to protect the green space in a park.
9 Designated towns are the towns designated with urban status, usually the seats of township government, which is different from rural market towns.
10 See Yeh and Wu (1999, pp. 183–184) for a detailed explanation.
11 This was in fact introduced into China in the era of Republican China but became formalized in the 1950s (Lu, 2006).
12 For details of the experiments, see Yeh and Wu (1999).
13 See Olds (2001) and Wu (2000) for place promotion.
14 These firms included Skidmore, Owings & Merrill Ltd., Johnson Fain Partners and NBBJ from the U.S., Kuiper Compagnons from Holland, Von Gerkan, Marg und Partner Architects (GMP) from Germany, the Urban Environmental Institute of Japan, and other domestic planning institutes. The MVA group, an international consultancy firm, carried out the Beijing CBD transport planning study.
15 The editorial was published in *City Planning Review* 25(3): 1.
16 This was revealed by a general manager of a major foreign planning consultancy firm, November 2013.
17 The director of the planning bureau of Xiamen, Mr. Zhao Yanjing, describes this irrationality of the local government from his many years of experience in planning consultancies and now as a senior government official, see Zhao (2013).

18   Zhang (2002a) described the expert team in Shanghai. Many local and overseas academics may serve various expert teams of the planning project or even act as advisors to the mayor.

19   See Chapter 4 for the operation of land development and its mechanism as a planning-directed growth machine.

20   The revenue of typical planning institutes ranges from 800,000 yuan per planner to 1.2 million yuan per planner.

21   Ye and Zhao (2013) described the role of the center as the fourth force together with administration, academia, and the planning institute.

22   This was debated in Chinese *weibo* (Twitter) and summarized in a paper presented at the annual conference of UPSC in 2013; see Tang (2013).

23   See Raco, Parker, and Doak (2006) for the change in the British planning system. See Gunder (2010) for a general critique of planning under neoliberal ideology.

24   Zhang and Luo (2013) described three types of planning board: executive, coordinative, and consultative. In reality, however, even for the executive type, the planning board is still heavily influenced by the administrative system.

25   Although this does not mean it has to be 'expansionist'; for example, in the strategic plan of Shenzhen 2030, the plan does not pursue urban expansion for the goal of competitiveness, because in fact the problem is the opposite: Shenzhen has very limited land remaining for growth and needs to seek a different approach.

4
Planning Under Urban Entrepreneurialism

In the Western market economy, the turn to urban entrepreneurialism has had a severe impact on the planning system. U.K. planning experienced streamlining and became more project-led rather than using a form of comprehensive land use regulation. The later development of 'spatial plans' shows a fuzzy boundary in post-political planning (Allmendinger and Haughton, 2012). In China, planning thrived, rather than diminished, under urban entrepreneurialism (Wu, 2007). This chapter first explains the unique institutional set-up that has turned the city into a growth machine in China, then certain planning practices that help enhance the position of the entrepreneurial city are discussed. This chapter also explains how urban entrepreneurialism became hegemonic in so-called 'socialist countryside planning.' Finally, the emergence of the non-statutory conceptual plan or 'strategic plan' is reviewed. The chapter concludes that planning under urban entrepreneurialism is in essence expansionist, and has been captured by the growth machine. But, interestingly, the development of this kind of planning has to be understood within the complex interface between the state and the market. Ironically, planning practices under the impact of market transition are not aimed at the market but rather at the regulatory state. The grand plan is used more to convince the central government of the need for developmental space than to convince investors, because the latter are mainly attracted by development opportunities and the favorable conditions created by strategic policies.

The making of the Chinese land-driven growth machine

The Chinese 'growth machine'[1] has been built upon the mechanism of the land market and the decentralized tax-sharing system. For the turn of Chinese local governance towards entrepreneurialism (Wu, 2003a), there are two different but not necessarily mutually exclusive explanations. First, the official evaluation system that emphasizes the performance of the local economy drives officials to pursue GDP growth rates. Local leaders, although they are public officials, become virtual CEOs of 'urban development corporations' (Chien, 2008). Second, the pressure on local public finance drives the government to initiate mega urban development projects to gain land revenue to fill the gap between budgetary fiscal income and expenditure. Since 1994, China has operated a tax-sharing system (*feng shui zhi*), in which the central and local governments have separate tax sources. The policy was designed originally to cope with the decline in tax share; the central government set up its own tax base, leaving land income to the local government. At the same time, with economic devolution, the central government managed to download social and public service expenditure to the local government. This policy created a fiscal deficit for the local government. Fiscal reform in the 1990s effectively raised the ratio of government revenue to GDP and the proportion of central government revenue to total revenue. The local government only keeps 25 percent of value added tax but is able to keep all extra-budgetary revenue and land revenue from 'selling' state land. The fiscal system has profoundly changed the behavior of local government, which now pays more attention to land development because land revenue has become an important source of local revenue (Tao et al., 2010). The fiscal change has led to the increasing role of local government in spatial development during political and economic decentralization.[2]

Another feature of the land-driven growth machine is the willingness to release industrial land at a lower price, even a zero price. The explanation is that while the local government does not get the full higher land value, the development of industry will expand the local economy, and the local government will then receive value-added tax and corporate tax from the development. This effectively converts once-for-all land income into a long-term source of revenue (Tao et al., 2010). However, this is not the ultimate gain from promoting industrial land development, because the local government can only retain 25 percent of value-added tax under the current system. The aim is to use industrial development to stimulate the local economy as a whole, and use the 'spill-over effect' to increase demand for housing and for commercial and retail space. The local government can retain the retail sales tax and the profit from land development. Inflated residential and commercial land values can expand local revenue through raising land values in the primary land market, where the local government is a monopolistic supplier. The Land Administration Act gives compulsory purchase power to the local government, which can buy land from farmers at a low price and then sell it at a higher market price.[3] The price gap is an important source of revenue, and lays down the foundation of the entrepreneurial city.

Under this institutional arrangement, land becomes the major asset under the control of local government. Existing land users (e.g. farmers) cannot convert their land from agricultural and residential uses into commercial or residential uses in marketable form (e.g. 'commodity housing' or private rentals). Planning helps to strengthen the power of the local government in maintaining its monopolistic position, because without going through an initial land sale to the local government, the developer cannot obtain the deeds of the land. Some villagers informally developed their properties and sold them illegally on the market, which is not recognized by the state. This special type of property is known as partial property right housing (*xiao chan quan fang*).[4]

The formation of the local growth machine aimed at attracting not only foreign investment but also domestic capital from other regions. Aggressive plans for a development project can lead to an influx of capital from other places to the city, inflating land and property values, which in turn attracts more investment. To effectively mobilize investment, the local government sets up various 'local financing and investment platforms' (*difang rongzi he touzi pingtai*), because it is not allowed to borrow money directly from the market based on public finance. These investment platforms are state-owned enterprises backed by the local government, or more precisely guaranteed by local government credit. The urban construction and investment corporation (in essence the land corporation) and the land banking center are the usual investment platforms. In order to secure loans, the investment platform needs to possess some assets as collateral. Thus, land development corporations and land banking centers are the most effective platforms because they own the land. The development corporation borrows money from the bank, develops the infrastructure, and converts the land into serviced land, which is for sale. Pioneered in the development of the new district of Pudong in Shanghai, this model is known as 'virtual capital circulation' (*ziben kongzhuan*), which means the land corporation had no initial capital but used undeveloped land as collateral to draw capital from the banks. After land development, the profit is used to pay back the loan, or to roll over loans for the next phase of development. When the loan is paid back, the capital circulation is complete. The development of land operates in the following stages:[5] 1) the development corporation uses cheap and subsidized land to attract investment in manufacturing industries; 2) it expands the overall GDP volume and in turn raises the land values of the city through industrial development; 3) the government leases the serviced land to commercial and residential markets to capture the differential rent between rural land and serviced land; 4) the government uses the land revenue to invest in infrastructure while covering the fiscal deficit because the expenditure exceeds the revenue; and 5) the government acquires rural land through compulsory purchase at a lower value and converts the required rural land into serviced land so as to raise the land value, which leads to a premium price for commercial and residential development. This is a form of 'financial innovation' similar to the 'securitization of subprime mortgages.'[6] Local government debt is thus a potential risk because the land development corporations are backed by the credit of the local governments, and the liability of commercial land development is thus transferred to the government. It is estimated that total local government debt could be as high as 20,000 billion yuan.[7] Fluctuation in property markets could jeopardize local public finances.

The heavy reliance on land development for public finance in China is known as the 'land-driven fiscal regime' (*tudi caizheng*). The regime has attracted wide criticism because it leads to overbuilding, social inequality, and financial risk. This regime can be seen as a Chinese form of urban entrepreneurialism. What are its distinctive features? Here, the entrepreneurial city is not an entirely autonomous agent, subject to the control of the upper level government through the personnel appointment system and the allocation of land quotas. The role of the state is a salient feature.[8] There are complex dynamics between central and local governments. For example, the central government tries to use various planning methods to intervene in local development (see Chapter 5). On the other hand, local governments prepare various plans for central approval. These plans often aim to defend the local government and create more development space for the city. In the next section, planning practices under entrepreneurialism will be examined.

An exemplar of entrepreneurial city planning: Kunshan's strategic plan and master plan

The entrepreneurial city and inter-city competition

Kunshan is located on the lower reaches of the Yangtze River Delta, on the edge of Shanghai. Travel by inter-city train from Shanghai to Kunshan only takes 20 minutes (Plate 4.1). However, they are separated by a provincial-level administrative boundary between Jiangsu province and Shanghai municipality, which is under the direct jurisdiction of the central government. The administrative rank of Kunshan is very low. It is a county-level city under the municipality of Suzhou. However, its low administrative rank gave Kunshan great freedom to adopt an entrepreneurial approach to governance, and to a lesser extent its governance has been affected by top-down policies. A rural county for many years, Kunshan gained the status of city in 1989.[9] Subsequently, the objective of Kunshan was to transform this rural county into an industrial district through a strategy of export-oriented growth. The development of Kunshan was locally initiated, following a bottom-up process of urbanization.[10] Located in southern Jiangsu, characterized by collective rural economies, and known for its 'sunan model' of rural industrialization and urbanization from below, Kunshan had not really been at the core of rural industrialization for many years. It lagged behind and was ranked last among six county-level cities in Suzhou, and hence was known as the 'little sixth.' After the collapse

Plate 4.1 The high-speed railway station at Kunshan.

of the rural township and village enterprises in the 1990s, the Yangtze River Delta began to experience mass privatization and turned to foreign investment. Because of its proximity to Shanghai and available high-quality land, Kunshan began to capture opportunities for industrial development in the 1990s.

Kunshan started industrialization by absorbing relocated industries that could not enter Shanghai. Factories developed in the 1960s and 1970s in the interior region of China (the so-called 'third front' during the Cold War) wished to relocate back to Shanghai, but because of tight controls they could not enter the municipality. Instead they settled in Kunshan. But the main thrust of growth came from investment from overseas, especially Taiwan, in labor-intensive manufacturing industries.

The advantage of Kunshan is that it is located near Shanghai but with much lower land costs and more flexible governance. Control is more lax because Kunshan is an administrative unit within Jiangsu Province rather than Shanghai, and has a low administrative rank. Its entrepreneurial governance is exemplified by its self-funding of a development zone without the approval of upper tiers of government.[11] That is, Kunshan's development zone was initially 'illegal.' However, later on the development zone had great success and was eventually recognized by the central government. In 1992, the Kunshan Development Zone was granted the status of a national-level economic and technological development zone. Industrial development in

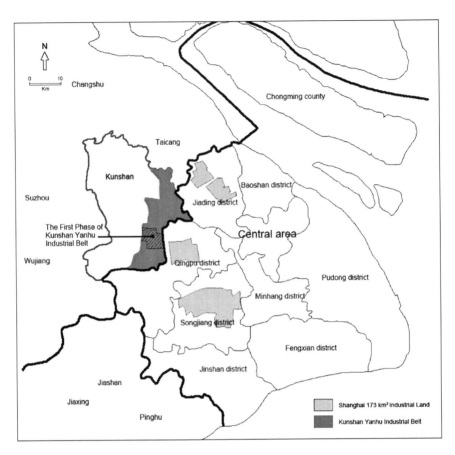

Figure 4.1 The original plan for industrial development in Kunshan, near Shanghai. The figure shows that Kunshan and Shanghai designated industrial development zones to compete with each other.

Source: Li and Wu, 2012a

Kunshan triggered fierce competition between Kunshan and Shanghai (Figure 4.1). Kunshan's strategy was to use cheaper land to attract industrial projects, especially in ICT, and it began to outbid some suburban districts of Shanghai such as Jiading and Songjiang. In the 1990s, Shanghai faced economic restructuring and was having some difficulty in upgrading its industrial structure to a service-based one, and also wished to attract ICT industries. These high-end manufacturing industries were attractive to Shanghai. To counter the advantage of cheaper land in Kunshan, in 2003, Shanghai launched Project 173 along the border with Kunshan. The project designated an industrial area of 173 square kilometers to offer cheaper land to investors in the preferred manufacturing sectors. There was even a slogan allegedly saying '173 fighting Kunshan.'[12] Nevertheless, competition between Kunshan and Shanghai escalated when Jiangsu province announced Project 1730—with an area of 1,730 square kilometers—for the same purpose.[13]

The turning point towards sprawl: Kunshan Master Plan (2002–2020)

In 2002, Kunshan commissioned two consultancy companies[14] to prepare conceptual master plan research. Confronting the danger of widespread and uncoordinated industrial development in Kunshan, the study proposed a novel concept, *pianqu*, possibly best translated as 'functional zone,' for the overall structure of Kunshan (Figure 4.2). The intention was to assign different functions to various jurisdiction areas within Kunshan. For example, in the north, the Yangchenghu Lake recreational and leisure zone was proposed, and in the east, the zone of a 'transport corridor' was recommended. The proposal, however, was more for functional differentiation within the municipality so as to concentrate industrial development in particular areas. It is alleged that the master plan of Kunshan (2002–2020) 'adopted' this functional zone proposal and divided the whole jurisdiction area into seven zones. But in reality, the master plan made critical modifications that overturned the rationale of functional differentiation. For example, the plan changed the function zone of a new town along Wusongjiang River to Wusongjiang industrial area, leading to the expansion of industrial land uses to the south of the core urban area. In reality, industrial development has grown out of control and is scattered over Kunshan. The master plan decided that 'the whole territory of Kunshan should be treated as a single city' (*shiyu ji chengshi*) and applied the approach of urban land use planning to the vast area of 927 square kilometers (Kunshan Planning Bureau, 2010). This was most problematic. That is, the plan literally treated a county that is equivalent in size to Singapore as a single city to distribute land uses over this space, under so-called 'coverage of planning to the whole area' (*guihua quan fugai*). Before the extension of planning coverage, an urban system plan would be prepared for the jurisdiction area of the county, treating the central city plus towns and rural settlements as a hierarchical system rather than as urban districts. Ironically, so-called coverage of planning to the whole area was intended to impose better land use control in rural areas, which had been outside the scope of conventional urban planning until the 2008 Planning Act. However, under the expansionist plan, the extension of coverage actually justified land development in otherwise impossible places. The master plan in essence treated various towns as urban districts, when they were in fact rural areas at that time.

For the core urban area, Kunshan consists of two administrative bodies, Yushanzhen town where the city government is located and Kunshan ETDZ. Interestingly, the planning bureaus of Kunshan and Kunshan ETDZ are of the

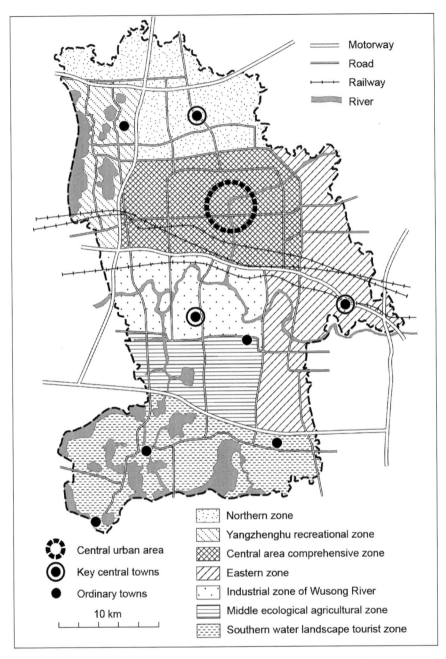

Figure 4.2 The concept of *pianqu* ('functional zones') adopted in the Kunshan Master
Plan (2002–2020). The structure in fact led to a wide sprawl of industrial land
uses in the whole territory of Kunshan, because the plan treats the whole
territory as the built-up area of a single city.

Source: Kunshan Planning Bureau, 2010

same administrative rank, which means there is no supervisory relationship between them. The conceptual master plan study proposed the concentration of industrial development in Kunshan ETDZ, while the central business and retail functions were to be concentrated in the central area of Kunshan. This was, however, not realized. In reality, separate government bodies under entrepreneurial governance (as an extreme version of localism)[15] wished to develop their own areas. The master plan made another critical modification: for the central area it proposed to develop 'one main city center and two subcenters' or so-called 'one center plus two wings' (*yiti liangyi*), which means the development of the central area. The central area includes a vast region from Yushanzhen (the town where the old Kunshan city proper was located) to Kunshan ETDZ, which spans 15 to 20 kilometers. Kunshan ETDZ also aimed to develop its own CBD as a subcenter. The proposal for a polycentric structure effectively meant the lack of a central area. The whole of Kunshan is like a gigantic factory zone rather than an integrated city.

In addition to *pianqu* (functional zones) applied to the county jurisdiction area and polycentric urban centers applied to the core urban area, the competition between Shanghai and Kunshan led to the designation of 'an industrial belt that encircles Shanghai' in 2003. This further promoted the dispersal of industrial development. In 2005, the Huaqiao Business Park was established at the nearest location to Shanghai, marking another turning point of development away from Kunshan proper and Kunshan ETDZ. In the subsequent master plan (2009–2030), Kunshan city proper (which had now become Kunshan High-Tech Development Zone), Kunshan ETDZ, and Huaqiao Business Park are treated as the gigantic urban core of Kunshan.

Dispersed urban form and governance fragmentation

Why has Kunshan seen such a dispersed pattern of land development? Besides the widely known reason that the government wished to use cheaper land to attract investment, there are specific reasons related to urban entrepreneurial governance and its planning regime. First, the conversion of agricultural land to industrial uses and the development of industrial areas are tactically deployed to compete with other cities. To counter the Shanghai's 173 Project and to benefit from the spillover effect of Shanghai, Kunshan, with the support of the provincial government, initiated the development of an industrial belt encircling the borders of Shanghai. The designation of the industrial belt changed the status of Qiandeng—an ancient tourist town that was under preservation. Industrial development was directed beyond the main urban area of Kunshan and Kunshan ETDZ.[16] This strategy has led to the wide spread of industrial land uses.

Second, the dispersed pattern of land development is related to fragmented governance. Despite the overarching city government of Kunshan, there are several government bodies in the territory. The city of Kunshan is located in the old county seat. Kunshan ETDZ is a relatively independent and powerful development zone that is responsible for its own planning and development. In addition, Huaqiao Business Park is another quasi-independent administration unit which has the status of a development zone. It absorbed the former town of Huaqiao and is considering "annexing" the town of Lujia. In short, various designated towns under the city of Kunshan have power to organize their land development. That is, despite being a county-level city, Kunshan acts like a municipality, under which there are ten town-level governments plus Kunshan ETDZ, which is listed separately in government statistics. This governance structure greatly mobilized lower level governments, but the city of Kunshan has to give development space to each of the designated towns, because under land-driven industrialization, each government needs to develop industrial areas to promote its economy and sustain public finance. In other words, if the city government concentrated industrial development in one or two towns, other towns would experience stress on their public finances, because land development is essentially a way to subsidize public finances and maintain fiscal balance. Even historical tourist towns have to develop their own industrial areas. Tourism alone does not generate sufficient income.[17] This growth incentive plus the 'strategic' consideration of inter-city competition has led to a scattered pattern of growth, as every town government wants its own space for development.

Third, to make the dispersed pattern of land development even worse, urban planning usually tries to fill the gap between the clusters of development under so-called 'inter-city integration.' The grand plan of a vast area between Zhengzhou and Kaifeng to merge these two cities is such an example (see the case in the next section). The objective sounds plausible, that is, to integrate different areas or even two cities. But the result is always the same—significant urban expansion. For example, there are integration plans for the two adjacent cities of Guangzhou and Foshan, for Xi'an and Xianyang, as well as for Zhengzhou and Kaifeng, which are separated by a vast rural area (see the case of the Zheng-Bian Strategic Plan in this chapter). In the case of the city of Zhenjiang, after it absorbed the county of Dantu as its new urban district, there were two built-up areas. The new district of Dantu is still largely separate from the old city center. However, the current round of master planning not only ambitiously tries to integrate these two areas but also plans to fill the gap between the main urban area and another county-level city under its jurisdiction, Danyang, by proposing a new eco-town between them (for the development of new towns in general, see Chapter 6). In short, just like planning in Chinese cities, the master plan in Kunshan has facilitated the significant expansion of urban areas.

Compromise between the thrust of expansion and development constraints: Kunshan Master Plan (2009–2030)

In early 2008, Kunshan launched a study of urban strategic vision, which led to the preparation of the Kunshan Strategic Plan by CAUPD Shenzhen Institute, because Kunshan wished to learn from the 'pioneering' city of Shenzhen. The preparation of a strategic plan was intended to introduce new concepts and widen perspectives. It is not a necessary step for a master plan, although in practice many cities prefer to use this approach to reflect local vision beyond the more restrictive master plan approach (see later in this chapter for the emergence of strategic plans). Immediately following the strategic plan, Kunshan commissioned the Jiangsu and Shanghai Institutes of Urban Planning and Design to jointly prepare the urban master plan. The Jiangsu Institute of Urban Planning and Design took the lead. The Shanghai Institute of Planning and Design had prepared the earlier master plan and was familiar with the local situation in southern Jiangsu. As for Jiangsu, it understands the policy of the provincial government and is close to the Department of Construction of the provincial government that approved the master plan. Both are very strong planning institutes in China.

The new master plan (2009–2030) recognizes the problem of uncoordinated development and aims to provide an overall development framework for the whole jurisdiction of Kunshan, rather than leaving individual town governments to organize land development. In the two decades after 1990, Kunshan experienced frenetic land development. In 2009, the built-up area of Kunshan reached around 400 square kilometers, accounting for almost half its territory of 927 square kilometers.[18] Rapid urban expansion caused the loss of agricultural land and a scattered spatial pattern of development, with industrial land uses spread all over small towns and various development zones set up by town governments. Some historical towns such as Qiandeng, Zhouzhuang, and Jinxi, known for their southern Jiangsu water landscapes, have been encroached upon by industrial developments.

Kunshan now faces constraints on future development. Under the protection of basic agricultural land, 280 square kilometers of agricultural land are reserved for protection. The development of basic agricultural land is forbidden. Water covers another 176 square kilometers of Kunshan, as the area is rich in water landscapes. There are only 129 square kilometers of developable land remaining in Kunshan. At the current pace of development, this will only meet the need for five or six years. The lack of land resources has thus become a serious constraint, forcing Kunshan to transform its development approach. Kunshan wanted to use the preparation of a new master plan to consolidate its growth pattern. However, it faced a dilemma: it wished to grow but lacked the land for massive expansion; it wished to control the speed of land development but did not want to suffocate development opportunities. The result of the master plan is a compromise between an expansionist thrust and development constraints. The master plan in the end adopts an ambiguous position. On the one hand, it requires more efficient use of land and sets a compulsory requirement for minimum investment intensity for land. On the other hand, it does not impose constraints on development, reflected in the designation of a vast urban area (see the spatial structure).

The master plan adopts a hybrid approach between a land use plan and a spatial plan. It sets up three major zones for the spatial structure of Kunshan, similar to the so-called 'main functional area plan' (see Chapter 5). In terms of implementation, the plan tries to relate the performance of officials to functional zones. Officials used to be mainly evaluated on their achievement of GDP growth rates. Now, for town governments within the designated zones of recreation and tourism, their performance emphasizes environmental protection and greening above the rate of GDP growth. The new master plan even proposes a set of key performance indicators, including the ratio of research and development expenditure to GDP, unemployment rate, energy consumption, and the coverage of green space and forest area. It is not clear how these indicators could be enforced through planning management. But the formulation index indicates the desire for regulatory control. Moreover, the master plan experimented with public participation. Interestingly, this was organized by a consultancy firm that specializes in organizing public affairs and events. The preparation of the master plan tried to reach the public and collected some feedback, but the extent to which these opinions can affect power negotiations and the interest of stakeholders is limited. Nevertheless, because of these novelties, the master plan received the national prize for the best urban and rural plan in China in 2009 and further received the ISOCARP prize of the year in 2011.

The new master plan adopts a quite pragmatic approach to urban expansion and is realistic about development control. The spatial structure of the metropolitan region is astonishingly straightforward (Figure 4.3). The whole municipal area is divided into three zones: the central urban area, a recreational and holiday resort area, and a water landscape and historical town tourism area. The central urban area is formed by the central city, together with an economic and technological development zone, a new business satellite town, and industrial areas in the nearby town. The plan requires that new development is concentrated in the central area, because in this central area there are several railway stations, including three inter-city railway stations within the jurisdiction of Kunshan and a high-speed train station. This area is therefore a major transport corridor. Moreover, both Shanghai and Kunshan realized that their relationship necessitated not just competition but also collaboration. With negotiation between the provincial and Shanghai municipalities,

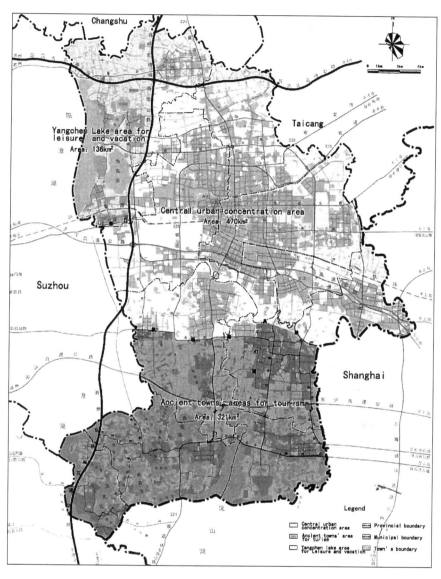

Figure 4.3 The spatial form of the Kunshan Master Plan. The spatial structure is surprisingly realistic about urban expansion. It designated the whole core area as a single urban area. However, traveling from the Huaqiao Business Park to the city proper of Kunshan by private automobile can take up to about one hour and involves crossing industrial and open spaces in between these urban centers, indicating this is less likely to be an integrated city.

Shanghai's No. 11 Metro Line was finally extended to connect with Huaqiao in Kunshan in 2013, closing the critical gap of 400 meters between the Huaqiao station and a cross-border station on the Shanghai side. Three metro stations have been set up within the territory of Kunshan.

The development in the central area is justified by 'transit-oriented development,' which surrounds the inter-city stations. The other two zones will be protected from land development. The plan seems to advocate a compact urban form. The whole central area thus becomes a gigantic city occupying 470 square kilometers. The gaps between the urbanized areas in this region will be filled so as to form a single built-up area. The boundary of this central urban area seems to designate a limit for metropolitan growth management.[19] However, in reality, developments have already occurred outside this gigantic urban area. Within the built-up area, there are mixed use areas. The areas outside this central urban area in the metropolitan region are obvious places to preserve. To the north, near the lake of Yangchenghu, a recreation area of 136 square kilometers is planned; and to the south, a water landscape and historical town tourism zone, accounting for 321 square kilometers, is designated. The plan recognizes the reality of fast urban expansion. Basically, leaving aside the requirements for basic agricultural land and a tourist zone, the plan maximizes space for urban development. Despite an essentially expansionist master plan, the plan is presented as a transit-oriented development[20] and an application of eco-cities. The presentation of the former deputy director of the Department of Construction of Jiangsu province is entitled 'Low-carbon Kunshan: towards a sustainable future' (Zhang Q., 2010). According to Chinese planning standards, the population in this central area should be around 4.7 million so as to fill the vast area of 470 square kilometers.[21] The Jiangsu provincial government approved the master plan for a population of 2.7 million in 2030. However, the plan does designate zones to protect the area near the lake and ancient town and water landscape areas. This is a compromise between compact urban development discourse and urban expansion reality.

The territory of Kunshan is almost equivalent to the size of Singapore. Kunshan is very keen to learn about new town development from Singapore and about the quality of urban development. However, as can be seen from the above spatial strategy, Kunshan has adopted an expansionist approach. The boundary of the designated 'central urban area' does not contain land development. Outside this designated gigantic urban area there is a still fairly densely populated urbanized area, with many small towns and much rural industrial land. For example, the town of Qiandeng lies just outside the boundary of this 'central urban area' but has still seen significant industrial areas developed near the town. To the east, large parcels of industrial land uses were created. To the south, this area was initially a town-level jurisdiction, Zhangpu along the Wusong River; now it has been created as an industrial area within the central urban area. Despite some green space, Zhangpu has already been developed. Towards the east, Huaqiao, under the initiative of Jiangsu, is becoming a business satellite town of Shanghai (see Chapter 6). But even outside this central urban area, the town of Qingdeng had already been developed during the encircling Shanghai industrial belt initiative. Bacheng, a town on the lake of Yangchenghu, has been designated as a residential area.

Expansionist planning under entrepreneurialism: from Zhengdong to Zhengbian

Design-led master planning in Zhengdong new district

Zhengdong, literally the East of Zhengzhou, is a newly designated district. Although the Zhengzhou High-Tech Development Zone had been developed in the west of Zhengzhou, the new municipal government leader wished to develop a different strategy and decided to use the opportunity of the relocation of the military airport in the east of Zhengzhou to develop a new district. Zhengdong district was planned to be the new CBD. The development of Zhengdong added a dramatic 150 square kilometers to the existing 133 square kilometers of built-up area in Zhengzhou. That is, the new development strived to double the existing size of the urban area.

In 2001, a design competition was launched, and the well-known Japanese architect, Kisho Kurokawa, won first prize. Kurokawa is known for his idea of metabolism and symbiosis, and was critical of functional Western modernism but at the same time keen to use utopian vision and iconic form (Xue, Wang, and Tsai, 2013). The scheme for Zhengdong is a grand design, with a cluster of over 60 high-rises in two rows surrounding a CBD. The inner ring consists of residential buildings 80 meters in height and the outer row of 120-meter-high office buildings. An artificial lake is located in the center. Beside the lake is the Convention and Exhibition Center and a 280-meter-high hotel (Plate 4.2).

The plan for Zhengdong new district reflects a new feature of city planning in China. Covering an area of 150 square kilometers, larger than the city area, the new district is more than a collection of skyscrapers. The plan is 'master planned' by an architect, focusing on design and morphology. This is very different from the conventional master plan, which focuses on land uses and the relationship between functional areas. In a sense, this is a design-led 'master plan.' This approach was welcomed because of the pressure of rapid urban development and the need to create a visual effect through mega urban

Plate 4.2　The central area of Zhengdong New District. This is a Convention and Exhibition Center. The core area is beside an artificial lake, surrounded by a circular distribution of office towers.

projects. The physical forms presented by illustrations and models are good for drawing attention and particularly attractive to leaders who are in a fixed-term office and wish to achieve a record for their political careers.

Following the plan, Zhengdong has become a new district of Zhengzhou. The development of Zhengdong represents another feature of urban development in China—development through the 'mega urban project.' The mega urban project is financed through entrepreneurial land development. At the beginning of the development, the government lacked investment in infrastructure construction and had only 1.05 billion yuan as compensation for moving the old airport (Xue et al., 2013). A development corporation was set up to raise funds from the capital market. It did this in two ways. First, the development corporation leased the land along roads to developers, and in return developers constructed the roads for the development corporation (the government).[22] Second, the development corporation used the land as collateral and obtained loans directly from the bank (Hsing, 2010). After constructing the infrastructure, the government sold the land at a higher price and paid back the loans. Through these entrepreneurial land developments, the new district managed to invest 18 billion yuan and earned 12 billion yuan in five years of development (Xue et al., 2013, p. 229). Because this mechanism of entrepreneurial land development continues to draw capital from the banks to invest in land and relies on the income from land sales to pay back the loan, the land price was raised tenfold by the land-driven growth machine in Zhengdong between 2003 and 2010 (*ibid*).

The design of Zhengdong has received some criticism. For example, it is not easy for pedestrians to cross the fast lanes of the circular road system surrounding the center to enter the central area, and the commercial blocks inserted between the two residential rings are not ideal as a shopping environment. Other than that, the main criticism is directed towards the use of water landscapes. Although located near the Yellow River, Zhengzhou is not a place with rich water resources, and in fact has only one tenth of the national average. The Yellow River has severe constraints on water supply, and the regions along the river compete for water resources. Yet the master plan created a huge artificial lake excavated into an area of 6 square kilometers, surrounding the island of the CBD. The 'dragon lake' forms a water landscape but at a severe environmental cost. Xue et al. commented, "The strong iconic effect and shallow 'cultural meaning' were easily understood and appreciated by the decision-makers in contemporary China but their technological implications were rarely considered" and added that this is a "heroic plan with little respect of local context." (2013, p. 226)

The land-driven development relied on the acquisition of a massive amount of rural land. From 2003 to 2006, the city of Zhengzhou acquired a large amount of rural land for the construction of university campuses in Zhengdong new district. Despite the requirement from MLR in 2005 to stop 'illegal acquisition,' the local governments (Henan province and Zhengzhou city) continued to speed up land acquisition. From the above discussion on the funding mechanism it is clear that once started, the development of a mega project requires a supply of land to sustain the capital flow. Eventually, the central government (the State Council) decided to give the deputy provincial governor and the mayor of Zhengzhou the penalty of a 'serious caution.' The tightening of land quotas has constrained the expansion of the university campus area. During the inter-city and region competition, Henan province felt that it had insufficient land quotas, which hampered its attempt to attract large industrial investment. A mega urban project requires not only local entrepreneurialism but also support from the central government. Design-led planning played an important role in the land-driven growth machine. It facilitated land development and achieved its objective of creating an iconic environment. In the same political economic context, the development approach of Zhengzhou has not changed. In subsequent years, the city, with the support of the provincial government, proposed an even more ambitious plan: Zhengdong is a 150-square-kilometer new district, while

Zhengbian—the new area—is a 400-square-kilometer built-up 'composite city' in a vast area of more than 2,100 square kilometers between two cities. Essentially, the scale of development requires a strategic planning approach. More importantly, the grand vision must conform to national policy, following lessons learnt from earlier local entrepreneurialism. The theme of this national policy, especially under the initiative of MOHURD, is 'low carbon' cities.[23] The city therefore developed a new strategic plan and strived to be recognized by the central government. But by the nature of planning, the new strategic plan was still driven by entrepreneurial governance rather than being formulated as a top-down coordination plan, to which the next section will turn.

Inter-city integration under Zhengbian Strategic Plan

Zhengbian Strategic Plan is a spatial plan applied to the vast area between the city of Zhengzhou and the city of Kaifeng, an ancient capital known as *bian*. The famous Chinese painting in the Song dynasty—*Spring on the River*—depicts a prosperous capital at that time. The plan uses a master plan approach for a region that is much larger than an urban area. The Zhengbian New District covers an area of 2,127 square kilometers but is not a unified jurisdiction. That is, it is not itself a 'new district,' as the notion refers to a rather loosely governed area, consisting of Zhengdong new district and Kaifeng new district (Figure 4.4). As mentioned earlier, the ambitious Zhengdong new district has an area of 150 square kilometers. However, the strategic plan aspires to a grand vision to create a 'composite urban area' with a population of 5 million and a built-up area of 410 square kilometers by 2020. The meaning of this gigantic 'composite city' will be seen later from its spatial structure.

The development of Zhengbian New District is not just based on the entrepreneurial city but also driven by the provincial government. The development has become the No. 1 project of the Henan provincial government. Henan has long been a major developing region specializing in agricultural production. The provincial government strived to promote industrial development and urbanization but lacked an instrument. To cope with the external constraints (which deemed the province to be an agricultural area), the provincial government proposed the concept of 'urban clusters of central China' that were centered on the city of Zhengzhou.

In fact, before the preparation of the new Zhengbian Strategic District Plan, the provincial government considered coordination between the cities of Zhengzhou and Kaifeng in a Zhengbian Industrial Development Plan, which was published in 2007. The notion of the 'integration of Zhengzhou and Kaifeng' was raised to coordinate these local governments. In 2008, the

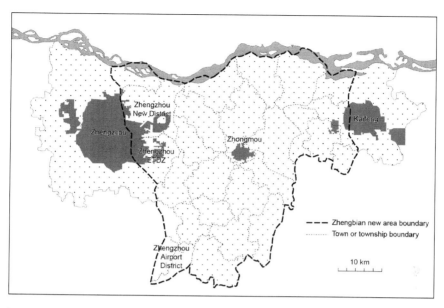

Figure 4.4 The vast rural area between Zhengzhou and Kaifeng is proposed to be set up as Zhengbian New District to integrate these two cities under the Zhengbian Strategic Plan.

provincial government set up the 'Zhengbian urban–rural reform and development experiment zone.' Further, in the new Zhengbian Strategic Plan, the scope was expanded to build a core area of 'the urban cluster of central China.' The strategic plan of Zhengbian New District facilitates the creation of a so-called 'central China economic region.' It centers on Henan province but spans nearby provinces including Hebei, Shandong, Shanxi, and Anhui. In 2010, the regional strategic plan of the central China economic region was completed and approved, and was recognized by the National Main Functional Area Plan in 2011(for this type of plan, see Chapter 5). Therefore, the preparation of the Zhengbian Strategic Plan goes beyond the issue of 'intercity integration' and is in fact an integral step towards building a regional growth pole.

In 2009, the Zhengzhou municipal government organized an international planning competition for the vast Zhengbian new area. However, there is no single administrative body for this area. Among the schemes prepared by six planning institutes and consultancy firms, the London-headquartered Arup, with the front work conducted by its China office, was chosen as the winner. The plan then received the International Society of City and Regional Planners (ISOCARP) Award for Excellence 2010. The Arup scheme, entitled 'Planning for low carbon urban system: the Zhengbian New District Plan,' was presented at the ISOCARP Congress in 2010. The case was reported to 'set up a series of spatial planning strategies based on: energy management, water resources, waste management, ecology, green transport, compact urban form, urban–rural coordinated development, ecological agriculture, as well as sustainable urban economic development.'[24] The plan is said to apply

> two innovative planning methodologies: the assessment of carrying capacity of the environmental system of the whole region to determine the limit of urban growth and population capacity and the setting up of a carbon dioxide emission audit framework based on land use planning parameters and decision rules for land use strategies, for the comparison and assessment of the impact of the planning options on greenhouse gas emission levels.[25]

The Arup proposal injected a concept of 'low carbon development,' an agenda that was being advocated by MOHURD at the time, into a grand development scheme. This is a more sophisticated method of place promotion, which defends the development of vast rural areas on the basis of ecological and low-carbon development. The strength of the Arup Plan is that it presents unprecedented technological details of the calculation of carbon emissions and ecological indexes, as it did successfully for Wuxi Taihu new town. Here the strategic plan uses a sound technical approach to deal with quite complex development politics. As can be seen in the earlier discussion, the demand for making such a strategic plan originated outside the sphere of technical rationality. It would be unfair to ask the consultant to fundamentally challenge the assignment of the 'client.' After all, many strategic plans are made on demand as a technical service under entrepreneurial governance. In this sense, despite the notion of a 'strategic plan,' the solution is often less than strategic.

The position of the plan can be better understood when it is situated in the specific political economic context, where local entrepreneurialism utilizes 'spatial plans' to pursue perceived local 'competitiveness.' Here, 'competitiveness' is only perceived, because there is no proof that an ambitious urban expansion plan contributes to its economic attractiveness to investors. However, it does eliminate regulatory constraints on developmental space. For example, in 2010, Zhengzhou managed to receive investment from Foxconn, a major contract manufacturer for Apple, to set up its massive iPhone production plant with a capacity of 200,000 employees.[26] However, the audience for the strategic plan was not only the investors but also, more importantly, the central government. The provincial government together with Zhengzhou municipal government tried many times to use spatial plans to convince the central government that the local economy would need space for development, and eventually managed to get the central China economic region recognized by the National Reform and Development Commission (NDRC)-dominated National Main Functional Area Plan. Although various plans have been resorted to and justified by technical rationality, the underlying expansion thrust was quite political.

The hegemony of urban entrepreneurialism in the new 'socialist countryside'

The urban–rural integration plan

The previous section examined an example of the inter-city integration plan. Since the mid-2000s, a new type of integration plan has been invented—the so-called 'urban–rural integration plan' which is not an independent plan outside the planning system. Rather, it has been created in response to the rhetoric of the 'new socialist countryside' by the leadership of Hu Jintao and Wen Jiabao (known as the Hu–Wen leadership). The intention was to reduce urban and rural inequalities by modernizing the countryside. The expansionist approach under urban entrepreneurialism in the 1990s and early 2000s led to the expropriation of rural land and the under-provision of public services in rural areas. The rhetoric was intended to reduce the urban–rural gap and encourage city governments to support the development of the countryside. Another unspoken economic reason is that China was facing surplus production capacity. Up to that time, exports had been the only way to absorb surplus capacity. The development of the countryside was thought of as a way to boost domestic consumption. For example, favorable policies were formulated to promote the use of household appliances such as refrigerators and washing machines in the countryside. Physical planning was thought of as a key instrument to deliver the urban–rural integration strategy (Qian and Wong, 2012). In the past, urban planning had focused on urban areas, while rural areas were largely left 'unplanned' except for land use planning which protects agricultural land. From the mid-2000s, city planning was extended to rural areas, and eventually the former 1990 City Planning Act was revised to include rural areas in the 2008 City and Countryside Planning Act. After its enactment, some cities began to prepare a specific urban–rural integration plan in addition to the conventional master plan. However, master plans prepared after the new planning act still did not fully include the countryside. That is, there was no specific countryside plan. The master plan considered the development of towns in rural areas as well as issues such as agricultural land protection and the preservation of ecological areas. Against this background, the urban–rural integration plan aims to extend the coverage of urban planning to the countryside.

It can be seen that the emergence of the urban–rural integration plan reflects multiple and even contradictory intentions. On the one hand, it emphasizes the need to modernize the countryside so as to 'balance urban and rural systems.' On the other hand, the central city continues to use this policy to 'assimilate' rural areas for urban development. The driver is 'land quotas.' Under the strict policy of farmland protection, the amount of farmland that could be converted to non-agricultural and built-up areas was subject to a development quota. The urban–rural integration plan is now an instrument to obtain development land quotas from the countryside. This is achieved through merging scattered rural villages and converting the land used for farmers' houses to agricultural land. The creation of agricultural land means that the city government is allowed to develop agricultural land elsewhere. In essence, land development quotas are created in the countryside and used for urban and industrial development. Therefore, these urban–rural integration plans are always characterized by the aggressive removal of rural villages and the resettlement of farmers. Qian and Wong (2012, p. 417) observed that

> the fiscal revenue of many cities has become over-dependent on the profits from land sales and the gains from using rural land played an important part. This, to some extent, perpetuated the rural land problems and in the longer term, it would endanger the exhaustion of basic farmland.

Demolition and relocation is particularly intense in the peri-urban areas (Wu et al., 2013).

To become an official strategy, the urban–rural integration plan is often part of the urban master plan. Just like other non-statutory plans such as the 'strategic plan,' these plans all serve the statutory plan in order to gain formal approval. An example is the master plan of Nanjing (2007–2020). Following the strategic plan (see later in this chapter) in 2000, which was absorbed into the revision of the master plan (1991–2010, revised in 2001),[27] the spatial structure of the municipality has been transformed from the compact urban area proper to one that consists of the central city and three new towns. The new master plan of Nanjing under the concept of 'urban–rural integration' continues to promote a polycentric urban structure on the basis of 'one central area, three new urban districts, many new cities, and new towns' (in contrast to rural settlements) and villages in the whole territory of Nanjing (Figure 4.5). Since 2001, when the master plan was revised, the built-up area of Nanjing has been expanding at an annual rate of 40 to 50 square kilometers (Qian and Wong, 2012). This is a significant figure, considering that the built-up area of Nanjing in 1982 was only 120 square kilometers. The strategy promotes the suburbanization of population and industries while in the suburbs, the concentrations of industries in industrial parks and places in three new districts

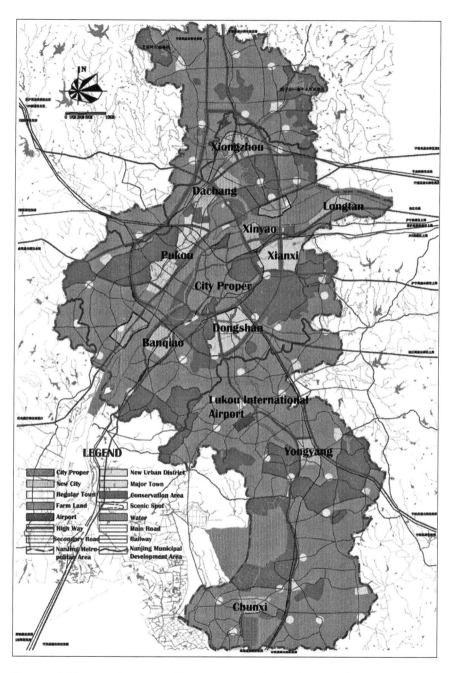

Figure 4.5 The spatial structure of Nanjing municipality under comprehensive urban and rural management. The plan extends the dominance of the city into the countryside.

Source: Qian, 2013

(Jiangbei, Dongshan, and Xianlin) act as suburban growth poles. In other words, in the suburbs the new master plan intends to consolidate industrial development and concentrate population in new towns and villages through 'government-led urbanization.' According to this vision, the former rural settlements (rural towns) in the countryside would become new towns to absorb rural industries and population. The implementation of rural–urban integration in many places reflects the continuation of urban entrepreneurialism in the countryside, and the use of physical planning, known as 'comprehensive urban and rural management' (*chengxiang tongchou*), as a tool to realize this transformation. Chinese planners hoped to introduce a scientific planning approach but were manipulated by the politics for growth (Wang, 2012).

Market-driven rural eco-tourism

Chinese rural areas have long been subject to a disadvantaged status. In the socialist period, rural areas were required to supply agricultural products through compulsory state purchase to support state-led industrialization. Following the

Plate 4.3 Improved village housing in Gaochun, near the city of Nanjing. Some houses have been converted into small hotels and hostels. The rural landscape has been improved to meet the demands of urban residents for eco-tourism and rural life experiences. The transformation is promoted by the local government as a way of promoting economic growth.

market transformation, the role of rural areas has been transformed to supplying land for urban expansion and urbanization. Along with increasing personal wealth, tourism has become a new area of consumption. Recently, eco-tourism in rural areas, as well as 'experiencing the life of rural areas' (*nongjiale*), has created new tourism markets.[28] Seeing the emergence of the rural and eco-tourism market, local governments began to facilitate the transformation of rural areas from living spaces to spaces of consumption. In addition to the commodification of rural, natural, and heritage resources,[29] the benevolent motivation is to improve social services and facilities in rural areas, as seen in Jiangsu's village improvement program (Wu and Zhou, 2013). For rural areas near large cities, the pressure for development is high, but because of the eco-tourism and rural tourism markets, the government may deliberately encourage the preservation of rural lifestyles. For example, about 80 kilometers from the city of Nanjing, Gaochun has preserved its landscape of a traditional rural town. Since it received endorsement as China's first slow town by the international *cittaslow*—a worldwide organization originating in Italy—planning policy has been very keen to renovate the rural town landscape, restore ancestral halls, add decorative furniture, and deliberately arrange performances of rural life such as girls dressed in traditional costumes picking up tea leaves. These arrangements target consumers from the city and transform rural areas[30] (Plate 4.3).

The emergence of the 'non-statutory plan': the 'strategic plan'

Earlier in this chapter, the Kunshan and Zhengbian Strategic Plans were reviewed. However, these plans are not listed in the Chinese statutory planning system, and the local governments funded them. Since 2001, China has seen the emergence of 'non-statutory plans,' or so-called 'conceptual plans.' In this section, the origins and implications of this phenomenon are examined.

The origins of non-statutory plans

The conceptual plan of Guangzhou was the first experiment with non-statutory plans in China. It was prepared in response to the challenges faced by the city. As the capital of Guangdong province and the gateway to southern China, Guangzhou is the central city connecting two urban corridors from Guangzhou and Shenzhen to Hong Kong and from Guangzhou and Zhuhai to Macau. Guangzhou had been an undisputed political and economic center. However, since economic reform, the economic development of the Pearl River Delta has been driven by foreign investment, and its economy has become export-oriented. The link with Hong Kong became a determinant of regional development. The pattern of urbanization has become more decentralized. Guangzhou faced competition from Shenzhen and other cities in the region. Seen from a wider geographical perspective, the Pearl River Delta as a whole also faced competition from the Yangtze River Delta. The growth of Guangzhou towards the heartland of the Pearl River Delta was augmented by another city, Panyu, which did not belong to the municipality of Guangzhou. In 2000, Guangzhou managed to annex the city of Panyu and turned it into one of its urban districts. At the same time, the city of Huadu in the north was converted into an urban district of Guangzhou.[31] The expansion significantly increased the jurisdiction area of Guangzhou and opened up access to the coast in the south and the mountains in the north. This change in jurisdiction boundaries required the development of a new spatial strategy. However, the preparation of a conventional master plan is very time-consuming. It was deemed too slow to suit the rapid pace of urban expansion. Thus, the city of Guangzhou began to explore a new planning approach, fairly similar to the style of the 'spatial plan.' However, at that time, few people were aware of the development of 'spatial plans' in Europe or the U.K.[32] The new planning approach was tentatively referred to as the 'conceptual plan,' suggesting that it should focus not on land uses but rather on formulating the 'concept' of metropolitan development.

In 2000, Guangzhou City Planning Bureau invited five planning and design institutes[33] to prepare the Guangzhou Urban Strategic Development Plan, which was also known as the 'conceptual plan.' In terms of content, format, and method, the Guangzhou government did not impose any specific requirements, because it was not defined by the planning system. The planning bureau suggested that this was not a master plan, but asked the planning teams to find a new planning approach that was suitable for the current situation of Guangzhou. After the five plans were submitted, the planning bureau organized an evaluation meeting with the participation of different government departments, the Chinese Communist Party, the municipal People's Congress, and the municipal Political Consultation Committee.[34] Then a team was set up to synthesize and reconcile the planning scenarios into the final Guangzhou Strategic Plan (Figure 4.6).

The plan focuses on a new spatial strategy, that is, a polycentric form of urban development. It directs urban expansion towards the east and the south along two major growth corridors. In particular, the southern growth corridor was proposed to shift the development of Guangzhou from the old city to new development clusters in the south, reflecting the opening up of growth space after the annexation of Panyu. The plan proposes a slogan for spatial development: 'containing the north, fine-tuning the west, shifting to the east, and expanding the south'; that is, the key strategy in the new urban areas included the following elements. The strategy requires the preservation of

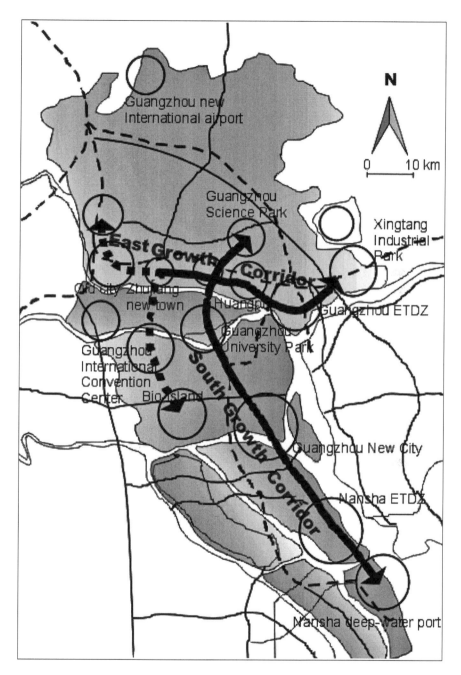

Figure 4.6 The spatial structure of the Guangzhou Urban Strategic Development Plan, which is also known as the 'conceptual plan of Guangzhou.'

Source: Wu, 2007

ecologically sensitive areas in the north, because this area is at the upper reaches of the water system. Only limited growth would be allowed, including a logistics hub near Beiyun international airport. The major direction of future growth is redirected towards the south along the planned metro line and the Guangzhou–Zhuhai highway. Along this growth corridor are several major development areas, including IT industrial parks, Guangzhou Science Park, an international convention centre, Guangzhou university town, Guangzhou new town, the Nansha Economic and Technological Development Zone, and a deep-water port in Nansha. Green belts are planned to prevent the built-up areas from merging into a gigantic contiguous area. The waterfront along the Pearl River would be converted from industrial and warehouse uses to residential and recreational uses. Besides the preserved mountainous area in the north, the plan emphasized access to waterfront areas. The vision is elegantly presented as the 'mountainous and water city,' often seen as a theme of Chinese poems and paintings. The conceptual plan of Guangzhou is an urban strategic plan. The objectives are very practical: for the municipal government to develop a strategic view of its enlarged territory. Unlike the other strategic plans that proliferated later in China, the plan did not pursue an ambitious spatial strategy so as to gain a title of 'strategic experimental zone' from the central government. In other words, the plan was largely prepared for the local government rather than for the approval of the central government in order to gain special policies and recognition. The conceptual plan opened up growth space for Guangzhou. Although it is a non-statutory plan, it contributed to the formation of the Guangzhou Master Plan (2003–2020), which was approved by the State Council in 2005. The preparation of the strategic plan helped overcome the usual limitation of the master plan, which overemphasized detailed land uses. The strategic plan divided Guangzhou into three major clusters: the central cluster, the Panyu cluster, and the Huadu cluster, and disaggregated the growth target at the municipal level into these three clusters helping to realize and reconcile long-term and short-term objectives.[35] The evaluation of the implementation of urban plans in Guangzhou suggests the limited role of planning in guiding market activities (Tian and Shen, 2011).

Another early experiment with strategic plans was in the city of Hangzhou located in the Yangtze River Delta (Wu and Zhang, 2007). The city had an opportunity similar to Guangzhou to expand its jurisdiction area. Hangzhou is known for its scenic landscape and cultural heritage. However, the city lacked development space because nearly half of the territory was used for tourism and preservation areas. The lack of space was a serious constraint on its economic growth. In 2001, the city of Hangzhou annexed two nearby counties, Xiaoshan and Yuhang, which opened up space for Hangzhou to expand towards the south and north. Like Guangzhou, the city swiftly organized the preparation of a conceptual plan. Three planning and design institutes[36] were asked to prepare their schemes, which were later synthesized into the Hangzhou Conceptual Plan. The plan proposed to develop a larger metropolis of Hangzhou together with the annexed counties. Further, the plan tried to relocate the central area from the old city center to the 'border area' between Hangzhou and Xiaoshan. The border area is along the Qiantangjiang River. Because the river is very wide, the two cities had each built their own infrastructure and had never managed to grow together. Hangzhou was not a cross-river city and did not use the waterfront area much. The new conceptual plan, however, asked the municipal government to relocate to this new cross-river area and develop it into a new CBD area (see also Qian, 2011). Moreover, in a wider region— the newly enlarged jurisdiction area of Hangzhou—the conceptual plan proposed the formation of a cluster of cities. The plan suggested that the city should avoid direct competition with Shanghai and should find 'differentiated sectors' in high-tech industries and develop provincial level producer services. It was believed that the high-quality natural and cultural environments were the main advantages for the city of Hangzhou to attract investors and, most importantly, talent in these sectors.

The planning of Nanjing is another exemplar (Wu, 2007). Nanjing annexed the county of Jiangning in 2000 and thus expanded its jurisdiction area from 1,026 to 4,728 square kilometers. The slogan of Nanjing is "Make the city stronger, bigger, finer, and prettier."[37] The aim of the strategic plan is to achieve the goal of making the central city stronger. The Nanjing Strategic Plan— another one prepared in the first wave of strategic plans—proposed a drastic expansion of the urban areas with one new urban district, Hexi new town (see Chapter 6 for new towns in China), and three new suburban areas (Xianxi, Dongshan, and Jiangbei) (Figure 4.7). The plan also proposed an extended transport network, which significantly transformed the city of Nanjing from a traditional compact city to a polycentric metropolis. New economic development zones were established within these new areas, including the Nanjing High-Tech Development Zone, the Nanjing Economic and Technological Development Zone, and the Jiangning Economic and Technological Development Zone. The plan proposed to develop a metropolitan area with a population of 10 million, a waterfront development, a belt of heavy industries to the north of the Yangtze River, and new high-tech industries to the south of the Yangtze River.

As can be seen from these earlier experiments, in contrast to the master plan which focuses on land uses, the strategic plan emphasizes economic functions and new development, and is more growth-oriented. Inevitably, strategic plans are all expansionist plans. For example, the Nanjing Urban Strategic Development Plan proposed to develop a new business center, Hexi new town (see Chapter 6). The plan was led by culture, sport, and business development. Old Nanjing was developed along the east of the Qinghuai River.

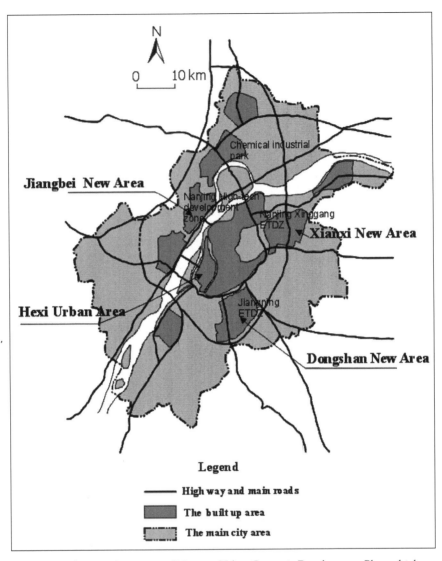

Figure 4.7 The spatial structure of Nanjing Urban Strategic Development Plan, which significantly extended the extent of the development area. The plan can be regarded as a metropolitan regional plan.

Source: Wu, 2007

Hexi, literally 'the west of the river [of Qinghuai],' remained undeveloped because of high underground water levels and poor geological conditions. However, the area is not far from the city center and became attractive because it was a large area of vacant land near the Yangtze River. Hexi thus is a major waterfront development. For the other three new towns, new functions were proposed. For Xianxi new town, one of the largest university towns in the nation was planned. On the eastern side of the university town, a science park was planned, incorporating multiple functions of education, research and development, as well as technological services.

The proliferation of strategic plans in the early 2000s was accompanied by a wave of administrative boundary changes in China. From 2000 to 2003, Guangzhou, Nanjing, Hangzhou, Hefei, Harbin, Xiamen, Suzhou, Haikou, Shijiazhuang, and Quanzhou all prepared strategic plans.[38] In total, 43 cities annexed nearby counties and converted them into urban districts.[39] Guangzhou, Hangzhou, and Nanjing are typical examples of administrative annexation in this period. For these plans, although the municipal government did not specify the format of presentation, which created a flexible environment for plan-making, the ultimate goal was pre-defined and not challengeable in a political decision-making process. In short, plan-making is a technical process, though the questions concerned are strategic and long-term. Because the local government is the 'client' of planning and design institutes, it remains in control of the strategic plan. It can also influence the strategic plan by choosing the planning scenario that fits its purpose. Because there are usually many different scenarios, the municipality usually selects one scenario or picks elements from different schemes to synthesize a new scheme that is most in line with its development aspiration.

Making strategic plans as place promotion

Although the strategic plan attempts to be 'scientific' and to find a 'practical' solution to development problems, in practice it only seeks a development vision or concept of the local elite (Zhang, 2002a). Because there is such a close relationship with the political leader, the local government has never before been so closely involved in concrete plan-making as it is now. The influence of political leaders over strategic plans has been very strong. For example, the mayor of Hangzhou proposed the concept of 'building a paradise metropolis' at the time of strategic plan-making, and this became a key objective of the plan. However, this also led to uncertainty over the strategic plan. Once the local leadership changes, the strategic plan may be abandoned, because the new leader usually wishes to find a different vision for the city out of consideration of his/her own political career prospects.

In the 2000s, there was a sudden proliferation of strategic plans, not because they had a proven effect on economic competiveness but rather because the main purpose of the strategic plan was place promotion.[40] The strategic plan helps produce a set of discourses that fit the requirements of place promotion. Second, the making of a strategic plan provides a channel for the local leader to influence the plans for development. Third, the strategic plan can be used to influence the urban master plan according to its desired direction of development. Because the strategic plan is a non-statutory plan, it is not constrained by planning standards and time horizons. But a formal plan-making process helps justify a different or even controversial solution that might be deemed inappropriate by the master plan. For example, a key suggestion of the Hangzhou Strategic Plan to build a new CBD was later absorbed into the master plan. The drastic southward development proposed by the Guangzhou Strategic Plan helped formulate a different development trajectory. Fourth, the process of making the strategic plan may itself serve as a way to steer the opinions of lower government departments. It is a more informal way, outside the formal government process. The preparation of the strategic plan may provide a vehicle for making other government officials aware of the aspirations of the leader. Finally, the plan-making process includes wide publicity events, which serve the purpose of city marketing. Slogans are invented during plan-making. For example, Hangzhou proposed to build a 'silicon valley in the city of heaven.' Many strategic plans propose easy and memorable slogans, which can be used for city marketing. Shantou Strategic Plan has two different Chinese and English slogans. The English slogan suggests the development of a 'coastal metropolitan garden city,'[41] but the Chinese slogan is an elegant expression: 'the city of Chao Chinese; elegant and exquisite Shantou; an international, coastal, landscaping, humanity metropolis.' The slogan is displayed in many places in the city, creating an atmosphere of new Shantou. The preparation of a strategic plan attracts wide media attention. In particular, the award of an international planning prize raises confidence in excellent planning work and local pride. The preparation of the Kunshan Strategic Plan deliberately commissioned a public relations consultancy firm to organize publicity activities and to involve the general public in the plan-making process. The public consultation was therefore seamlessly orchestrated and non-confrontational. The overall rationale of development, however, was not challenged. It may be unfair to simply regard this kind of activity as window-dressing, but in essence it does not fundamentally empower civil society. Nevertheless, its purpose is quite propagandist.

Characteristics of strategic plans

The imperative of enhancing competitiveness dictates the rationale for making a strategic plan. Following this imperative, there are some salient features of strategic plans. First, the strategic plan usually carries out a development stage analysis, to benchmark the city against other competitors, and accordingly propose 'strategic actions.' For example, the Guangzhou Strategic Plan believes that the city is at the stage of rapid urbanization and globalization and thus should adopt a 'leapfrogging' approach to capture development opportunities in the Pearl River Delta region. For Hangzhou, the strategic plan suggests that the city is in transition from the early to the mature industrialization stage, and thus the city should develop producer services on the basis of its advantages in the natural environment.

Second, the strategic plan pays attention to 'regional analysis,' that is, the position of the city in the region, compared with other cities. This then leads to the identification of threats and opportunities. For example, the Guangzhou Strategic Plan aims to turn the threat of Shenzhen into an opportunity to upgrade its economic structure and regain the status of the economic center in the region. It believes that Guangzhou still has a competitive edge because of wider links with other cities in southern China. The regional analysis of Hangzhou identifies its proximity to Shanghai and its excellent natural environment, and thus suggests that the city should move towards high-tech industries. Also, the plan advises Hangzhou not to compete directly with Shanghai but rather to strive to become a regional and provincial production service center. For Kunshan, the regional perspective suggests that the city could benefit from its geographical proximity to Shanghai, and develop a business satellite town. In particular, with the high-speed railway, the travel time from central Shanghai has been reduced to only 20 minutes. It is believed that the city could strive to become 'an edge city' of Shanghai. The strategic plan for Guangzhou advises the city to 'occupy the central location' of the region, namely to build the city towards the south, through a so-called 'southern expansion strategy.' Through some rudimentary gravity analysis, it is believed that the center of gravity of the Pearl River Delta core region is Nansha—a district located in the southern area under Guangzhou. Therefore, if Guangzhou could 'strategically occupy' the center of gravity and develop a focus of linkage, it could capture the growth momentum of the region.

Third, as noted above, the strategic plan has a spatial concern and aims to develop a spatial strategy. Unlike the focus on land uses in the master plan, the strategic plan tries to propose action in spatial terms. The spatial concern is to enhance economic competitiveness rather than to avoid incompatible land uses and to reduce externalities. The new spatial structure is formulated to direct future urban expansion and major infrastructure projects. For example, Guangzhou proposed to build a new CBD in the southern area so as to strengthen its control over the newly acquired district of Panyu. For Hangzhou, a cross-river waterfront CBD was proposed to turn the city strategically from a city located near the lake to a cross-river city. For Kunshan under the jurisdiction of the municipality of Suzhou, it aimed to develop its connectivity with the global production network and become a node in the network. In this topography, the lower rank of county-level city does not matter, because it does not rely on resource allocation from the formal administrative system. This explains why the city government is less concerned about various top-down regional plans, as it does not aim to gain 'experimental zone' status.

Compared with conventional master plans, the strategic plan emphasizes policy that can be put into action. Actions may include countermeasures to threats from competitors and tactics to enhance competitiveness, for example, repositioning the city in the region, and defining an aspiration for growth and the pathway to realize the aspiration. The latter is often represented in catchy slogans for the media. Shenzhen, in its Shenzhen 2030 Strategic Plan, aims to become a 'global pioneering city.'[42] However, a renowned Chinese urban geographer at Beijing University, Professor Yixing Zhou, sharply criticized this notion of the 'pioneering city'. Zhou (2013) argued that Shenzhen should pay more attention to building a habitable city for migrants, as in 2000 the migrant population accounted for 82 percent according to the definition of the fifth population census. Zhou maintained that the slogan of the 'global pioneering city' was not properly defined. However, to his disappointment, the media reported his speech in the Shenzhen 2030 Urban Development Strategy Forum as an endorsement (Zhou, 2013, p. 113). He had to write to the mayor to clarify his viewpoint. It is shown in this case that such a forum may often be used to promote an already decided policy rather than to generate policy debates. In a sense, it has the purpose of place promotion. Indeed, such a slogan triggered some interest. In 2008, when Kunshan prepared its urban master plan, the local planners were trying to learn from Shenzhen. They invited the Gongzongli (public participation) Business Consultancy Ltd. based in Shenzhen to organize the publicity for the process of strategic and master planning.

Further, the strategic plan pays more attention to governance, and even sometimes proposes institutional changes and innovations needed to implement the vision. In this sense, the strategic plan is less like a physical plan and more like a 'spatial' or action plan. For example, the Hangzhou Strategic Plan points out the importance of developing a cooperative relationship between the central city of Hangzhou and its two subordinate districts, Xiaoshan and Yuhang, which had been converted from former county status, and suggests giving them more autonomy in order to maintain their economic vitality. The plan diagnoses the weakness of a 'laid-back' local culture and urges a 'new spirit for competition.' The plan regards the fragmentation of municipal governance as a major obstacle to the city rejuvenating itself to compete with other cities in the region. The strategic plan is also a kind of study, which suggests very concrete proposals to adjust administrative structures.[43]

More recently, Wuhan in central China ambitiously prepared a new strategic plan called the Wuhan 2049 Strategic Development Plan. CAUPD was commissioned to prepare the strategic plan. In the conference organized to disseminate the mid-term report, the government of Wuhan was extremely excited to report the recognition of Saskia Sassen. In the official English web-site of the municipal government,[44] it is reported that experts "discussed the interim results of Wuhan 2049 Long-term Development Strategic Planning. Saskia Sassen, world famous master of planning, predicted that Wuhan would be an 'undiscovered global city.'" This verdict was widely disseminated by local and national media and triggered interesting discussion on Chinese *weibo* among the Chinese professionals.

A brief verdict

The emergence of strategic plans reflects the shift of city planning from a resource allocation tool to a development instrument. It is not a result of deregulation but rather of the strengthened role of the local government in pursuing its development target. The local government feels the conventional master planning approach is top-down and too restrictive and the master plan cannot meet its need to enhance economic competitiveness. Therefore, the strategic plan was invented, reflecting the desire of the city to outbid its competitors. In the planned economy, cities were not geared up to compete against each other. The purpose of city planning was to remove competition by administratively based resource allocation, which emphasized self-sufficiency. At that time, the city was fragmented by different state work-units, which belonged to different levels of government. The city was not regarded as a whole entity that should achieve an independent development goal. Now, entrepreneurial governance has emerged after economic devolution and, in particular, the establishment of a tax-sharing system. So the mindset that cities compete against each other is relatively new. To further the interests of the city, the new non-statutory plan entirely funded by the local government has been created outside the formal planning system. With a weak civil society and a strong 'mayor' (in fact the Party secretary is usually the top leader), professional planners are asked to produce a strategic plan in a short period. In essence, the plan reflects the vision of political leaders rather than an outcome of stakeholders' negotiations. The vision is visualized by planning rather than created by planners because the process of plan-making does not suit the fundamental mentality of growth. The long-term strategy is often produced in response to short-term imperatives such as the adjustment of administrative boundaries or change in the local leadership. Its preparation is separated from the political process through which the city is built and regulated (Wu and Zhang, 2007).

Finally, the strategic plan opens up the process of plan-making. Non-local consultants and design institutes are invited to prepare their scenarios for the strategic plan. Through commercial contracts, the input of external consultancy firms is brought into the planning process, which makes the plan-making process more complicated. Consequently, their involvement has to be managed in commercial terms, which changes the dynamics of plan-making because this in turn requires a more formal approach and following certain procedures. It is believed that non-local consultants are detached from the local politics of development and therefore can be more objective in the proposal of development scenarios. The 'client'—the municipality—often uses the expert view and strategic plan to justify its vision to the upper government. In fact, the external consultants may sometimes be tactically selected based on consideration of their connections with the government department that is in charge of planning, or at least some key urban planning and design institutes that have close relations with the upper government may indirectly help to influence the view of the upper government. The local government sometimes deliberately uses this plan-making approach as a way of coping with 'up-scaling governance' (see Chapter 5), and asks for preferential policies from the upper government. On the other hand, the detachment of planning from the statutory system makes it more difficult to produce a realistic development scenario, because the politics of administration and inter-government coordination are important factors in the direction of future urban development. The scenarios become more or less the brainchild of key consultants in the plan-making process. To produce a more 'realistic' scenario, the planning consultant tries to grasp 'local politics,' especially the preference of key politicians such as the mayor or the Party leader. More experienced planners grasp the importance of understanding the 'hidden' agenda and try very hard to find out why they have been appointed to carry out the task. Besides the formal channel of communication, which is limited, planners in the plan-making process resort to various informal approaches such as having tea with the assistants of political leaders or local planning bureau directors to grasp the 'real' motivation and possible intentions. Insider information is vital. Because plans produced from external consultation may not be easily implemented due to this communication gap, after multiple scenarios have been produced, the municipal planning bureau (the 'client' of the strategic plan, *jiafang*) has to pick one local planning institute and assign it the task of synthesizing and generalizing these scenarios to produce an implementable plan. But before this, the client may organize a consultation meeting to evaluate these plans. More external consultants or experts are brought into the process to compare these planning scenarios and produce a verdict. Compared with the more enclosed process of plan-making in the statutory plan, the preparation of a strategic plan is more flexible and involves more participants. Despite this openness in the process, public participation is procedural rather than substantial, because the stakeholders involved are mainly confined to the elites, and the parameters of planning evaluation are set. Some non-statutory plans may pass a formal evaluation process, despite obvious flaws. It does not require professional knowledge to spot the problem—for example, the design of an imaginary and geometrically shaped 'eco-city' in a vast rural area. The public should have the right to be asked if this is what they want. But in reality, planning is such a closed system that the decision-making process is not open to them.

The introduction of strategic plans creates tension and even conflict with the statutory master plan. The legal status of the strategic plan is undefined and not recognized by the upper government. There are two different opinions regarding the future of strategic planning. First, the strategic plan could be standardized and incorporated into the existing planning system. In practice, the strategic plan has been widely prepared before the process of master plan revision, and the approach to preparing the strategic plan has become less idiosyncratic and more standardized. In order to obtain recognition, the local government may try to use it as a stage before making or revising the master plan. In a sense, the research in strategic planning is not wasted and key recommendations are absorbed into the master plan. In the case of Shantou, the strategic plan and master plan were commissioned to the same planning institute, because the same design institute took on the task of making the urban master plan after completion of the strategic plan. However, in many other cases, the link between the strategic plan and the master plan is assumed rather than guaranteed. The strategic plan is not officially required to prepare the master plan, and the requirements set by the strategic plan do not directly influence the master plan.

The second opinion is that the strategic plan has to be standalone to maintain its flexibility, because this flexibility is very much required by changing local conditions. Once the strategic plan is formalized, it is argued by those who insist on its merit as an independent type of plan, it would lose its flexibility, and the local government would invent another new plan to suit their needs. The justification for the strategic plan is not just due to its strategic perspective and flexibility but also to its role as a growth tool under the control of entrepreneurial governance. In essence, the strategic plan is not a product of the process of negotiation among stakeholders but rather an instrument of the entrepreneurial local state. It is based on the interest of the central city. Although currently the municipality-funded strategic plan is used for inter-city competition, the approach of strategic planning, especially regional analysis (rather than city-focused design), the spatial strategic view (rather than land use focus), and action-oriented policy recommendations (rather than blueprint style) are very appealing to governments at different levels. As can be seen in the next chapter, this approach has been adopted by central and regional governments to up-scale urban governance and consolidate central control over localities.

Conclusion

Planning under urban entrepreneurialism is essentially expansionist planning. It has been captured by the local growth machine, which is built upon land revenue and the career prospects of key politicians. Planning has adapted to the new environment and reinvented itself as a growth tool. In the West, urban entrepreneurialism is associated with the 'streamlining' of planning (Allmendinger and Haughton, 2012), and consequent reorientation of planning towards the support of mega urban projects. Planning has become project-oriented.[45] In contrast, Chinese planning has not become an obstacle to economic growth. It evolved quickly into part of the growth machine. Rather than removing land use plans to suit the market, the Chinese growth machine is highly contingent upon a complex central and local relationship. The central state maintains and has even strengthened some aspects of control—for example, macroeconomic aspects and land management. This forces the local state to resort to a planning approach to bargain for more land for development. Land becomes an asset to exchange for capital investment. All these operations require an action plan to propose a concept (through non-statutory planning) and the specification of land to be sold in the market (which is achieved through the 'detailed development control plan,' see Chapter 3). The purpose of planning is thus not to contain growth. Planning is, on the whole, not a regulatory device for control. The three planning projects discussed in this chapter are all incidentally recognized by ISOCARP for the best practice award, but they tell essentially the same story of planning for growth, albeit in slightly different ways. The use of 'zones' (*pianqu*) in the Kunshan Master Plan in the 1990s did not serve the purpose of containing industrial land in designated zones but rather led to the spread of land uses into a greater geographical area, intentionally or unintentionally. For Huaqiao, a town under the jurisdiction of Kunshan but near Shanghai, the use of the notion of transit-oriented development opened up the possibility of developing the land in a further away place. Zhengdong new district is a project to expand the city through CBD development. The design has been applied to the whole new area, as an urban design of a mega project. Later, the city of Zhengzhou ambitiously designated the whole area from Zhengzhou to Kaifeng as a regional integration project. But this regional integration project is not a top-down regional plan (see Chapter 5 for up-scaling regional governance). It is an entrepreneurial driver for strengthening the position of Zhengzhou as the core of the so-called 'central China urban cluster.' To fulfill the desire of entrepreneurial governance, the non-statutory plan was invented. But ten years later after the invention of the conceptual plan, the application of the Shantou Strategic Plan shows some sophistication. While growth is still a major objective, the strategic plan proposes a more incremental approach (Wang and Dubbeling, 2013).

This indicates that planning under entrepreneurialism is also evolving. Despite this sophistication, the non-statutory plan remains an attractive and flexible approach to reflect local desires and absorb external advice in a competitive environment.

Notes

1   For the concept of the growth machine, see Logan and Molotch (1987).
2   See Yang and Li (2014) for an example, and also Wang, Potter, and Li (2014).
3   That is, only the local government can acquire farmers' land to release as the first source of land to land users. See Yeh and Wu (1996); Lin and Ho (2005), and Hsing (2010).
4   See Deng (2009) and Hsing (2010).
5   These steps are described in detail in Wu (2012c, p. 241).
6   See Aalbers (2012) for a description of the subprime mortgage crisis from the perspective of financialization; Wu (2012a) for a summary of the housing market under globalization; and Wu (2014) for an assessment of the implication of commodification on housing market cycles.
7   Information from China Central Television news, March 2013.
8   Wu and Phelps (2011) coined the term 'state entrepreneurialism' to denote the combination of strong state governance and market-driven land development methods.
9   For the early development of Kunshan, refer to McGee et al. (2007) and Wei (2002); for urbanization from below in Jiangsu, see Ma and Fan (1994); and for more recent developments, see Chien (2007) and Wu and Phelps (2008).
10   For the bottom-up urbanization process in southern Jiangsu, see Ma and Fan (1994), Shen and Ma (2005); see Shen (2005) for an earlier study of scale changes.
11   See Chien (2007) for more information about the development of the ETDZ; also Wu and Phelps (2008) for the development of Kunshan as an edge city in Shanghai city-region.
12   The phonetic pronunciation of the number '3' in Chinese is 'shan', which makes the slogan very amusing.
13   See Zhang (2006, p. 48) and Li and Wu (2012a).
14   These were Huahui Engineering and Architecture Design Ltd. and Jingqun International Planning and Consultant Ltd. (the English name is actually EDS international), which is based in Taiwan.
15   Localism has been promoted in the U.K. under the Coalition Government but there is still strong local resistance to development.
16   See Li and Wu (2012a, p. 186).
17   This is particularly the case because these historic towns are quite near to Shanghai, and most tourists come for a day tour and do not bring sufficient income to the local government. The local government is less keen to develop 'properties' (using property-led development) in this area because there is no property tax and thus no sustained income for the government.
18   See Zhang Q. (2010) for a general description of the master plan.
19   Metropolitan growth management is applied in the U.S.
20   This is because the central area is mainly along the railway and planned transit.
21   This is based on 100 square meters of the total construction land use per capita.
22   This is called using the 'land to develop the road,' which has been widely used (see Zhang and Wu (2006)) but because the negotiation between the developer and the

municipal government is not transparent, the MLR has required since 2004 that all land sales should be on the open land market. Since then this 'betterment' has been suspended, see Wu et al. (2007).

23   This will be discussed in detail in Chapter 6.

24   See the case study brief at http://www.isocarp.net/projects/case_studies/cases/cs_info.asp?ID=1700 (accessed Jan. 15, 2014).

25   *Ibid*, the case study brief.

26   Reported in news.xinhuanet.com/english2010/china/2010–08/02/c_13426617.htm (accessed Jan. 20, 2014).

27   For the revision of the master plan in Nanjing, also see Qian (2013).

28   See Newtown and Franklin (2011) and Marsden, Yu, and Flynn (2011) for eco-tourism and the implications for rural livelihood.

29   See Su (2014) for the commodification of heritage in China.

30   Gao, Zhang, and Luo (2014) provides a full account of the case.

31   See Zhang and Wu (2006) for administrative annexation as a new approach to consolidating the role of municipalities.

32   See Dühr, Colomb, and Nadin (2010) and Healey (2004).

33   These five planning institutes include the Chinese Academy of Urban Planning and Design, the Institute of Urban Planning and Design of Qinghua University, the School of Architecture and Urban Planning of Tongji University, the Center of Urban and Regional Research of Sun Yat-Sen University, and the Guangzhou Academy of Urban Planning and Design.

34   These include a full spectrum of Chinese formal governance organizations.

35   The former mayor, Lin Shusen, published a book (Lin, 2013) and fully recognized the contribution of the strategic plan to the making of the statutory master plan in 2003. The Guangzhou Strategic Plan created a precedent of using external consultancies to widen the perspective before the statutory master plan is made.

36   These included Nanjing University, the Shanghai Academy of Urban Planning and Design, and the Chinese Academy of Urban Planning and Design.

37   This was suggested by the former director of the City Planning Bureau, Zhou Lan, see Zhou (2002).

38   See Wu and Zhang (2007, pp. 720–722), for a list of these plans.

39   See Zhang and Luo (2013, p. 147), and Zhang and Wu (2006) for a general discussion of administrative annexation.

40   For the concept of 'place promotion' or 'city marketing', please refer to Short et al. (1993). Wu (2000) provides an example of place promotion in Shanghai. See also Berg and Björner (2014).

41   Wang and Dubbeling (2013) summarize the background and process of Shantou Strategic Plan preparation. The plan also received an ISOCARP Award, see Chapter 6 for a related plan for its new town.

42   See Ng and Tang (2004), and Zacharias and Tang (2010) for the history of Shenzhen development and planning.

43   See Zhang and Wu (2006) for a discussion of the use of administrative changes such as annexation and conversion of jurisdiction status.

44   The English version can be seen at: http://english.wh.gov.cn/publish/english/2013–07/15/1201307150906530043.html. For the Chinese version, there are hundreds of news reports, simply Google or Baidu, "Sassen and Wuhan" in Chinese. One example is at: http://www.chinacity.org.cn/csfz/csxw/109914.html.

45   See Allmendinger and Tewdwr-Jones (2000) and Lord and Tewdwr-Jones (2014).

5
National and Regional Planning

China's rapid urban growth has been accompanied by economic evolution. The decentralization of economic decision-making and the rise of 'urban entrepreneurialism' are widely noted.[1] The promotion of market development seems to resonate with neoliberalism in the West. However, the state is still dominant in every aspect of political and social life, and plays an important role in economic development. In this sense, the Chinese state is quite different from the notion of neoliberalism. The Chinese state seems to learn from the 'developmental state'—a concept largely derived from the East Asian countries.[2] The developmental state influences economic development through state-led comprehensive and territorial planning. The developmental state approach created a special pathway to the global city as shown in Singapore (Olds and Yeung, 2004). However, unlike the developmental state, Chinese governance has seen the transformation of scale from central to local governments since economic reform. It is the local state that proposes growth-oriented targets and drives local economic growth. Derived from rural China is the concept of so-called 'local state corporatism,'[3] which emphasizes the role of the local state in economic regulation, as decentralized fiscal policy incentivizes the local state to build its own tax base, especially through coalition with enterprises under its control.[4]

The previous chapter described local planning activities of the entre-preneurial city. This urban entrepreneurism has become a powerful driving force to transform the local state into a market agent. As seen in the previous chapter, urban planning has been transformed by the transfer of power from the central to the local governments, which is known as 'state rescaling.' However, the lack of development control has led to a series of social and environmental crises (Wu and Zhang, 2010, p. 60). Inter-city competition exacerbates redundant and rampant development; land encroachment jeopard-izes ecological security; social inequality is enlarged and creates tensions and alienation. In response to these crises, we have seen a new trend of up-scaling governance and the re-emergence of national and regional planning. To make matters more complicated, the re-appearance of planning at the national and regional levels is not just a result of strengthened control by the central government. It also results from the tactic of local government to 'jump the scale' to gain strategic support from the central government. The regional plan, especially the so-called urban cluster plan, can be used for place promotion.[5] In particular, gaining the title of 'special zone' or 'experimental zone' for the national strategy can allow application for preferential policies and stimulate the inflow of investment. In this chapter, the recent trend of emerging national and regional policies is reviewed.

Region building: the re-emergence of 'regional policies'

Before we discuss national and regional planning, it is useful to contextualize the concept of the region to see how it has changed in the history of the Chinese political economy. Table 5.1 provides a succinct summary of the three stages. In the planned economy, because of the top-down hierarchical control, cities were organized into a regional system, with their division of labor defined by the state. Industrial policies required collaboration between different sectors across the region, and regional policies acted as a redistributive policy to constrain inequality between regions. However, as with urban–rural dualism, the socialist state did not manage to eliminate regional inequality, because industrial policy supported specific divisions of labor that were not favorable to underdeveloped regions. But because cities did not have independent interests or motivation, they did not compete as autonomous agents. However, economic reform has transformed the centrally planned economy. In particular since the 1990s, hierarchical control has been weakened, and the downscaling of governance has been a major contributory factor.[6] Cities since then have aggressively used their new power to promote local development, which has led to fierce inter-city competition. At a later stage, especially after entry to the WTO, export-oriented industrialization, on the one hand, led to a boom in coastal areas, especially in the Pearl River Delta, the Yangtze River Delta, and the region around Beijing and Tianjin. In essence, a regional scale of economic production is under formation. On the other hand, cities pursue GDP growth. GDPism is created by the promotion system of government officials. To some extent there is a mismatch between the regionalization of production and downscaled urban governance. The entrepreneurial city encountered serious challenges and crises, and as a coping strategy the state began to recentralize certain aspects of regulation. For example, land management has been strengthened by a new top-down approach through which central government allocates land quotas to local governments.[7] The land management system also requires the designation of 'basic agricultural land' to enforce protection. Further, a process of region-building has started to reverse the process of diminishing the regions following economic devolution.

Table 5.1 The conceptual framework of region-building in different historical periods in China.

Historical formation	Form of state spatial selectivity	Form of urban-regional regulation	Major contradictions
State socialism 1949–1978	The national scale of statehood as over-arching governance	Managerialism achieved through hierarchical economic planning	Urban–rural dualism
Early market reformist regime 1979–2001	Rising localities and the dominance of central cities	Urban entrepreneurialism and devolution of planning control	Fierce inter-city competition and uncoordinated development
Post-WTO market society 2001–present	Up-scaling towards the city–region	Strategic plans, centrally initiated regional coordination plan, soft institutions, and 'national new districts'	Inter-region competition for national entitlements

Source: Adapted from Wu and Zhang (2010)

Along with the changing scales of governance, the relationship between the city and its functional region has also changed. In the planned economy, the functions of the city and its region were arranged by economic planning. For example, Shanghai was the center of manufacturing, while the region supplied raw materials. In the early stages of export-driven manufacturing development, cities near Shanghai began to 'compete' with the central city for investment, leading to tension between the central city and its region. Nationwide, the adoption of so-called 'city leading counties'[8] consolidated the status of the central city at the expense of its region. However, this hostile relationship between the central city and its region changed when economic restructuring imposed a new regional order. Shanghai strives to upgrade to become a center of producer services. Other cities see geographical proximity to the central city as a new opportunity. For example, the city of Kunshan developed a business park near Shanghai and aimed to transform its rural town Huaqiao to become a 'business satellite town' of Shanghai (see Chapter 6). More recently, Shanghai received a new policy from the central government to become 'China (Shanghai) Pilot Free Trade Zone' in 2013. Other cities in Jiangsu and Zhejiang began to consider the implications and how to benefit from this new development. The development could therefore be regarded as a new 'regionalism' in the lower Yangtze River Delta. However, the establishment of regional governance has been difficult and hampered by administrative division. In the following section, major national and regional plans are examined.

The National Urban System Plan (2005–2020)

The concept of the 'urban system' was originally imported from geographical studies. In the 1980s, the urban system plan was created as a new type of plan. In the 1990 City Planning Act, the urban system plan is recognized as a component of, and usually approved together with, the statutory urban master plan. At the regional level, even before the development of the National Urban System Plan, provincial urban system plans were widely prepared. The problem with provincial urban system plans is that they are all based on administrative boundaries; they usually recognize the provincial capital as the center of the region and pay little attention to the cross-border relations between cities in different provinces. In a word, they are much more inward looking. The 1990 City Planning Act requires MOHURD, in charge of urban and regional planning, to prepare a national urban system plan in order to provide 'necessary guidance' to provincial urban system plans and urban master plans, and grants the State Council the power to approve the National Urban System Plan.

Against the backdrop of 'up-scaling' governance, MOHURD started to prepare the National Urban System Plan (2005–2020) in 2005. The plan was the first national-level plan on urbanization and spatial development to re-insert top-down regulation (Li and Wu, 2012b, p. 95). The plan identifies major cities and urban clusters, and potential areas for development. It then formulates different urbanization strategies, for example, to reduce over-concentration in the coastal area. An infrastructure framework is proposed to support the overall pattern of urban development. The plan also gives consideration to natural resources and ecological conditions, and sets guidelines on spatial development at the provincial level. The guidelines stress the role of core city-regions (or so-called urban clusters, *chengshiqun*). Figure 5.1 shows the distribution of these city-regions. The plan also considers coordination in trans-border areas and inter-regional infrastructure. The National Urban System Plan strives to achieve balanced development and to reduce inter-region competition. As can be seen from Figure 5.1, the urban system plan has become more strategic, which is different from previous urban plans that focused on construction and development.

The Chinese Academy of Urban Planning and Design prepared the National Urban System Plan. It is more a study than a statutory plan, because the plan adopts a scientific approach, heavily influenced by geographical studies, with due attention paid to the natural environment and socioeconomic conditions, but there is no mechanism to implement the plan in national macroeconomic management. In particular, in terms of resource allocation, the National Reform and Development Commission (NDRC) plays a significant role. The plan prepared by MOHURD has limited or virtually no influence over this NDRC-

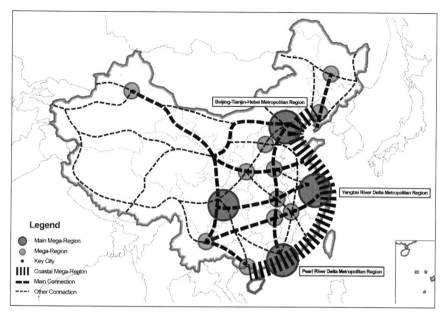

Figure 5.1 The distribution of city-regions in the National Urban System Plan
(2005–2020).

Source: China Society for Urban Studies, 2013; originally in MOHURD and CAUPD (2010)

centered national strategy formulation. Its implementation relies on the
translation of the rank–size distribution of the urban system, functions of the
core cities, and infrastructure framework into the approval procedure of
individual provincial plans or the master plans of key cities listed in the
National Urban System Plan. Although MOHURD is in charge of the approval
of these provincial and local plans, it is not clear how this requirement could
be embedded into the procedure. Moreover, in essence the implementation of
the urban system plan requires the up-scaling of the plan into a national
economic development strategy, which goes beyond the remit of MOHURD
and enters the 'territory' of other departments of the central government,
especially NDRC. Inter-departmental politics make it difficult for this plan
to become a national economic development strategy.[9] It could be said that
the initiative under MOHURD correctly sensed the turn from the 'growth-
first' mentality to a 'scientific approach' to a 'harmonious society' under the
new generation leadership of Hu-Wen, and strove to up-scale both in terms
of geographical scale (from individual cities to a system of cities) and
functionality (from urban expansion to regional distribution). However, the
plan ignores the complex institutional dynamics of governance (between the
departments of central government and between central and provincial and
local governments) and underestimated the momentum initiated under 'state

entrepreneurialism.'[10] The formation of urban clusters is part of local government strategy to enhance their competitiveness, and is not directed by the national guidelines. In this process, NDRC managed to distribute various titles of so-called 'reform experimental zones' and 'national strategic areas' and hence maintains some directives over local governments, while MOHURD, as a sector-based department of the central government, lacks such a power of comprehensive policy intervention. In 2010, the plan was published as a book[11] without a statutory status, and it has not been implemented.

The main functional area plan

A major planning development at the national and regional level is the evolution of the system of five-year plans towards 'spatial plans.' The market reform has reduced the role of the five-year plan as an economic program. The National Planning Commission (NPC) evolved into the powerful National Development and Reform Commission (NDRC), which has become a de facto small State Council (cabinet) in charge of economic development and resource allocation. In the 1980s, 'territorial planning' (*guotu guihua*) was imported from Japan and Western Europe to insert a 'spatial' element into the system of five-year plans. Various levels of local planning commissions above the county level were instructed to prepare territorial plans, and the national territorial plan was prepared by NPC (Wang and Hague, 1993; Li and Wu, 2012b). The plan paid particular attention to 'territory,' namely natural resource preservation (through land use regulation). However, territorial plans ceased in 1996, because against the backdrop of economic devolution, top-down control had been greatly reduced. The territorial plan can be regarded as a five-year plan with some spatial presentation, aiming at resource allocation and redistribution. Simultaneously with the decline of the functionality of resource distribution, the role of the territorial plan was very limited.

However, after the frenetic growth of the early 2000s, the central government increasingly felt that there was a need to place a nationwide spatial order upon economic growth. Furthermore, after the new generation leadership of Hu Jintao and Wen Jiabao took office, a slogan of 'scientific approach to development' was created to make a change from the growth-first approach under Deng Xiaoping. The new approach required a stronger role from the central government (under the State Council) and subsequently, NDRC became a major government body in economic intervention. In 2006, the State Council officially required NDRC to prepare the National Main Functional Area Plan (Figure 5.2). In 2010, the plan was completed and released. The 'scientific' base of the plan originated from geographical research at the Institute of Geographic Research of the Chinese Academy of Sciences (CAS). There is an interesting link between the research institute and the government

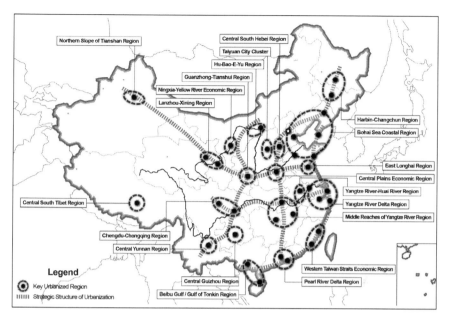

Figure 5.2 The main urban areas of the National Main Functional Area Plan. This plan
categorizes the national territory into four zones, with each having a particular
type of policy.

Source: Redrawn from Zhang and Luo, 2013, p. 187

planning commission, because the institute was under the dual governance of
NDRC and CAS. The key person behind the creation of the main functional
area plan was Professor Fan Jie.[12] In contrast to resource allocation in the five-
year plan, the new plan was intended to control undesirable development,
especially in ecologically sensitive areas.

The plan divides the national territory into 'four main functional areas': a
'prioritized development area, optimized development area, constrained
development area and forbidden development area.' The functional area is
linked to a spatial unit equivalent to a jurisdiction area (except for the forbidden
area which follows the boundary of a natural reservation area). Therefore, in
theory, these main functional areas are also policy target areas, which can be
applied to the jurisdiction assigned to one of the categories.

For each category, there is a specific set of policies.[13] For the 'prioritized
development area,' the policy encourages the acceleration of industrialization
and urban development, often through development of new industrial sectors
and growth poles. In a sense, this applies to 'industrializing' areas. For the
'optimized development area,' the policy aims to transform the current mode
of resource-intensive development and promotes the upgrading of industrial
structures. This means that the category mainly applies to more industrialized

areas. For the 'constrained development area,' the scale and pace of development is regulated according to ecological capacity, and for the 'forbidden area,' development is not permitted.

But how are spatial units assigned to one of these four categories? Here the 'scientific geographical approach' comes in. For the 'forbidden area,' the boundary simply follows the national 'natural and cultural protection zones.' For the other three types, an index system is used to define their categories, which consists of '10 index terms, 28 factors and a total of nearly 100 variables' (Fan et al., 2012, p. 89). These indexes range from land availability and water resources to ecological vulnerability. Thus the national plan seems to be prepared entirely under a 'scientific rationale.' The categorization of these policy areas is a result of a scientific procedure similar to factorial analysis[14] (Figure 5.3).

Owing to the appeal of the ability to associate a spatial unit with a set of targeted 'regional' policies, the main functional area plan is replicated on different scales. That is, the same approach has been used to divide provinces, municipalities, and counties into the four categories. So in theory, it is possible

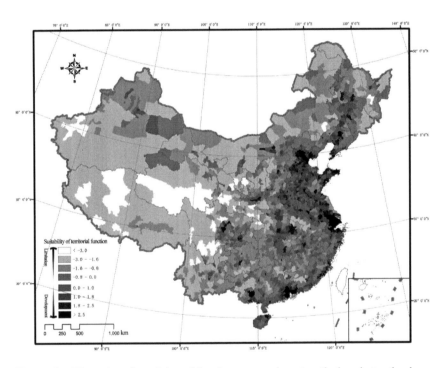

Figure 5.3 The index of suitability of development as the scientific foundation for the main functional area plan.

Source: Fan et al. 2012, p. 92

for a municipality located in a constrained development area, and a county underneath the municipality, to be listed as a prioritized development area. At these lower levels, the spatial unit is smaller. For example, for the city level, the unit of town is used.

The main functional area plan thus represents a change of planning rationale from promotion to containment at a larger regional scale. The control imposed varies for different jurisdictions. The link between jurisdiction and policies through categorization is a desirable feature of the plan, because it represents an effort to set different targets for the regions according to their different conditions. Compared with the previous, more growth-oriented economic plans, the intention of the main functional area plan is to identify the respective 'main functions' of the jurisdiction and formulate different goals to match their main functions rather than pursuing GDP growth at all costs. Designating the categories of 'constrained development areas and forbidden areas' strengthens the control role of the plan. The link also helps to address the expansion thrust, because of the evaluation of government officials. For jurisdictions in the categories of constrained area and forbidden area, officials should not be evaluated by growth achievements but rather by the task of perseverance. This is, however, an ideal situation. The actual performance evaluation of officials is more complicated. The four categories of development area are not directly mapped onto the evaluation system.

The creation of the main functional area plan reflects the effort to apply a so-called 'scientific development approach' to urban and regional planning. The method relies on the use of indexes and pays attention to natural conditions and regional endowment. The approach is largely divorced from national and regional politics; the adoption of the main functional area plan helps strengthen the role of the NDRC, but it lacks a statutory status, and is essentially a government development program. Many localities are keen to fund development plans in order to gain recognition for 'strategic areas' or 'experimental areas.' With the complex dynamics between the central and local governments, the plan is inevitably stretched and serves different purposes at different times.

The Pearl River Delta Urban Cluster Coordination Plan

The Pearl River Delta is known for its bottom-up urbanization.[15] The process is characterized by so-called 'exo-urbanization' (Sit and Yang, 1997), which is driven by export-oriented industrial development. The result is a rather scattered and rampant pattern of regional development (Xu and Yeh, 2005). The provincial government has tried to regulate development through strategic planning but without success. In 1989 and 1994, the Guangdong provincial government (specifically led by the construction commission) prepared two urban system plans. The 1994 Urban System Plan, entitled the 'PRD Economic Region Urban Cluster Plan,' was quite influential and received a national planning award. However, as seen in Chapter 3, the urban system plan lacked an implementation mechanism and became ineffective under the general trend of economic decentralization in China at the time. In 2004, the Guangdong provincial government and MOHURD jointly prepared the Pearl River Delta Urban Cluster Coordination Plan. The plan was influential in China at the time, because it differed from the previous physical planning approach and used a regulatory approach to govern the spatial pattern of regional development. In other words, it was a kind of 'spatial plan,' similar to an urban strategic plan but applied at the regional scale. In contrast to the locally initiated urban strategic plan under entrepreneurial governance, this new type of regional plan reflected a more top-down process to maintain a more coordinated order of spatial development in the face of intense inter-city competition. The format of the plan involved more than just presenting land use: a regulatory document that consisting of 10 chapters had to be prepared. The plan also had a subtitle—'Towards a Great Global Metropolitan Region,' reflecting its ambition (Xu, 2008).

One novelty of this plan is that it adopts a policy of 'spatial governance.' For the Pearl River Delta region, the plan emphasizes the development of general guidance (for example, designation of key development areas) and compulsory requirements (for example, the definition of preservation of green belts and transport corridors). The four types of governance mechanism include control, governance, coordination, and guidance[16] (Table 5.2). The control mechanism sets up legislation enforcement and is implemented through administrative management. It is applied to defined open spaces and transport corridors that have to be compulsorily enforced. The governance mechanism specifies building standards and other environmental requirements. It is an index control, and is applied to regulate unsuitable activities and uses. The coordination mechanism helps municipalities within the region achieve better coordination through defining cross-border areas and cooperation, and allows the provincial government to issue notices to reduce any negative impact on nearby cities. Finally, the guidance mechanism is not restrictive and provides a policy guide to lower tier plans.

Other than its policy novelty, the plan is known for its effort to achieve regional competitiveness rather than the competitiveness of individual cities. The plan attempts to impose a spatial order upon scattered developments in the region, and proposes a spatial structure that consists of one core area, three development belts, and five development axes (Figure 5.4). Despite similar spatial manifestations, these belts and axes are different from those terms as used in urban strategic plans, because they aim to direct development into specific areas rather than leaving them to sprawl. More importantly, the plan

Table 5.2 The four major governance mechanisms proposed by the Pearl River Delta Urban Cluster Coordination Plan.

Governance mechanism	Policy areas	Key instruments
Control	Regional green space and transport corridor	Green line and red line
Governance	Regional industries and transport hub	Index and targets
Coordination	Inter-city area	Joint meetings
Guidance	Special region support	Lower tier spatial plans

Source: Adapted and simplified from Xu, 2008

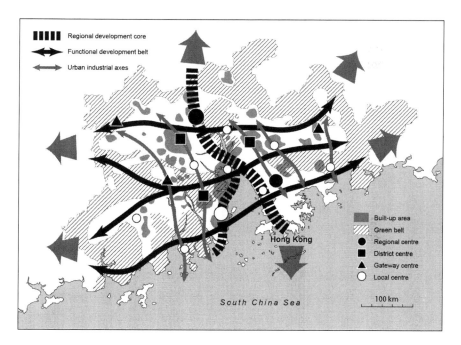

Figure 5.4 The Pearl River Delta Urban Cluster Coordination Plan, which aimed to create a spatial order for rampant urban development caused by export-oriented manufacturing industrial development and bottom-up urbanization in the delta.

has led to the establishment of a coordination office under the construction department of the provincial government. In 2006, the Guangdong People's Congress endorsed the PRD Urban Cluster Planning Ordinance, which became the first local legislation document for regional plans in China (Xu, 2008, p. 178). The ordinance affected the coordination of regional infrastructure development such as inter-city railways. In addition, the PRD has to consider the cross-border issue of development. Regional governance continued to be a major issue for the region. In 2006, the Great Pearl River Delta Urban Cluster Coordination and Development Study was launched, consisting of not only the cities in the core PRD but also cross-border Hong Kong and Macau, two special administrative regions in China.

However, at the level of the central government, the plan was in an awkward situation. Inter-departmental conflict of interests meant the State Council had not approved the plan. The powerful NDRC that was in charge of capital allocation, for example, believed that regional planning should be its role. Thanks to the Party secretary who sat in the Politburo of the CCP at the time, the Guangdong government managed to invite NDRC to prepare a regional plan in 2009, which was approved by the State Council. The spatial plan, however, was more a generalization of regional development and lacked spatial policies and guiding mechanisms (Xu, 2008). The preparation of the regional plan for the Pearl River Delta reveals a complex dynamic of governance and inter-ministerial rivalries that hampered the development of coordinated regional policies in the area. Regional policies and planning should concern not only different jurisdictional bodies but also different government departments. The Pearl River Delta Regional Plan is less well known. In contrast, the Yangtze River Delta Regional Plan is widely known. Although MOHURD led the Yangtze River Delta Urban Cluster Plan (2007–2020), NDRC clearly had an advantage and prepared the Yangtze River Delta Regional Plan, which became more widely noted and influential. The next section examines another round of regional plan-making in the Yangtze River Delta.

The Yangtze River Delta Regional Plan

As with the competition between the National Urban System Plan and the National Main Functional Area Plan, there was competition between NDRC and MOHURD at the regional level. They both initiated regional plans for the Yangtze River Delta. In 2005, NDRC initiated the Yangtze River Delta Regional Plan, while MOHURD started the Yangtze River Delta Urban Cluster Plan Project. The former was approved in 2010 and has now become relatively well known, while the latter did not manage to become a major plan for the region, as was the case with the MOHURD-led Pearl River Delta Urban Cluster Coordination Plan. NDRC funded the preparation of the regional plan and appointed a vice-director as the project leader, suggesting the importance of the plan. The preparation was the responsibility of the Department of Regional Economic Development of NDRC but involved researchers from the Nanjing Institute of Geography and Limnology of the Chinese Academy of

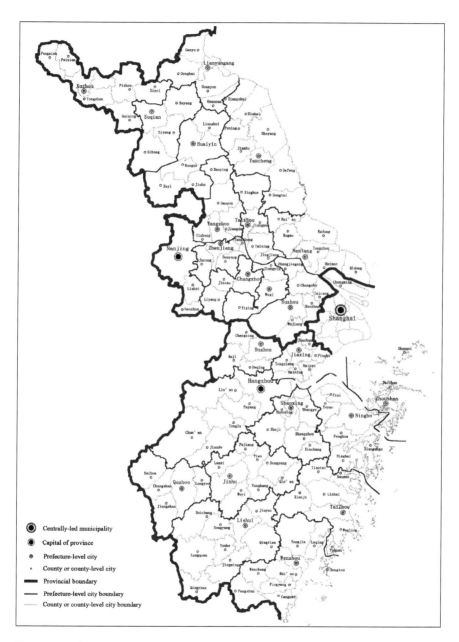

Figure 5.5 The administrative units of the Yangtze River Delta Regional Plan show this is a highly developed city-region with two major development axes from Shanghai to Nanjing and Shanghai to Hangzhou.

Source: Li and Wu, 2013

Science and representatives of the 'reform and development commissions' of various local governments in the region.

The Yangtze River Delta Regional Plan covers two provinces (Jiangsu and Zhejiang) and one municipality under the direct jurisdiction of the central government (Shanghai). The region includes three provincial-level governments, 24 prefecture-level urban governments, 49 county-level city governments, and 61 county governments (Figure 5.5). Inter-region and inter-city competition is severe.[17] Administrative fragmentation is a major problem, although along the axes from Shanghai to Nanjing and Shanghai to Hangzhou, urban built-up areas are almost contiguous, forming a gigantic 'megalopolis.'

The plan examined the challenges and opportunities facing the region and proposed a regional strategy. It defines the development target (the level of GDP), and promotes the development of service industries. To enhance *regional* competitiveness, the plan encourages economic restructuring and upgrading export-oriented manufacturing industries. Most importantly, differently from conventional five-year plans, it envisages a regional spatial structure (Figure 5.6) as 'one core with six belts' and designates functional roles for the cities. The influence of the plan over the region is achieved through its status as an official document approved by the State Council, although the plan itself is not a statutory one. For example, when NDRC approves large projects, it can refer to the plan for justification. The plan reveals the preference of the central government for particular local developments, which can be useful to local governments. For example, to protect the environment, metallurgical plants are banned or restricted to certain areas. NDRC uses the plan to reduce the over-capacity of metallurgical industries in the region.

The regional plan is quite comprehensive, covering land uses, the local economy, the environment, and infrastructure projects (for example, roads and inter-city railways), urbanization and patterns of urban development, social development, and public services. For each city, the plan proposes a develop-ment strategy, but the strategy is developed in the regional context, different from the urban plans made by individual cities, which are usually prepared from their local perspective. The regional plan is thus a top-down requirement, although local governments contributed to the process of plan-making. It is hoped that through this approach, better regional coordination and integration can be achieved. For example, the plan hopes to address the long-standing issue of industrial over-capacity, because individual cities all wish to develop profitable industrial sectors and hence invest heavily in particular sectors such as the iron and steel and petrochemical industries. The result is the 'assimilation of industrial structure' (*chanye tonggou*) in the region (Zhang and Wu, 2006). But obviously the influence of the central government over the region still relies heavily on project approval. As for regional transport infrastructure, the

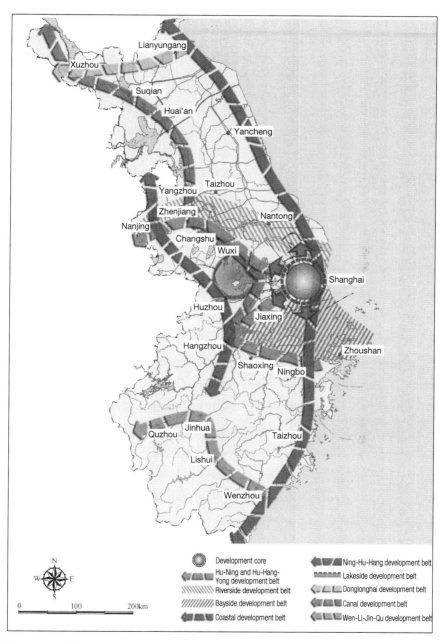

Figure 5.6 The spatial structure of the Yangtze River Delta Regional Plan. It designates 'one core with six belts.'

Source: Li and Wu, 2013

central government plays a significant role, as by the nature of these projects, an integrated regional perspective is necessary. For the Yangtze River Delta, the plan encourages the development of inter-city and high-speed railways, because land is in short supply and highways occupy too much land. The central government helps coordination between provinces and municipalities through central initiatives and filling the gap between inter-city infrastructures.

The plan also aims to overcome administrative fragmentation. For example, land protection is the responsibility of MLR, while urban construction and management is regulated by MOHURD. The new regional scale designated by NDRC is intended to provide overall guidance in relation to the regional strategy and structure. The intention is to achieve regional coordination through regional plans rather than a level of government (for example, in this case it would be a 'southeast region'). In other words, development is coordinated through a coherent plan rather than many administrative orders from a regional government body. It is argued that the regional plan reflects the 'new state space' introduced by the central government to govern the region without inserting another level of regional government body into the existing hierarchy (Li and Wu, 2013: p. 143). This new state space is a 'soft' space built up not by jurisdiction boundaries, but rather by being bounded by the spatial plan. But this state space is soft, and the implementation of the regional plan requires the cooperation of local governments. This may work well if the local governments in the region wish to collaborate, but it proves difficult when there is competition between local governments. As shown in the fragmentation of spatial plans at the national level, the regional level has multiple plans originating from different sectors of government. It is not clear whether the regional plan is consulted or referred to when local governments prepare their urban master plans or when MOHURD approves their master plans, because they belong to different departments. The local governments may selectively use the plan to justify their local proposals for their own interests (Li and Wu, 2013, p. 145). In other words, the regional plan itself does not have an implementation mechanism directly linked to the local governments. Because of administrative fragmentation, it has limited influence over the actual preparation of local urban plans. Its influence is mainly in macroeconomic policy.

The capacity of the central government has been greatly strengthened since the global financial crisis in 2008. The central government is in charge of capital liquidity, and injected 4 trillion yuan into a stimulus package. The investment is heavily oriented towards infrastructure development and large state-owned enterprises. With the sudden expansion of resources, NDRC is in charge of the distribution of capital and thus possesses significant power. Local governments strive to be listed as national strategic areas so as to receive policy support. However, the dynamics between central and local governments are more complicated than what is specified in the regional plan. The implementation of the regional plan is still a major challenge, as local governments often use the plan to fulfill their own vision, as the evaluation of government officials is still largely by GDP growth, and the tax-sharing system, which lays down the institutional foundation of local state entrepreneurialism, is still in operation.

To sum up, the 'renaissance' of regional and national plans reflects a process of up-scaling governance by the central government to cope with rampant urbanization and uncoordinated industrial development initiated by entrepreneurial local governments under economic devolution. The discourse is centered on the notions of sustainability, harmony, and 'scientific approaches.' However, the scientific approach as exemplified by the National Urban System Plan or the National Main Functional Area Plan cannot deal effectively with the dynamism of governance. Although the main functional area plans have some merit, for example, introducing regional perspectives and consideration for the natural environment, they are largely a product of planners or researchers. At the national level, various spatial plans cannot reconcile themselves to form a unified spatial framework, due to the fragmentation of the central government departments (NDRC, MOHURD, and MLR). These plans have no clear implementation mechanism. It is difficult to implement them through administrative procedure. The involvement of multiple central government departments further complicates possible implementation, as the National Spatial Plan requires governance beyond government sectors. On the other hand, the development of regional and national plans does facilitate the up-scaling process of governance and strengthens the influence of the central government in the process of planning.

Region building and the revival of city-region planning

Region building is achieved through both the adjustment of administrative boundaries and the development of 'soft regional institutions.' First, economic reform has been accompanied by changes in administrative boundaries. The so-called 'city-leading-county' system was adopted in the earlier stage of reform to strengthen the core city (Ma, 2005). The result was that core cities began to absorb the resources of counties under their control to build up the competitiveness of the central city. In the 2000s, there was widespread 'administrative annexation' through converting counties adjacent to the core city into districts of the core city to expand the territory of urban development (Zhang and Wu, 2006). The intention was more than just concentrating resources and support on the core city. Rather, administrative annexation was a response to inter-city conflicts or contentious relations between the core city and the counties under its jurisdiction. In a sense, the motivation goes beyond the building of the 'entrepreneurial city'; rather it wishes to use administrative annexation to solve the problem of the entrepreneurial city—the conflict between the central city and its nearby counties. The city-leading-county system and subsequent administrative annexation have consolidated the status of the central city and formed a larger municipal region. This process is in fact 'metropolitanization.' The lowest administrative units of urban district and county have joined to form the metropolitan region. In the intensely developed coastal region, the metropolitan regions have become adjacent, no longer separated by 'rural' counties, and have formed a large city-region. However, administrative annexation led to rapid expansion of the urban area. It did not solve the problem of the entrepreneurial city but rather aggravated low-density development under 'government-led urbanization' (see Chapter 4 for examples and details).

In the late 2000s, administrative adjustment again gained momentum. This later phase is characterized by the development of strategic areas in the municipalities under the direct jurisdiction of the central government (Shanghai, Tianjin, and Chongqing), consolidation of central urban districts, and the expansion of special economic zones (Shenzhen, Xiamen, and Zhuhai). For example, the new district of Pudong in Shanghai annexed the nearby Nanhui district, which expanded its development hinterland. Tianjin set up a new Binhai district, which merged three districts (Tanggu, Hangu, and Dagang) in 2009. In Chongqing, a new Liangjiang district ('two rivers district') was set up in 2010. For municipalities with the status of special economic zone, the policy of special zone was actually only applied to a designated zone within the metropolitan region. Now, for Shenzhen, Xiamen, and Zhuhai, the special zone policy has been expanded to cover the whole municipal region. In other words, the whole municipal region is a special economic zone. The expansion eased the spatial constraints on development. Another example of radical administrative change is the abolition of the municipality of Chaohu in Anhui province in 2011. The counties under the municipality were distributed to three municipalities (Hefei, Ma'anshan, and Wuhu) in the region (Zhang and Luo, 2013, p. 191). The three municipalities thus gained new territory, which facilitated the formation of two major urban clusters in the province (one centered on Hefei and the other based on the two cities of Wuhu and Ma'anshan). It is hoped that administrative change can also solve the problem of fragmentation of resource management, in particular, to better manage Chaohu Lake, which is one of the five major lakes in China. As can be seen from the above examples, consolidation and annexation expanded the territory of urban areas and facilitated 'building the region.' The motivation for the change is quite complex, a mixture of the desire to enhance urban competitiveness and the need to strengthen regional coordination. The result has been change in the unilateral direction of devolution and the up-scaling of governance towards a particular scale of governance—the city-region in China.

Second, the formation of the 'soft institution,' for example, regional associations and mayors' forums, helps with the building of regions. Under entrepreneurial urban governance, cities are driven towards inter-city competition. However, individual cities began to recognize the problem of excessive competition. Although they may not be able to change the situation entirely, there has been a spontaneous initiative to develop some coordination mechanisms and turn 'urban competitiveness' into 'regional competitiveness,' especially in the later phase of development. Larger city-regions are increasingly recognized as single entities by external investors. For example, the choice of investment location is not necessarily between Dongguan or Guangzhou, or between Suzhou or Shanghai, but rather the trade-off may be between the Pearl River Delta and Yangtze River Delta.[18] Initially, cities began to develop an interest in seeking collaboration with other cities. For example, in the Yangtze River Delta, an association of urban economies was formed as early as 1996, which consisted of the mayors of the cities in the region (Luo and Shen, 2007; 2009). They hoped to cooperate in regional transport infrastructure development, tourism, and human resources management. In 2000, between Shanghai, Jiangsu, and Zhejiang, a forum of economic collaboration was formed at the provincial-level governments. But these soft mechanisms lack a tier of regional government and thus are not binding in regulatory control (Wong, Qian, and Zhou , 2008). Regional collaboration may also result from the proposals of key politicians. For example, there was a 'Pan-Pearl River Delta' initiative, including nine provinces and two special administrative regions (Hong Kong and Macao).[19] But a regional initiative needs to be considered in the national context. The initiative of the Pan-Pearl River Delta or other large regions may have an impact on the political landscape of the nation. The central government is less likely to support the development of formal governance in a large region. The cities in a larger region hoped to collaborate on a voluntary basis for mutual benefits. The loosely assembled parties lacked binding and enforcement mechanisms (Wu and Zhang, 2010, p. 63). Nevertheless, the regional initiatives do reflect the fact that individual cities are now aware of the limits of inter-city competition and the importance of regional collaboration. For the provincial government, there is a strong desire to unify the core city-region under the banner of 'regional competitiveness.' However, the process of region building is subject to the politics of development.[20] In the underdeveloped eastern region of Guangdong province, three municipalities (Chaozhou, Shantou, and Jieyang) used to belong to a single municipality. Economic devolution led to the fragmentation of regional governance and created three independent municipalities. Now the provincial government, especially under the initiative of its new leader, requires them to collaborate

Plate 5.1 The Lianjiang River in southern Shantou is seriously polluted; as shown here, it is pitch black. The treatment of the river requires collaboration between different cities. There is a need for regional cooperation in water management.

to be regionally competitive. Although the municipalities recognize the need to collaborate, they each tend to use the opportunity to gain more benefits so as to be the central city in the region. In both regional infrastructure and environmental protection (e.g. water management), each municipality pursues its own interest, which does not lead to effective regional governance. The lack of cooperation in the regional water treatment became clear (Plate 5.1).

Overall, as can be seen from region building, we are seeing the revival of 'regional' policies and planning, but these regional plans are constructed at a different scale—the city-region rather than the macroeconomic regional scale between the developed coastal region, the industrializing central region, and the underdeveloped western region. A city region is built upon core cities, forming a cluster of cities within a densely interlocked area. There are two different logics that both contribute to the formation of a city-region. First, entrepreneurial governance continues to dominate in individual cities but they wish to collaborate to form 'regional' competitiveness. The provincial government particularly wishes to promote the development of core regions in its territory. Second, the state reacts to the ramifications of entrepreneurial governance and consolidates its regulatory power. This regulatory control is also implemented at the city-region scale, as seen in the Yangtze River Delta

Regional Plan. As a result, the city-region becomes an interface between the central and local governments. At this particular scale, we have seen the emergence of various spatial plans to reverse the trend of diminishing regional policies in the aftermath of economic devolution.

A brief verdict on the regional plan

In response to the crisis of entrepreneurial planning, China has seen the revival of regional plans. One particular type of regional plan is the urban system plan, which is defined by the Planning Act. It is a component of the statutory urban master plan at the city level. The plan aims to coordinate urban development within a region. Nevertheless, the planning approach is detached from the actual process of regional development and politics. The focus of this type of plan is placed on so-called 'rank–size structure, functional structure and spatial structure.' It is more like the plan of a particular government department (in this case the system of construction) and does not have sufficient influence over resource allocation. In essence, the urban system plan lacks the capacity to implement these structures. The major limit of the plan is that it presents a 'scientific' outcome without defining strategic policies, or the pathway that could lead to the desired outcome. This limitation is even more obvious at the national level and cross-regional scale. The National Urban System Plan is more a study than a plan, because, unlike the provincial urban system, which can at least try to persuade the provincial government to take up some recommendations, the national level has not established a link with policy. At the cross-regional scale, for example, the area covering different municipalities or provinces, there is no administrative instrument to implement the plan. The making of the plan lacks sufficient involvement of and negotiation between stakeholders. The outcome has no binding power on these administrative units.

In contrast to the detachment of the urban system plan from corresponding administrative units, the main functional area plan aims to assign a main function to an administrative unit. It tries to set development targets in accordance with the natural and socioeconomic conditions of the jurisdiction, and hence accordingly evaluates the performance of their officials. This intention to differentiate regional development targets and link targets with performance evaluation is plausible. However, in reality, the translation of the plan into regional policies, industrial policies, and fiscal policies is not straightforward. Because the plan originated from the system of NDRC, which has been in charge of resource allocation dating back to the planned economy and is responsible for preparing five-year plans on different scales, it has some effect on regional policies. But the impact is not achieved through regional

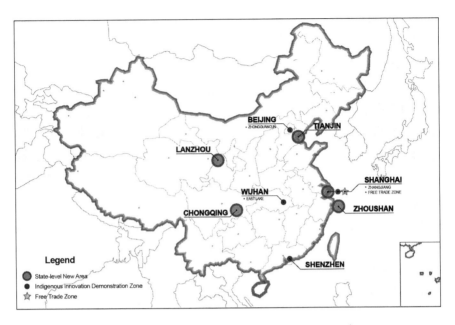

Figure 5.7 The national new districts and the indigenous innovation demonstration zones approved in recent years. These districts and zones constitute a new spatial form of development in China, representing a shift from the differential coastal, inner, and western macroeconomic regions to the city-regions.

plans such as the main functional area plan. Rather, NDRC designates strategic areas to which special policies and investment preferences are given. To some extent, NDRC orchestrates regional plans which reflect the characteristics of 'planning for production forces' in the era of the planned economy. The plan reveals the role of the state in China's market development. This role has been strengthened by the global financial crisis as the state (rather than the local government) controls monetary policies and injects capital liquidity. What we have seen in the aftermath of the global financial crisis is the development of mechanisms of regional coordination by the state. The top-down spatial plan reflects the strengthening of state capacities. But these plans still cannot be effectively implemented. What has been in operation is strengthened policy targeting specific special development zones. As a result, although the intention of regional plans is to provide better coordination and balance between different regions, in reality, a differentiated regional policy targets strategic areas, and zones of exception still dominate. Figure 5.7 shows the recently approved nine 'national new districts' (*guojia xinqu*) that are administratively ranked as deputy provincial status, plus four 'national indigenous innovation demonstration zones' (Zhongguanchun of Beijing, East Lake of Wuhan, Zhangjiang of Shanghai, and the most recent one—the whole municipal area of Shenzhen, approved on June 4, 2014; the zone has an administrative area of 397 square kilometers. In addition to the China (Shanghai) Pilot Free Trade Zone located in Pudong new district of Shanghai, these new centrally approved spaces constitute new spaces for institutional change. However, the objective of enhancing regional coordination cannot be easily achieved through strengthening administrative control, because the problem of the lack of coordination is caused by administrative-dominated local growth and inter-jurisdictional competition. To develop an effective regional plan, better negotiation and coordination between stakeholders would be needed.

Notes

1　See Harvey (1989) for his seminal study of the transformation from urban managerialism to entrepreneurialism in Western market economies. Jessop and Sum (2000) elaborated the concept of the entrepreneurial city and applied the concept to Hong Kong. Wu (2003a) examined the concept in the Chinese context, and, more recently, Chien (2013) discussed urban entrepreneurialism at the county-level city Kunshan. Cochrane (2007, pp. 85–107) provided a critique of the notion.
2　See Wade (1990), Woo-Cumings (1999), and Olds and Yeung (2004).
3　See Oi (1992, 1995).
4　See also Walder (1995).
5　Zhang and Luo (2013, p. 188).
6　See sociological analysis, Walder (1995); or economic analysis of so-called economic federalism (Qian and Weingast, 1997).
7　See Xu, Yeh, and Wu (2009) for the review of new land use management.
8　See Ma (2005) for discussion on the changing administrative system. See also Zhang and Wu (2006) on regional governance.
9　According to the Xinhua News Agency journalist, Wang Jun, who wrote many articles on the city of Beijing and urban development, the plan was resisted by other departments, in particular NDRC, because the latter believed the making of spatial plans is now under its remit (Wang, 2011b).
10　For the term 'state entrepreneurialism,' see Wu and Phelps (2011) in which the concept is applied to describing the development of a new town in Beijing.
11　The book is in Chinese by MOHURD and CAUPD (2010).
12　Most publications are in Chinese. However, there is one paper about this type of plan by Fan et al. (2012) in English.
13　Please refer to Fan et al. (2012, p. 88) for further explanation and Li and Wu (2012) for a detailed table of policies.
14　It is not clear, though, at the provincial and municipal levels, whether the same standard and approach have been followed, as the collection of these variables is quite time-consuming, and at the local level where smaller building units such as towns are used, some variables might not be available.
15　See Shen, Feng, and Wong (2006) for a discussion of 'bottom-up' and 'top-down' urbanization.
16　Xu (2008, p. 177) provided a different set of translation: supervisory governance (*jianguan xing guanzhi*), regulative governance (*tiaokong xing guanzhi*), coordinative governance (*xietiao xing guanzhi*), and conductive governance (*zhiying xing guanzhi*).

17 See Li and Wu (2012a) for the competition between county-level cities—Kunshan and Shanghai.
18 See Yang (2009) for a comparison of Suzhou and Dongguan, and the relocation of investment from the Pearl River Delta to the Yangtze River Delta.
19 See Xu and Yeh (2011), and Cheung (2012).
20 See Luo and Shen (2008) for the failed case of Su-Xi-Chang regional plan.

6
New Practices: New Town and Eco-city Planning

As revealed in earlier chapters, the rationale of planning in China is for growth. In Chinese terms, planning is always to create a new development, no matter whether it is a workers' village in the socialist period or a new estate of commodity housing in the post-reform era. The role of coordination, e.g. solving land use disputes among neighbors, is limited. This growth-oriented rationale is particularly salient in the planning of new towns (*xincheng*) and, more recently, eco-cities—a particular type of new development with a focus on ecological and low-carbon development. This chapter will discuss some new planning practices as seen in the development of new towns and eco-cities.

The origin of Chinese new towns

New towns in the socialist period were proposed as industrial satellite towns. The concept of satellite towns was not in fact a brand new invention. In Shanghai, new towns were proposed in the 1948 Metropolitan Plan in the period of Republican China (see Chapter 1). In 1958, the Shanghai Master Plan followed the proposal and confirmed five satellite towns (Minhang, Wujin, Anting, Songjiang, and Jiading). In the 1970s, large petrochemical industries developed in Jinshanwei south of Shanghai, and iron and steel industries in Baoshan north of Shanghai. To support these large state-owned enterprises and benefit from the new developments, Shanghai planned two additional comprehensive new towns for these places. The 1980 Master Plan further defined an urban system and specified two growth corridors. The north corridor was along the Wusong River and the Yangtze River towards the new town at Baoshan, while the south corridor developed towards Wujin, Minhang, finally reaching the new town of Jinshanwei in the south. Within the metropolitan area, a hierarchy of the urban system was also planned. Up to this stage, the development of satellite towns had been mainly driven by state investment in industries and public housing.

Similarly, in Beijing an industrial complex was planned in the suburbs in the 1950s, which later evolved into industrial satellite towns. These satellite towns were not too far from the city proper and were known as 'dispersed clusters' (*fengsan jituan*) or 'fringe clusters' (*bianyuan jituan*), which means that new developments are clustered in specific locations but the distribution of these clusters is dispersed across the urban area. In 1990, the Beijing Master Plan recognized ten clusters in the peri-urban area, which were in fact satellite towns. However, except for large state-owned enterprises that had the capacity to develop their infrastructure in the suburbs, the lack of funding mechanisms meant that Chinese cities were quite compact and did not see large-scale dispersal or urban sprawl. The planning practices for new towns were quite limited in the socialist period, because planning was abandoned during the Cultural Revolution (1966–1976). Even in the period immediately after economic reform, the planning of new developments in the suburbs remained constrained until the introduction of the land market.

The major changes in new town planning came in the 2000s, when Chinese cities experienced accelerated suburbanization.[1] The Shanghai Master Plan (1999–2020) proposed to consolidate satellite towns in the suburbs into larger new towns. The purpose of these new towns was to accommodate both industrial and residential uses and to provide better public services. In fact, these new towns were expected to become more or less independent cities. In the municipal region, according to the master plan, the urban system comprises four levels: the central city of Shanghai with a population of 8 million, 11 new towns with a population of 200,000 to 400,000 each, 22 central towns with a population of 50,000 each, and 88 market towns with a population of 20,000 to 30,000 each.[2] Later, in 2001, the municipal government of Shanghai announced its No. 1 decree to accelerate suburban new town development. The scheme was known as 'one city and nine towns,' and reduced the number of new towns from 11 to 9. The most outstanding feature of this scheme was that the new towns were to be built in distinctive Western styles to promote a cosmopolitan image in the Shanghai metropolis. For example, Songjiang was to be developed with an English style, Anting in Jiading with a German style, Pujiang in Minhang with an Italian style, Luodian in Baoshan with a Scandinavian style, Fengjing in Jinshan with a North American style, Gaoqiao in Pudong in a Dutch style, Fengcheng in Fengxian in a Spanish style, Baozhen in Chongming with an Australian style, and Zhu-jiajiao in Qingpu in a traditional Chinese style. Besides financial incentives, the municipal government gave the district governments more power to prepare their plans. The district governments led and managed the development of their new towns. In practice, new town development corporations became the major developers in the primary land market, and then real estate companies

Table 6.1 The growth of major new towns in Shanghai.

	Population in 2000	Population in 2010	Annual growth rate	Planned population	Percentage of migrant population
Songjiang new town	271,000	684,000	9.69%	1,100,000	69.6%
Jiading new town (town proper)	266,000	473,000	5.94%	520,000	78.8%
Qingpu new town	188,000	349,000	6.38%	700,000	65.5%
Linggang new town	156,000	212,000	3.08%	800,000	78.8%
Nanqiao new town	158,000	303,000	6.72%	750,000*	46.8%
Jinshan new town	143,000	205,000	3.67%	400,000	66.3%

Note: * up to 1 million.
Source: Adapted from Deng, 2014

obtained the serviced land to build 'master-planned communities,' as can be seen in the flagship project of Thames Town in Songjiang new town. Table 6.1 shows the growth of major new towns in Shanghai. It can be seen that the annual growth rate for these new towns from 2000 to 2010 ranged from 3.1 to 9.7 percent. Songjiang comes at the top of the list. However, the growth is driven by the influx of migrants (*wailai renkou*, literally 'non-local population').

The table shows that the influx of migrant population is a major driving force of new town growth. As observed in Songjiang in detail (Shen and Wu, 2013), suburban growth has diverse forms. The typical notion of 'suburbanization' refers to the relocation of residents from the central area to the suburb. However, in Chinese suburbs we have also seen the development of informal settlements in which rural migrants live.

The Beijing Master Plan (2004–2020) proposed the concept of a polycentric urban structure that comprised 'two axes, two belts and multiple centers' (see Figure 6.1). The master plan designated three major new towns in the eastern growth belt, namely a manufacturing base at Shunyi new town, comprehensive service industries at Tongzhou new town, and high-tech development at Yizhuang new town. Each of these new towns was planned to grow to a population of 700,000 to 900,000 by the year 2020. Therefore, they were regarded as major urban growth areas that would accept the relocation of residents from central Beijing.

Planning new towns in the post-reform era

The planning of new urban development under entrepreneurialism is discussed in Chapter 4. The Zhengdong New District of Zhengzhou and Kunshan, a

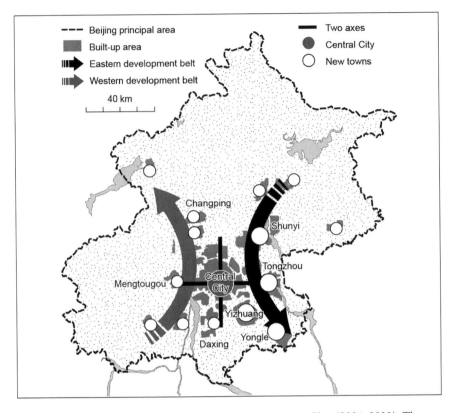

Figure 6.1 The polycentric spatial structure of Beijing Master Plan (2004–2020). This is the first plan that explicitly proposed multiple centers in which new towns were an important component to decentralize urban population and functions.

Source: Redrawn from the master plan

county-level city, are important exemplars. The new district of Zhengdong is in fact a new town built through master planning. The city of Kunshan could also be regarded as a new town at a lower level of the urban hierarchy. The economic and technological zone of Kunshan was similar to a new town. Besides these exemplars, in this chapter we examine other new towns to suggest that city planning in the post-reform era has been essentially for growth.

Yizhuang new town in Beijing

Yizhuang is one of the three major new towns in Beijing. It is located in the southeastern suburb 17 kilometers from the city center, along the 'eastern development belt' designated by the master plan. The planning of the new town scaled up the original Beijing Economic and Technological Development Zone (ETDZ) located at Yizhuang into a strategic urban growth area between

Plate 6.1 Yizhuang new town in the southeast suburb of Beijing. **(a)** The town center. The new town originated from a development zone, Beijing ETDZ, but has been scaled up by the urban master plan to become one of the three new towns in the metropolitan region of Beijing. **(b)** The new business park. Although the economic structure is still heavily oriented towards manufacturing industries, its business parks as shown here accommodate the headquarters of some multinationals in China such as DHL. The new town, connected to the central Beijing by light rail, has thus become an important city in itself along the development corridor from Beijing to Tianjin.

Source: Wu and Phelps, 2011

Beijing and Tianjin. In terms of the transport network, the new town is located between the cross sections of the Beijing–Tianjin highway and the fourth and fifth fast circular roads of Beijing. The new town plan was approved in 2007, aiming to develop high-tech modern manufacturing and producer services industries (Plate 6.1).

The role of planning can be clearly seen from the evolution of Yizhuang. The town was developed from a rural market town into a development zone dominated by industrial employment and land uses, and was then transformed into a new city with integrated residential areas, urban services, amenities, and transport uses through new town planning. This transformation includes the conversion of a large single-use industrial area into a more functionally mixed employment and commercial center. This was largely achieved through master planning both at the metropolitan and new town levels. Unlike 'spontaneous' residential-driven suburban development in the U.S., Chinese suburbs are planned on a large scale. While the suburbs of Beijing still accommodated large-scale residential relocation from the central area, the planned new towns started to become more like cities themselves, seeing a greater employment–residential balance. These new cities are quite different from the residential suburbs or industrial complexes in the socialist period. It is argued that this feature of new town development could be regarded as Chinese 'post-suburbia'[3] —a term coined to capture the 'edge city' type of suburban development in the U.S. and elsewhere. However, a significant challenge for new town planning is how to balance industrial growth and residential development (*zhi zhu ping heng*), and, more importantly, the matching of the two, because sometimes these two sectors are not well coordinated. For example, in Yizhuang, the lack of housing for lower skilled workers forced the new town government to develop so-called 'blue-collar [worker] apartments' to solve a housing shortage, while the villas and apartments of commodity housing were developed for those who commuted to central Beijing. On the other hand, Songjiang in Shanghai, a new town discussed later, found a need to develop new industries after the relocation of labor-intensive manufacturing industries to the western region of China. As a result, the suburban area is predominately residential and lacks economic vitality.

The designation of 'new town' additionally imposes a governance challenge (Wu and Phelps, 2011). Below the municipality of Beijing, there are 16 urban districts and 2 counties. But Yizhuang new town does not belong to any of these jurisdiction units. The new town is physically located in the Daxing District. The narrowly defined new town is Beijing ETDZ (with an area of 46.8 square kilometers), which is governed under a development agency that directly belongs to the municipality of Beijing rather than the district of Daxing where it is located. In other words, Yizhuang new town is not part of Daxing District. But more complicated is the fact that the actual functional area of the new town is much larger than that of Beijing ETDZ, and spills over into nearby areas. Some of the areas that are spilled into actually belong to a different district, the district of Tongzhou. There is no unified administrative body that is responsible for the whole area of Yizhuang new town. The governance of this new town area is thus quite fragmented. The new town has to negotiate constantly with two other district governments when it tries to provide social services. The planning area of the new town, however, is much larger, covering an area of 212 square kilometers (Figure 6.2). This planning area consists of three parts governed by two district governments and one municipal development agency (that is, the development zone). The new town plan has a spatial layout but lacks regulatory power over these separate parts. What is more difficult is that to plan the new town as a strategic growth area, it is necessary to develop even further to an area of 500 square kilometers. The strategic study of Beijing spatial development prepared by the Chinese Academy of Urban Planning and Design in 2006 proposed consolidation of

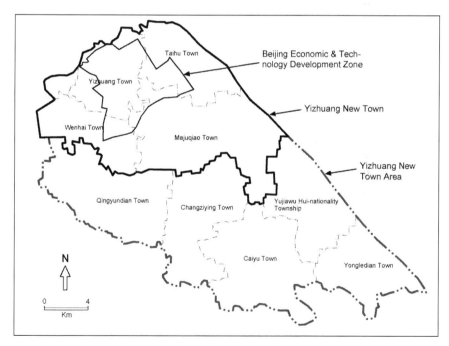

Figure 6.2 The jurisdiction area, planning area, and functional region of the new town of Yizhuang in Beijing. This shows administrative fragmentation, which is not dealt with effectively by spatial planning. The jurisdiction area of the new town is controlled by a development agency, while other two local district governments govern the actual functional areas. The new town plan, prepared in a top-down manner, is essentially a growth plan for its jurisdiction area.

Source: Wu and Phelps, 2011

the current fragmented governance of this region. But the implementation of this proposal would be quite a challenge.

The planning of Yizhuang shows what a new town plan can and cannot do—essentially as a growth plan for the new area, the new town plan lacks the capacity to coordinate different governments in the region, which reflects some fundamental features of Chinese planning: planning is for growth but is weak in coordination. In fact, the making of such a plan is not itself an outcome of negotiation between these different local governments or stake-holders. It is a top-down process organized by the municipal government and its development agency. Administrative fragmentation creates difficulties not only for service provision for the new town but also for the transformation from a development zone to a new town. The lack of governance intervention at a city-region scale has been a limitation of Chinese growth-oriented planning.[4]

Songjiang new town in Shanghai

Songjiang is located about 40 kilometers from the city center of Shanghai and is designated as a new town in English style. The new town is literally a new city, with a population size of 680,000 in 2010.[5] It was built on the site of an old satellite town and has been expanded with a 'university town' and clusters of master-planned communities built in the 2000s. Within the new town area, there are diverse residential types. Some are high-rise suburbs, such as the area near the stations of No. 9 Metro Line to Shanghai. Other areas are built to a lower density with a villa style, such as Thames Town in the western residential quarter of Songjiang (Figure 6.3). The reasons for relocating to these different suburban residential areas were quite diverse (Shen and Wu, 2013); for example, those who moved to the villa area were motivated by the lifestyle choice and planned to use their houses as second or holiday homes. For the 'white collar suburb,' high-rise apartment buildings near the metro line stations were chosen, because of their cheaper house prices compared to the central areas. Residents have to commute to central Shanghai for work. Rural migrants also moved to the suburban new town mainly because of the employment opportunities, hoping to work in nearby industrial parks.

In 2001, Shanghai organized a design competition for Songjiang new town, which attracted five international firms. Atkins, a British firm and also the first planning firm to enter the Chinese market, was the winner of the competition. Subsequently, it was asked to prepare a strategic plan for the whole of Songjiang new town, and an urban design for a pilot area of about 23 square kilometers. There were three flagship projects: the town center, the transport hub, and an English-style residential area. With a consultation fee of US$6 million,[6] the planning and design of Songjiang new town marked a new era in Chinese

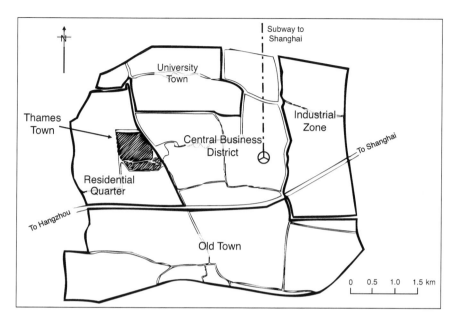

Figure 6.3 The location of Thames Town in Songjiang new town in Shanghai.
The spatial plan shows that Thames Town is in essence a cluster of gated
communities. The villa area is part of the designated residential area in the
new town in addition to other types such as high-rise apartment buildings
near the metro line stations and residential areas in university campuses.

Source: Shen and Wu, 2012b, p. 192

planning practices, which began to emphasize esthetic landscapes and lifestyles.[7]
The public spaces of Thames Town deliberately encompass buildings of Tudor,
Victorian, and Georgian styles, with a neo-Gothic church surrounded by lawns,
a castle by a man-made lake, and a plaza with red brick warehouses on the
waterfront (Plate 6.2).

Thames Town is in essence a cluster of gated communities (Shen and Wu,
2012b). The development was completed in 2005. But because the villa area
is located about 5 kilometers from both the town center and the Songjiang
station of No. 9 Metro Line to Shanghai, most residents are supposed to travel
by private car rather than public transport. The houses sold quickly but not
many buyers actually moved into Thames Town. They simply used the houses
as second homes or holiday resorts. Because of low occupancy, the shops
in the English-style town center lacked customers and became difficult to
maintain. This is in sharp contrast to a bustling English market town atmosphere. Faced with the difficulty of building the center of a market town, the
developer then repositioned the central area as an 'international art district'
and decided to develop cultural industries, conventions, exhibitions, and
wedding services. In the central area, the urban planning exhibition center

Plate 6.2 **(a)** The Thames Town at Songjiang new town. It is master planned to mimic an English market town style. But this cluster of gated communities dominated by villa styles is only part of the suburban new town landscape. The majority of housing in a new town is built as high-rise apartments, at a density higher than their Western counterparts, as shown in **(b)**. This shows the high-rise apartments at Jiading new town of Shanghai. This represents the 'ordinary' landscape of a Chinese new town in contrast to the branded and exotic style of Thames Town.

and art galleries are used to host public events and exhibitions. In particular, the wedding business has grown very successfully, with 19 wedding studios in the town, for those customers who seek a 'truly Western wedding.'

The development was carried out by Songjiang new town development corporation, which is a joint venture between the district government and three large municipal development companies. The municipal development companies provided 100 million yuan and the district government contributed the land. The new town development corporation carried out the initial plan and development tasks such as detailed design, land acquisition, and infrastructure construction, and then leased the land to other development companies to carry out housing development. The corporation itself invested and built schools, supermarkets, a sports center, an art gallery, and an exhibition center, while three other developers were each commissioned to construct a single villa-style residential subdivision. A fourth company—Henghe Property from Zhejiang province—was in charge of the development and management of the town center and commercial area. These companies paid a significant amount of capital to the corporation for the land, which became a major source of investment for the corporation. The new town development corporation itself also developed a gated residential subdivision, and reaped a substantial return.

As shown in the design of Thames Town, foreign consultants are used in planning processes for two reasons. First, the planning of a new town, in this case, and indeed city planning in general in China requires knowledge beyond the specific locality. When Shanghai aimed to designate a cosmopolitan style for new towns, local planners simply did not know how to achieve this. Second, using foreign planners who back the novel concept, be it 'new urbanism,' new town, or eco-city, can help make the story more convincing and authentic. On the completion of Thames Town, the mission of making Songjiang a distinctive English-style new town had been 'achieved,' as argued by the director of Songjiang planning authority,[8] because it had been quite challenging to plan the whole new town in an English style. In fact, the original plan for other places was not fully completed. Songjiang new town as a whole is distinctively Chinese—with numerous high-rise blocks in the suburbs and a building density higher than some central areas of Western cities. But designating a very small pilot area to adopt the English style made it possible to achieve a brand. As can be seen later, the development of eco-cities adopts a similar tactic. Within a vast ordinary housing area, some ecological technologies are applied to some buildings, which creates a significant impact and reputation. In Sino-Singapore Tianjin Eco-city, a large property developer, Shimao, developed an estate named 'British Land.' Planning here contributes to 'enchanting' the lifestyle of suburban new towns.[9] In contrast to the undesirable image of public housing estates in British new towns, new towns in Chinese suburbs are 'designer products' which bear some characteristics of middle and upper-class housing.

Hexi new town in Nanjing

Hexi new town in Nanjing is also known as Nanjing Olympic new town. The development originated from the designation of the area as a new CBD of Nanjing, in conjunction with organizing national sports games as a 'marketing mega-event' (Zhang and Wu, 2008). Hexi, literally 'west of the river,' is a vast area to the west of the Qinghuai River in Nanjing, similar to Pudong New District to the east of the Huangpu River in Shanghai. It is therefore a new city center rather than a new town. The whole Hexi new area is 56 square kilometers, with 24 square kilometers of the core area reserved for CBD development. The new town is therefore different from other suburban residential developments at a distance from the city center. Rather, like the Pearl River new town in Guangzhou, the core of the development is a new CBD for the entire city. This business district outside the planning area of Nanjing was the brainchild of Li Yuanchao,[10] then the Party leader of Nanjing, and later received support from the provincial government when Li Yuanchao became the Party leader of Jiangsu province, as one of three office parks in Jiangsu to avail itself of the new development opportunities of service industries.[11] The Hexi area is adjacent to the city proper of Nanjing (Figure 6.4). The place remained undeveloped, because of high underground water levels and weak physical foundations. In 2002, the new town development office was set up. To support new town development, some administrative adjustment was made to assign the area to Jianye District. The office of the district government was relocated to the new town. The aim was to develop this area as the prestigious area of Nanjing with 16 office towers. Residents from inner Nanjing were relocated to this new area. According to the recent plan, Hexi aimed to become the Bund of Shanghai. Its planned population size is 600,000 by 2020. To the south of the CBD area, a Youth Olympics new town was built to host the summer Youth Olympic Games in 2014.

The development required significant investment. In 2003 alone, the government spent more than its accumulated revenue from land development. The government had to go to the land market for continuing contribution to this mega urban project. It was estimated that about 70 percent of the cost came from the premiums of land leasing. To balance the budget, the government had to release land plots at a much faster pace than planned. The contribution to new town development was achieved through negotiation with the developers, through programs such as 'using land to support road construction,' a mechanism similar to planning gain.[12] This was possible at

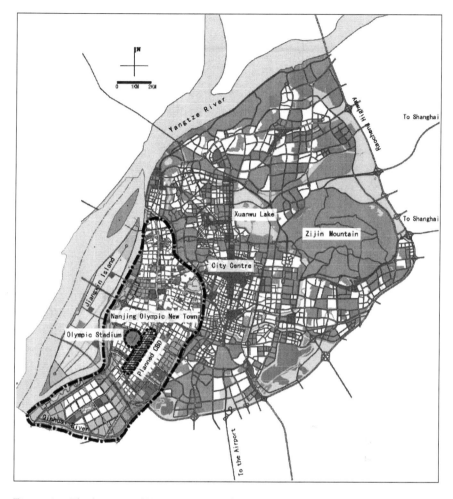

Figure 6.4 The location of Hexi new town. The new town is in essence a new district in which a new CBD is located. The development of a new CBD helps strengthen the concentration of producer services industries in Nanjing .

Source: Zhang and Wu, 2008

that time, before China adopted a transparent land bidding system in 2004. The development of a new town area attracted larger developers such as Vanke, China Ocean, Wanda, Shimao, and Shunchi. Initially the land price increased, and the government benefited from increased land value to fund the stadium, roads, public facilities, and landscaping projects. But nearer the time of the games the property market slowed down, because of the central government's control policy at that time. Moreover, the sudden release of new housing in a new area of Hexi led to the oversupply of properties. The government also saw a decline in income from land sales during the market downturn, which affected the confidence of developers and also delayed the auxiliary projects undertaken by the government. The tightening of macro-economic policy in 2004 created some difficulties for funding. An investment of approximately 40 billion yuan was planned in 2004, but only 5 billion was spent in addition to 12 billion yuan from the private sector. In 2005, after the completion of the National Sports Games, office buildings in the CBD remained empty. The government had to allow the developers to convert some offices into a residential development. The reuse of the stadium and other sports facilities became a challenge, as post-game legacies were not fully planned. The government had to subsidize the operation costs of these facilities.

The development of Hexi represents an entrepreneurial model of urban development. The development was organized by the new town development corporation to draw land income to fund infrastructure development. A growth coalition was formed for the new town development. Planning played a key role in project conceptualization, or more precisely, it facilitated the imple-mentation of the idea proposed by the political leader. Finally, Hexi new town

Plate 6.3 The central area of Nanjing Hexi new town. This place was left undeveloped for a long time and was outside the planning area of Nanjing, which means that development was not allowed. The development of the new town is attributed to the decision of key political leaders. Planning was passive at the beginning but was soon taken over by the leader and became part of the entrepreneurial mode of development.

has been generally successful because of its proximity to the city center. Key infrastructure such as the metro line was developed to link the CBD with the city center and railway stations. Now the new town has become the new CBD of Nanjing, the second largest CBD after Shanghai Pudong.

Huaqiao new town in Kunshan at the border of Shanghai

As discussed in Chapter 4, Kunshan as a county-level city adopted entrepreneurial governance and self-funded its development zone. Later, the development zone was recognized by the central government and became a national level ETDZ. The city of Kunshan is located at the edge of Shanghai municipality. It takes only about 20 minutes for inter-city trains to travel from Shanghai to Kunshan. Interestingly, when Shanghai built its outer ring road, the road cut across part of the territory of Kunshan at Huaqiao. That is, some of the area of Huaqiao is literally within the outer ring road of Shanghai. Kunshan took this opportunity to develop an edge city of Shanghai (Wu and Phelps, 2008). The local administrative status of Kunshan actually gave it more freedom to implement aggressive local entrepreneurialism. With the support of the provincial government, Huaqiao was planned as one of the three bases of Jiangsu province to promote outsourced office development. Learning from Shenzhen, Kunshan also strived to become a pioneering city in economic restructuring. The Huaqiao Business Park thus became the backbone of a business new town. It also aimed to fulfill the strategy formulated by the provincial government of Jiangsu in the development of service industries. It adopted the slogan 'Merging into Shanghai, facing the world, serving Jiangsu.' In a sense, Huaqiao was given a mission by the provincial government to open a door to Jiangsu to attract modern producer service industries. In so doing, it was hoped to promote the economic transition of Jiangsu. The planning of Huaqiao was specifically targeted at the development of information technology outsourcing, business process outsourcing, and logistics (Plate 6.4). The development of Huaqiao combined several sources of input: the support of a key provincial leader, entrepreneurial local government, and a business opportunity presented by its geographical proximity to Shanghai. The plan helped conceptualization and the formulation of spatial layout, designated land near the business park to guarantee the land supply, and also actively sought to develop key infrastructure, e.g. the metro line connection to Shanghai.

The coastal new town of Shantou

Shantou in southeast China is one of the four earliest special economic zones set up immediately after the economic reform.[13] But compared with the other three special economic zones, the economic development of Shantou has

Plate 6.4 (a) Huaqiao new town of Kunshan at the boundary of Shanghai. This new town aimed to become an edge city of Shanghai and attract office development. (b) The business park for information technologies. The opening of Shanghai No. 11 metro line to this new town improved its accessibility from Shanghai. However, the real estate sector played an important role. There is a risk that this business park-centered new town may become yet another property-driven development rather than a concentration of businesses.

lagged behind. Shantou, as part of Chaoshan culture, has a long tradition of trade, and its diaspora is distributed all over the world. Comparatively, it has less experience in industrial development. Shantou is partially constrained by high population density, even in its rural areas. It presents some feature of 'deskota.'[14] As the local culture is based on clans, there is a strong capacity for social mobility and self-organization. Shantou experienced a period of prosperity based on trade in the 1980s. But a case of smuggling led to the collapse of the trade-based local economy. In the aftermath of this case, Shantou wanted to strengthen its industrialization process. However, the external environment had changed. Dongguan in the Pearl River Delta experienced local industrialization but investment had moved to the Yangtze River Delta, to places such as Kunshan,[15] which relied on its strong collective economy and local governance capacity to develop a strong local entrepreneurism. The development in Kunshan proved to be successful, attracting, for example, Taiwanese investors in electronic industries at a higher order than small investors. As the latecomer, Shantou now faces tough competition. The development of Shantou has lagged behind. The development of the special economic zone has driven the city to expand towards the eastern seaboard, leading to the decline of the original city center in an inner harbor area. This is rare in the case of Chinese cities, because usually both suburban economies and the central city are experiencing fast growth (Plate 6.5).

Today, Shantou faces a much fiercer inter-city competition. The new phase of planning began to emphasize that planning should respect the local tradition of self-organization and recognize the fact that the local government has been relatively weak (Wang and Dubbeling, 2013). Because of weak local government and higher population density, it is difficult to acquire large parcels of land to attract major investment projects. Hence, the strategic plan prepared by Nanjing University[16] proposed an incremental approach rather than a familiar approach based on mega urban projects. The strategic plan aims to promote 'organic and incremental development' and transform Shantou into a 'bay area with two clusters.' The new vision was a 'coastal metropolitan garden city.' However, although the incremental approach to urban regeneration was promoted by the strategic plan, the funding for incremental change has been a challenge. Mega urban projects in China developed a funding mechanism by drawing capital from land development. However, for incremental improvement, it is difficult to generate sufficient land revenue to achieve infrastructure investment.

At the provincial level, the new provincial Party leader, Hu Chunhua, recognized the risk that Guangdong province might lag behind Jiangsu in terms of economic development, and urged the adoption of an expansionist approach. Specifically for cities outside the Pearl River Delta, planning was asked to

Plate 6.5 The dilapidated city center of Shantou. The old city center is located in the 'little park' (*xiaogongyuan*). The population moved very fast towards the new areas in the special economic zone, leading to population decline in the central area. This is rare in China, because the development of suburbs usually coexists with a prosperous city center, which remains an attractive location. The Chinese suburbanization process is in contrast to strong nostalgia for the countryside in Britain or white flight and inner city decline in the U.S.

enhance the capacity of the central cities (known as *kuorong*) by annexing nearby areas. For Shantou, the difficulty was that local government was relatively weak and found it challenging to control the land. Thus the coastal new town aimed to reclaim a large quantity of land from the sea, which was actually quite expensive. However, this approach at least circumvented regulatory control over the preservation of farmland. With investment from the National Development Bank, the city government refined the 'eastern economic belt' as a coastal new town.

Against this background, the coastal new town is being planned. The new town planning competition has been jointly commissioned by three parties: the Shantou Planning Bureau, the development office of the eastern economic belt (now new town), and China Transport Construction (Shantou) Ltd. The development office is a special department under the municipal government of Shantou and does not bear corporation status. This is different from other cities discussed earlier. In these cities, the development office and primary developer are usually combined into a state-owned development corporation. In the case of Shantou new town, the developer is a project company under a central state-owned enterprise (SOE). The SOE of the central government provides a credit guarantee for the debt of the Shantou branch to obtain a loan from the China National Development Bank. This is again unusual, because it is normal to use land as collateral for loans. In this case, land is to be reclaimed from the sea. The local government would benefit from the development of a new town as an achievement, but perhaps not directly in terms of land income.

The design competition was organized in 2013. With the help of ISCORP, in particular its deputy director, Martin Dubbeling, Shantou found three international firms to participate in the competition. These included Arup's office in Hong Kong, NBBJ from the U.S., and Kuiper. After four days of an international jury meeting, two schemes were chosen as the winners. One jury member admitted that 'this process was very intense.'[17]

Plate 6.6 The 'Shantou Cape'—a model of the coastal new town of Shantou. Paul Andreu, a French architect who planned the national theater in Beijing, stands beside the model developed jointly by the Dutch team and his firm.

Source: Photo taken by Ma Xiangming

What can we learn from the design competition of Shantou coastal new town? The original proposal was to develop the coastal area of Shantou as an 'economic growth belt.' However, after the change of city leadership, the emphasis has been shifted from an economic belt to a 'new town.' While service industries remain an important component, the adoption of a new town concept has expanded the scope. The development then began to focus on a new CBD. A new urban image was produced to strengthen this change. The 'Shantou Cape' of the winning scheme[18] is a designer space to put Shantou on the world map, with the aim of attracting overseas Chinese, as the strategic plan proposes that Shantou should become the home of overseas *Chaoshanese* (Plate 6.6). The award scheme is entitled 'The return of Shantou.' According to its chief planner, this is also 'The Return to Shantou.' The vision is that 'new Shantou will be a shining world-class garden city.'[19] The change from an economic belt to new town—the 'coastal garden city' as suggested by the winning scheme—reflects a substantial change in the development approach. Despite the call by the strategic plan for an incremental urban regeneration approach, the new town was proposed as a mega urban project. This is understandable, because under current development conditions, mega urban projects are probably the only effective way to promote development quickly. Shantou coastal new town has been planned and developed just like many other new towns in Chinese cities.

What are Chinese new towns?

From the analysis of these exemplars, it is now pertinent to critically examine the concept of the new town in China. The term 'new town' is used loosely in China, and can refer to both new settlements and large urban regeneration projects. In terms of land use, a new town in China could be a purely residential project, because of its large scale. It could also refer to a new financial center, an edge city of clustered office buildings, or a purposely designed university campus. In terms of location, the new town includes the development of a business district adjacent to a city's built-up area. Examples include the Pearl River new town of Guangzhou, Zhengdong New District of Zhengzhou, or Hexi new town of Nanjing. These are similar to Canary Wharf in London or La Défense in Paris, which are not normally known as 'new towns.' Other typical new towns, such as Yizhuang of Beijing or Songjiang in Shanghai, are located at some distance from the central area, and are literally independent new cities. Large new towns such as Yizhuang and Songjiang are not purely residential areas but rather contain a mix of residential, industrial, and office developments. The known villa area of Thames Town in Songjiang new town only occupies about 1 square kilometer, though it brings good publicity. In this sense, the Chinese new town is quite diverse and different from the widely known post-war British new towns[20] as it has been built as a growth pole (or 'anti-magnetic' pole) in the municipal region, to counter the attractiveness of the central city.[21]

In China, first and foremost, the new town is an investment and financing platform. The whole new town might be initially controlled as an asset of a single large company. The creation of new towns in this way can be seen in Guangzhou, which proposed to develop nine new towns in 2013. But these are not new towns, because the word 'town' is only used metaphorically here. The town indeed refers to any type of mega urban development as a single entity. But the 'town' is not simply a place without boundaries. The boundaries of these projects are clearly marked for the purpose of investment. Therefore, the so-called 'nine new towns' in Guangzhou are in fact new mega urban projects. As discussed earlier, urban governance in China is quite fragmented, especially in terms of planning and finance. These projects try to combine the processes of planning, project approval, resource allocation, and land regulation into a mega project that has a geographically identified area. But most importantly, the district government is seen to have ownership after the decentralization of planning and development into urban districts, because each district wishes to set up an investment and financing platform. The combination of planning, resource allocation on the lines of the Development and Reform Commission, and land regulation in the hands of the land authority resulted in the higher efficiency of these platforms.[22]

As shown by one of these nine 'new towns,' Guangzhou financial new town is an entirely urban redevelopment project (Plate 6.7). The project needs to demolish an old power station and villages to create a new district. Guangzhou paid a heavy cost for hosting the Asian Olympic Games in 2010. After the games, there was pressure on municipal finances. The resulting action was to further devolve planning powers to local district governments, each of which was asked to shoulder a financial burden and maintain a growth momentum. The key issue is to sustain financial capacity through the creation of new projects to raise capital. Against this background, these nine new towns were created as new investment and financing platforms. Planning plays an active role in the process of creating new development concepts, while the creation and operation of a new town relies on an investment and financing platform to raise capital based on land collateral. The use of an investment and financing platform by the local government is widespread and raises the concern of local financial debt. For example, in the Wujin New District of Changzhou, eight investment and financing platforms have been set up, ranging from a techno-city and tourist zone to eco-parks.[23]

Not all new towns have been successful. Some even failed at the beginning if there was a severe overbuild problem or they were built in the wrong location. The worst case was the 'ghost town,' such as Kangbashi New District of Ordos in Inner Mongolia (Plate 6.8) and Chenggong District in Kunming,

Plate 6.7 The planned Guangzhou 'financial new town' adjacent to the CBD—the Pearl River new town. This scheme aims to replicate Canary Wharf in Guangzhou. The whole new town is built as a mega urban project.

Source: Courtesy of Guangzhou Planning Bureau

Plate 6.8 The new Ordos in Inner Mongolia, which experienced a high property vacancy rate. Its new district is known as a ghost town in China. The risk of a real estate bubble increased in the early 2010s when manufacturing industries slowed down.

Source: Photo taken by Nicholas Jewell

which allegedly applied the concept of 'new urbanism.' Concepts such as new urbanism or transit-oriented development (TOD) may be used to expand a city into the suburbs. Without strong planning support and a land development driver behind these projects, development in these locations far away from the city center would be impossible.

A brief verdict

The power of planning is fully demonstrated in the creation of brand new master-planned developments such as Zhengdong New District of Zhengzhou, and Lingang new town in Shanghai. In the planning of Yizhuang new town of Beijing, the master plan upgraded the development zone into an entirely new urban area. Although there are spontaneous and informal developments in unplanned Chinese suburbs, new towns reflect a planned and formal development approach. The planning process uses various promotion tactics. Repositioning is an important approach; for example, Huaqiao new town in the jurisdiction of Kunshan fully utilized its geographical proximity to Shanghai and repositioned itself as a new 'edge city' with producer services for the Shanghai region. The development of new towns as mega urban projects has implications for the process of plan-making, which now has a defined objective to serve these projects. Planning is thus becoming more project-led instead of formulating a comprehensive land use plan. The new town plan focuses on 'investment and financing platforms' like the 'nine new towns' of Guangzhou, which are quite diverse projects ranging from a smart technology cluster to a financial center. The planning of a new town is in essence an expansionist plan rather than a way of constraining land uses. The plan serves as an interface between the market and the state, which facilitates project conceptualization and helps the government control the land as the primary developer. In short, the business model of planning is fully embodied in the planning of new towns.[24]

In this sense, the new town plan is a generic type. It operates across different scales, including strategic urban areas in a metropolitan region, specific large-scale projects within an existing urban area, or large master-planned communities. In fact, some urban regeneration projects have begun to take a new town development approach. For example, in Guangdong, the policy of so-called 'three types of old area regeneration'—old factories, old villages, and old urban areas (*sanjiu gaizao*)—designed the redevelopment scheme as a whole master-planned community. The area is divided into at least two parts. One part is used for resettlement housing, and the other is redeveloped into office and commercial buildings or housing sold in the market to generate capital for funding the redevelopment project.

As shown in the process of planning new towns, planning has become a market instrument. Consultants and 'experts' are brought in through 'contracts' and 'paid services.' Detached from a political process, new town planning remains more like a 'commercial service' in contrast to the top-down plans funded and organized by the central government. The local government shows little interest in top-down plans such as the Yangtze River Delta Regional Plan. Without the cooperation of local government, these top-down plans are very difficult to implement. For example, a city in southern Jiangsu was listed in the regional plan as a controlled 'optimizing zone' rather than a priority development area (see Chapter 5). When the leader was asked about the regional plan, he said he had not heard of it but "without us how could it be possible to implement it in this territory?"[25] The local government has its own vested interest in the growth agenda. Restraint of growth by the government itself is difficult to achieve.

Planning China's eco-cities

Although eco-cities by name are new to China, they are in essence a special type of new town that incorporates some technological and ecological features to achieve ecological targets. Such development was initially more focused on environmental and ecological qualities, and hence was branded mainly as 'green cities.' But later, at the national level, there has been increasing concern about greenhouse gas emission, as China faces international pressure. MOHURD therefore coined a new term—'low-carbon eco-cities'—to combine eco-cities and low-carbon policies. In the latter, green buildings and technologies are applied to reflect the new mission of carbon reduction. Interestingly, eco-cities are not entirely a top-down initiative. The movement combines at least three different kinds of input: national policies, local politics, and global policy mobility. At the national level, the eco-city concept is strongly supported by MOHURD, especially under Vice-minister Qiu Baoxin, and also the China Society for Urban Studies, of which the Vice-minister is also president. At the local government level, new initiatives are proposed to catch up with the new development opportunities supported by the central government.

Besides the early experiments of Huangbaiyu, a village in Liaoning province, to develop an eco-village (see May, 2011) or Dongtan (Wu, 2012d), eco-cities are now widespread in China. Just as with the frenzy of development zones in the 1990s and global cities in the 2000s, eco-cities became a new movement in Chinese urban development in the 2010s. By 2011, more than 259 cities in China had proposed to develop eco-cities or low-carbon cities.[26] The frenzy of eco-cities reached such a pitch that its policy master, Mr. Qiu, had to call for opposition to 'fake' eco-cities. Thus, MOHURD regarded the establishment of an evaluation system as an urgent task. In 2012, MOHURD approved a list of eight cities to be subsidized to the tune of 50 million yuan each for their eco-city development[27] (Table 6.2). The development of eco-

Table 6.2 The eight eco–cities supported by MOHURD pilot program.

	Planned area (sq. km.)	Population target	Per capita built-up area (sq. m.)	The time span of construction (years)
Sino-Singapore Tianjin Eco-city	30	350,000	58	10–15
Caofeidian International Eco-city	74.3	800,000	93	5
Guangming new district of Shenzhen	156	800,000– 1 mn.	90	n.a.
Wuxi Taihu new town	150	1 mn.	100	8
Chongqing Yuelai Eco-city	3.4	57,000	43	9
Changsha Meixihu new district	7.6	178,000	40	8
Guiyang Zhongtian Eco-city	9.5	172,000	41	5
Chenggong new district of Kunming	160	1.5 mn.	107	n.a.

Source: Adapted from China Society for Urban Studies, 2013

cities in China is thus an interesting combination of three trends: the emerging eco-state, which regulates carbon emission and justifies its existence by new regulatory functions; local entrepreneurialism, which uses the opportunities created by eco-cities to promote local growth; and policy mobility, which introduces various eco-city imagineering and environmental technologies from overseas. In planning practice, policy mobility is made possible by 'commodification' of planning as a contracted consultancy task.

Not all the plans for eco-cities are prepared by professional planners. For example, a city in southern Jiangsu commissioned a consultancy to develop its southern new town. The leading consultant was not a professional city planner.[28] In fact, the eco-city planning consultancy was commissioned and supervised by the system of the Development and Reform Commission. The plan is a non-statutory study, similar to a 'conceptual plan.' The study proposed to develop an imaginative layout of flower-shaped settlements (Figure 6.5). The proposal is quite unconventional and artistic, but has gained the support of its political leader. However, under the system of the Development and Reform Commission, there is also a formal type of plan, called the 'main functional area plan' (see Chapter 5). Immediately after the eco-city

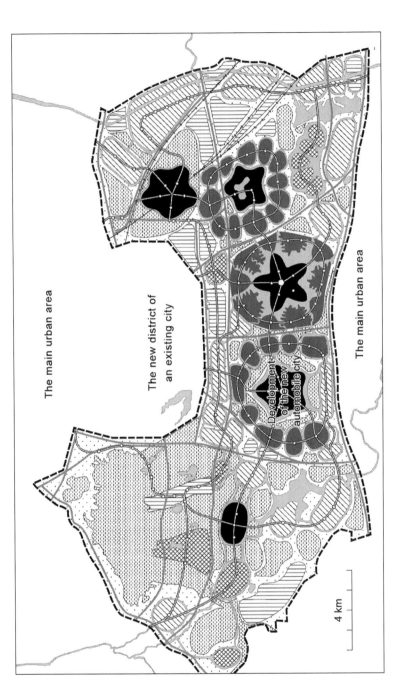

The main urban area

The new district of
an existing city

The main urban area

Development
of the new
automobile city

4 km

Figure 6.5 The new eco-city proposal for a city in southern Jiangsu. This new town is located in the southern area of the city. This grand imaginative proposal aims to develop an entirely new town that consists of flower-shaped settlements. The eco-city is mainly greenfield development on farm land. The area is subject to high development pressure. One of these 'flowers' on the left corner has already been occupied by a large automobile industrial project to develop an automobile city.

consultancy, the system commissioned an institute in the Chinese Academy of Sciences to prepare the main functional area plan. However, the formal plan ignored this proposal and conducted its own study of functional classification. At the same time, the process of urban master plan revision (2013–2030) started. The consultant's proposal for the southern eco-city has created an awkward situation for its new master plan. It is obviously difficult to absorb this consultant's proposal for a new town into the master plan, as the latter is subject to a technical index control, especially the regulation of the quantity of built-up land per capita. The master plan was not able to resist entirely the idea of building an eco-city in the southern area, but tried to use a scientific approach based on technical rationality to propose a 'recreational business district' as a large ecological park, which would reduce development intensity. But it is not clear how this development project can be financed. For the new town type of eco-cities, real estate development provides a major source of investment (see the case of Changxindian eco-community in Beijing later in this section). In this section, some examples of eco-city planning in China are reviewed in order to understand the institutional background of eco-city planning.

Dongtan Eco-city

The first experiment with eco-cities in China was perhaps the Dongtan project located on Chongming Island in Shanghai. In 2005, the landowner of Dongtan near the wetland of Chongming Island, the Shanghai Industrial Investment Corporation (SIIC), wished to develop the site but did not have a definite idea. The location was quite sensitive, and hence there might have been some constraint on large-scale development. The company needed a new planning concept to overcome the constraint. Interestingly, the use of planning to overcome development constraints has been successfully applied in the redevelopment of inner urban areas. At Xintiandi in Shanghai, where the First Chinese Communist Party Congress was held, the site was under building height restriction. The developer, Shui On group from Hong Kong, asked Benjamin Wood, based in Boston, to plan the area. The place was designed into a cultural and entertainment quarter by preserving the *shikumen* (stone portal gate) style housing and turning it into small restaurants, bars, and boutique shops (He and Wu, 2005). For Dongtan, a London-headquartered engineering consultancy firm, Arup, offered a concept of 'integrated urbanism' (see Pow and Neo, 2013) to turn the place into an eco-city.[29]

Arup then became the key partner in the Dongtan project and was asked to prepare a master plan for an area of 80 square kilometers. The project aimed to become the first eco-city in the world and attracted wide attention due to excellent information dissemination by the Arup design team. The first phase

Plate 6.9 The vision of Dongtan. **(a)** The landscape of Dongtan is designed to feature ecological modernization. **(b)** It also aims to provide an appealing landscape of Chinese urbanism, with the symbols of a pagoda and water landscape.

Source: These images were part of the 'Dongtan Eco–city urban concept,' which was awarded the Holcim Awards Acknowledgement Prize 2008 Asia Pacific. Courtesy of Holcim Foundation

of the project was planned to accommodate 10,000 residents to showcase the World Expo 2010 in Shanghai. The population target was 80,000 by 2020 and aimed to eventually reach half a million people. In essence, this would be a new city outside Shanghai city proper (Plate 6.9).

The project failed to be implemented. Despite the publicity, the Dongtan project has not been rescued (Plate 6.10). This is unlike the Sino-Singapore Suzhou Industrial Park or the Sino-Singapore Tianjin Eco-city, characterized by a developmental state approach and close collaboration between the government and state-owned enterprise. Arup is a master planner rather than an investor. However, investment was not the only constraint. The Dongtan project was not initiated by the central government, nor was it a project of the municipal government. It was the project of a large enterprise owned by Shanghai municipality. The development bypassed the county government of Chongming, which was lukewarm in its enthusiasm for the project. The county government would not give its land quotas to the project. As it was a mega project supported by the municipal government, the Shanghai government should have directly allocated land quotas to the Dongtan project. However, the issue of land quotas was not really a constraint, because in order to support the World Expo, the central government gave a green light to Shanghai and allowed Shanghai to prepare a package of key infrastructure projects that required land to be approved as a package. Approval was much easier and more straightforward. However, when the former mayor, Cheng Liangyu was jailed for corruption, the government no longer pursued any land quota allocation for the project.

Even though land quotas could have been a significant obstacle at that time, Dongtan was after all a commercial project. If SIIC had been determined to pursue the project, it would still have been possible to obtain approval for land allocation. However, first and foremost, Dongtan was a design project with some possibility of implementation. In fact, SIIC was not entirely sure about how to use the piece of land in Dongtan at the time. The planning of Dongtan

Plate 6.10 The site of Dongtan wetland at Chongming Island of Shanghai. The photo was taken in 2010 after the project was suspended

was thus a brainstorming exercise, although the consultancy was quite costly. The planning process of Dongtan project started with design, then master planning, and finally a business case for development. This is different from other mega projects, for example, West Kowloon cultural and recreational district (Raco and Gilliam, 2012) in Hong Kong, where the parameters for design consultancy are clearly defined. In fact, the design-led approach could occur anywhere. It happened in Dongtan, because SIIC possessed the development rights to this area. There was also a lack of contextual understanding of the location. This is also different from other eco-city projects, such as Wuxi Taihu new town, where a small area was designated for the eco-city project. The development of the new town was carried out irrespective of whether there was an eco-city project. The eco-city component simply added some ecological control indexes. For Dongtan, because of the absence of a profitable business model, investment was uncertain. Efforts were made to argue the case for the development of a low-carbon research academy as well as contacting HSBC as a potential investor. However, these potential investment opportunities did not come to fruition.

Why did Dongtan 'fail'? Or perhaps it is more precise to ask why Dongtan failed to be implemented, because to the planning consultant, this was not necessarily a failed project. As the landowner, SIIC, saw it, the project was not economically viable. The additional cost of green technology on top of the property price could not be internalized,[30] i.e. absorbed by the housing market. The project did not reach a stage where a co-funder was identified. The project had first to be a viable real estate project. Then, the ecological aspect of an eco-city could be added on. Dongtan was not really an ambitiously grand project. The initial size of the Dongtan project was a population of about 10,000 people. Featuring 'low impact development' for a total area of 80 square kilometers, development would be concentrated in about 1 square kilometer, according to the Chinese design standard, which is roughly the size of Thames Town in Songjiang. In other words, the project could be regarded simply as a cluster of gated communities. The properties in Thames Town sold out quickly after completion.[31] Therefore, the initial stage could be achieved without too much difficulty. The major problem, however, was the location of the project. It was still regarded as too far from the city center for this type of property.[32] The cost of green technologies could not be recovered from property development. The final stage of Dongtan was planned to reach a population of 500,000 in an area of 80 square kilometers. This would have meant that eventually Dongtan would become one of the major new towns (as identified in the scheme of 'one city and nine towns'), but compared with other new towns, job provision would be a challenge—jobs in the manufacturing sector would be unlikely. For a long time, another new town in Shanghai supported by the municipal government—Lingang new town—failed to attract residents. Although it is near enough to the Shanghai deep-water port to be developed into heavy equipment production and port industries, the distance from the city center was a constraint on the development of a new town. Even for producer services or creative industries, it is questionable whether the location of Dongtan (as compared with Songjiang, a university town, and Jiading, an automobile town) would be sufficiently attractive. The question was whether the business case for Dongtan was strong enough to attract investors or whether it was just seen as having a robust design. This engineering-led approach did not manage to fully cover the investment plan, while the owner did not have a development strategy at the stage of eco-city planning. This is a lesson for other technological developments such as smart cities.

Sino-Singapore Tianjin Eco-city

The failure of Dongtan did not stop China from experimenting with eco-cities. The Sino-Singapore Tianjin Eco-city is another example of collaboration between the Chinese government and the government of another country— Singapore in this case. But on the ground, the development was conducted by a joint venture between Tianjin TEDA Investment Holding Group and a Singapore state-owned enterprise that represented the Singapore government. The agreement of the two governments was ceremonial but laid down the institutional foundations for this eco-city project. The project is located quite far away (about 45 kilometers) from the center of Tianjin. The project is physically based in Tianjin Binhai New District, a new district that received strategic support from the central government after Pudong in Shanghai in 1990. The eco-city covers an area of 30 square kilometers, about 1/20 the size of Singapore. The development area was chosen to minimize land occupation. It is built upon 'unusable' land. One third of the land is deserted saltpan, one third is saline-alkaline non-arable land, and one third is an area polluted by the discharge of industrial wastewater in the past. This is quite different from the high-quality environment of Dongtan. The Tianjin Eco-city Project itself could be regarded as an attempt to promote an 'ecological fix' and pollution treatment. However, the project was controversial from a larger geographical perspective as to whether this place should be developed at all, because it is an ecologically sensitive area that connects the ecologically preserved northern mountainous area of Beijing–Tianjin–Hebei and the ecological corridor leading to the Bohai Bay. It is also a migration path for birds.[33]

The Tianjin Eco-city Master Plan was jointly prepared in 2008 by the Chinese and Singaporean teams. The China Academy of Urban Planning and Design was responsible for the overall design. The objective was to create an eco-city that could be practically replicable in other places. The planned

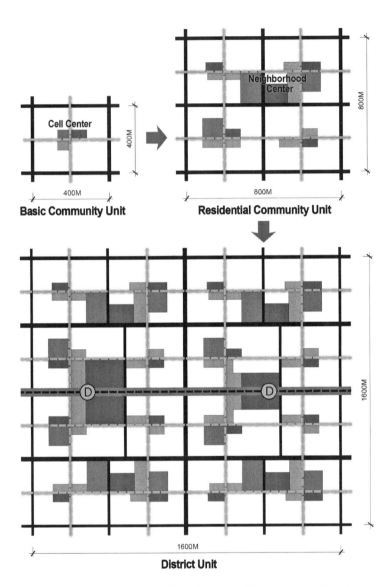

Figure 6.6 The residential structure of Sino-Singapore Tianjin Eco-city based on the
            Singaporean concept of eco-cells. This model seems alien to the Chinese
            planning practice as an imported concept from Singapore through the Chinese
            and Singaporean joint design team but in fact there has been a long tradition
            in China of using micro-districts, a concept that can be traced to the
            'neighborhood unit,' to plan its residential areas.

Source: Yang and Dong, 2008

population was 350,000 by 2020. In terms of density, this is slightly higher than the usual standard of 10,000 residents per square kilometer in China. The plan adopted the mass transit as the central development corridor and designed the city center and two district centers together with the transit stations. The spatial structure is thus characterized by 'one axis, three centers and four zones.'[34] An interesting feature is that the eco-city adopts a concept of specific 'neighborhood units,' known as Singaporean 'eco-cells' (Figure 6.6). The residential structure consists of three levels: the basic eco-cell as the neighborhood unit, the residential district, and urban development zones. The lowest level, the eco-cell, is a 400 meter by 400 meter superblock. The eco-cell has four to five buildings. The second level is in essence the commonly used micro-district or 'residential community' (*xiaoqu*), which in fact has a long tradition in Chinese planning.[35]

The eco-city adopts a wide range of technological fixes, for example, technologies for water saving and combined heat and power supply. The solar energy is required to exceed 60 percent of the total energy supply (Plate 6.11). Over 50 percent of water will be recycled. Sewage treatment should

Plate 6.11 The streetscape of Sino-Singapore Tianjin Eco-city, showing that solar panels have been used for street lights. The eco-city presents various technological fixes to advance the low-carbon agenda. The photo shows the buildings of an estate called 'British Land' which is designed in the style of a British market town and British castles.

Plate 6.12 The sales office of Shimao is combined with a low-carbon exhibition hall.
A buyer is browsing the list of released properties. Residential development is
a central feature of eco-cities.

reach 100 percent, with a sewage treatment plant with a daily capacity of
150,000 tons. This is particularly useful for areas with water shortages in
northern China.[36] Green buildings are planned to save energy. A system of
slow transport separates pedestrians and automobiles, and green transport
adopts the 'neighborhood unit' together with TOD. At the street and
community levels, parks are built within accessible distances. Green coverage
will be over 50 percent, and green corridors link the parks and squares.

Because the eco-city is relatively large, some land is assigned to industrial
uses. It is hoped to achieve a better job and housing balance. In the nearby
Tianjin Binhai New District, industrial developments provide additional jobs.
The eco-city is mainly driven by housing development. Large property
developers such as Shimao and Wantong have taken plots to develop residential properties. The sales office of Shimao is named and serves as a low-
carbon exhibition hall (Plate 6.12). New property developments include an
estate called 'British Land', designed in a hybrid Western style. However,
Sino-Singapore Eco-city is quite a long way from the center of the new
district. Whether or not residential properties in the new district will sell
remains to be seen.

Caofeidian International Eco-city

Caofeidian International Eco-city is located in the city of Tangshan near Beijing in northern China. The city is part of the widely known Beijing–Tianjian–Tangshan urban clusters. In 2005, Caofeidian was still a small city but the relocation of Capital Steels from Beijing to Caofeidian stimulated its development. The initial area of development was only 2.8 square kilometers, but this soon expanded to 74 square kilometers. The core start-up area accounts for 30 square kilometers. This aggressive expansion was due to the identification of eco-cities as a new growth impetus. A Swedish engineering firm, Sweco, was asked to prepare the conceptual plan for the start-up area in 2007, and the Tsinghua Planning and Design Institute prepared the detailed plan. In 2008, Hebei province formally approved the Tangshan Master Plan (2008–2020), which confirmed the status of Caofeidian as an eco-city. According to the master plan, Caofeidian will have a population of 800,000 by 2020. The eco-city partially serves as the living quarters of the state-owned enterprise, Capital Steels. The central area of Caofeidian and the new industrial area are the two wings of Tangshan, which serves as a main seaport for the capital Beijing (Figure 6.7). The eco-city features a 'circular economy,' which promotes the flows of industrial materials and energies between enterprises to make the best use of intermediate materials and reduce waste.

The most distinctive feature of Caofeidian is the adoption of a system of indicators. The Swedish company, Sweco, proposed 141 indicators. There are 109 indicators for planning, consisting of three levels. The first 68 indicators are set for the master plan level, then there are 16 at the development control plan level, and finally 25 indicators at site level. The remaining 32 indicators are management criteria (Joss and Molella, 2013, p. 125). The number of indicators is far more than for the conventional design codes in China. The data are not available for Chinese cities. It is not certain how the planning system can cope with this level of complexity. The reality is that these indicators are all proposed for the 'city of the future,' rather than regulating current settlements. In short, they just represent desired developments. The purpose of the indicators is to make the eco-city vision more concrete and 'operational.' Therefore, there is no need for extensive data collection.

Sweco have designed the new eco-city of Caofeidian as a 'techno-city,' which contains many technological features. It is noted that the term 'eco-city,' in this case at least, "appears to have a dual meaning – namely, relating to certain environmental measures and benefits (renewable energy generation, public transport etc.) and relating to a particular kind of planned, urban technological ecosystem" (Joss and Molella, 2013, p. 127). The indicators try to define the technological ecosystem. Although the Swedish side played a significant role in the planning of Caofeidian, for the Swedish government this was an

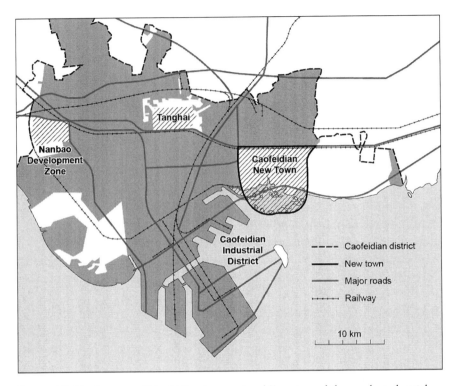

Figure 6.7 The location of Caofeidian International Eco-city and the nearby industrial
area and the city proper.

opprotunity to introduce Swedish technologies to China. It did not make any
investment in the city.[37] This was disappointing for Caofeidian, reminiscent
of the Dutch efforts to develop a joint project in Pingdi in Shenzhen without
investing in the development.[38] In the latter, the only support given was for
planning, which it was hoped would generate a market for environmental
technologies.

The development of Caofeidian was expensive. The land was reclaimed from
the sea, but increasingly this approach has become quite costly. Infrastructure
constitutes a huge cost. It is concerning that the Caofeidian's debt may well
exceed 60 billion yuan, while the total annual fiscal budgetary revenue for the
city of Tangshan was 30 billion yuan.[39] The original plan for Caofeidian
involved the development of four pillar industries—port industry, electricity,
steel, and petrochemical—which has not materialized. Investment in industrial
development significantly declined after 2011. There is a risk that the eco-city
may go bankrupt.

The Changxindian low-carbon eco-community in Beijing

Changxindian is another example of Arup's application of its concept of 'integrated urbanism' to low-carbon residential areas in China. The town is located at Fengtai District in the southwest of Beijing. After approval of the Beijing Master Plan (2004–2020) by the State Council, Beijing strived to develop a green strategy. The extension of Zhongguancun High-tech Park into multiple parks in Beijing gave Fengtai District an opportunity to to establish a zone to enjoy the same preferential treatment as the Beijing Indigenous Innovation Zone.[40] Three kilometers away from the old town, a new development zone of Changxindian was set up at that time. The area faces serious environmental problems and is one of the major areas being treated for pollution. The purpose of developing Changxindian was to explore ecological development, promote high-tech industries, and transform the previous development model. The low-carbon plan of Changxindian was jointly prepared by Arup and the Beijing Institute of Urban Planning and Design, and was started in 2008.[41] But the development of this eco-community project should be seen in the context of wider macroeconomic changes.

The developer, Vanion (the Chinese spelling literally is Wannian Jiye), managed to obtain the development rights to a piece of land near Changxindian town in 2006, but soon after that, in 2007, the central government suddenly tightened up real estate policy to cool down property speculation.[42] The developer therefore needed to find a new way to develop the land. Allegedly inspired by Dongtan, the developer commissioned an eco-development plan. The development was carried out by a joint venture of equal shares by Vanion and a local town-owned enterprise.[43] As has been shown earlier, this is a powerful Chinese model for development zones, because in essence it is a real estate project developed by real estate companies but with ecological and low-carbon themes. Officially, the developer, Vanion, together with Fengtai Planning Bureau and the park management committee jointly supervised the planning process. In reality, the 'client' of this eco-planning project was a large property developer. Later the project was also referred to as 'Changxindian Eco-city' or 'Vanion Eco-city.'[44] (See Plate 6.13.) The Changxindian project advertised the involvement of Arup and its track record in the design of the Bird's Nest Stadium, the Water Cube aquatic center, and Sydney Opera House. The developer, Vanion, also had a track record of planning eco-cities and involvement in the Caofeidian International Eco-city project.

The planning process of this eco-project had two stages. The first stage was a conceptual plan for sustainable development, and the second stage was the preparation of a detailed development control plan for low-carbon objectives. Again the eco-city concept was implemented through the combination of ecological objectives and development control plans. In Changxindian,

Plate 6.13 The Changxindian low-carbon eco-community in Beijing. This the name
that was used for its ISOCARP award in 2009, but it is also known as
Vanion Eco-city in the property advertisements, because its developer is
the Vanion Group. In essence, it is a real estate project themed with ecological
and low-carbon features. For example, about one square kilometer of wetland
has been created to enhance ecological quality. The buildings are equipped
with solar roof panels and arranged in such a way as to facilitate air
circulation. Just as many real estate projects use the town or city to represent
a large development scheme, the project shown here is the Garden Palace
estate of Vanion Eco-city.

eco-planning was built into the preparation of the detailed development
control plan at the street and land parcel levels. First, the objective was to
reduce CO_2 emission by 50 percent, and renewable energy usage should account
for more than 20 percent of the total energy use of buildings. Green space
coverage should be over 50 percent, with 40 square meters of green space per
capita. About 15 percent of housing was set aside as social security housing,
and the maximum distance from each housing unit to the bus station was
specified as 500 meters. A series of other indicators were designated. According
to the plan, the ecological footprint should be reduced by 27 percent compared
to the conventional urban model. Again, the plan for Changxindian stressed
the use of neighborhood units and tried to reduce commuting distance. Because
the development project is in a suburban area, to reduce the ecological footprint
it encourages a balance between jobs and residential uses. Changxindian is a
self-contained and independent development area. The plan tried to maximize
matches between jobs and housing, that is, the people living there are not

supposed to commute to the city center but rather to work in nearby industrial parks. This is not entirely new, as the rationale of socialist planning was to facilitate living near the workplace and commuting through walking and bicycles. What is novel here is the use of low-carbon indicators, including energy use indicators, renewable energy requirements, green roofs, and micro-climate designs. The project was a small-scale pilot scheme and only occupied about 5 square kilometers. After approval, the plan received the International Society of City and Regional Planners' (ISOCARP) 2009 best award.

Wuxi Taihu new town and the Sino-Swedish Wuxi low-carbon city

Wuxi low-carbon eco-city is another example of the use of planning instruments to promote local development. This eco-city project captured the national policy agenda for eco-cities and turned the requirement for ecological development from a potential constraint into a development driver. South of Wuxi, a vast area of 150 square kilometers was designated for a new town project. In 2007, the development office of Wuxi Taihu new town was established. The plan aimed to develop a sizable new town that combined multiple functions of government, office, finance and business, culture and entertainment, science and research, and residential areas. The target population size of the new town was 800,000 with 500,000 jobs. The new town has a high-density CBD (Plate 6.14). As with other Chinese cities, Wuxi new town is more compact than new towns in the U.K.

The development of Taihu new town attracted wide attention from large developers. SCII, the landowner of Dongtan, was one of the developers who showed interest. It recommended that the new district government should consider the eco-city as an attractive option. But the consultancy came with an extremely high price tag. The Wuxi New District government found out that it was Arup who had actually designed Dongtan Eco-city and therefore contacted the company directly for consultancy.[45] In 2009, Arup prepared an eco-city plan for Wuxi Taihu new town. At that time, MOHURD started to advocate eco-cities and later, low-carbon eco-cities. Wuxi took this opportunity to insert the low-carbon concept into its new town development and hoped that "through the development of an eco-city, [Wuxi] could enhance the quality of its city and competitiveness" (Feng and Yi, 2012, p. 83). In the same year, the new district government asked a Swedish architectural firm, Tengbom, to prepare the 'Sino-Swedish low carbon eco-city conceptual plan.' The success of Hammarby in Stockholm provided an attractive exemplar. Through swift planning actions but also, more importantly, the existence of a physical entity of a new town, Wuxi Taihu new town managed to gain the title of 'national demonstration zone of low-carbon eco-city' from MOHURD. Within the vast

Plate 6.14 Wuxi Taihu new town. The town center has a much higher density than its Western counterparts. The Sino-Swedish low-carbon city is part of the new town.

new town area, an area of 2.4 square kilometers was assigned to the pilot project of the Sino-Swedish low-carbon city in the memorandum jointly signed between the municipality of Wuxi and the Swedish government. The planned population size of this low-carbon city was 20,000. Through these entitlements, Wuxi successfully up-scaled its new town into a national and international project.

The unique feature of the Sino-Swedish low-carbon city is that it is actually a small pilot area within a much larger new town, which meant that the low-carbon project could be designed in detail. This low-carbon city planning practice was innovative in Chinese planning, because the new town government managed to 'graft' a set of eco-city development targets onto the existing detailed development control plan (see Chapter 3). Because a detailed development control plan is a statutory plan, this combination allowed the eco-city targets to be implementable through a set of control indexes extending from conventional plot ratio and setback requirement to the inclusion of ecological indicators. This, in theory, promotes eco-city development through planning requirements (Figure 6.8). In 2011, this practice was codified through the promulgation of Wuxi Taihu New Town Eco-city Ordinance—the first local legislation for eco-cities in China.

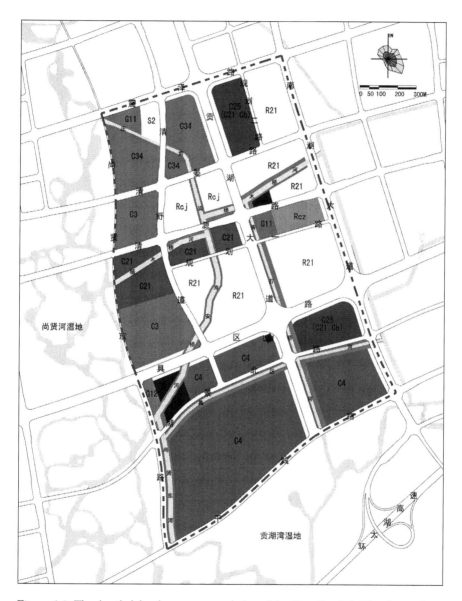

Figure 6.8 The detailed development control plan of the Sino-Swedish Wuxi low-carbon
city in Taihu new town. The figure shows that ecological indicators are used
together with conventional planning indexes in the statutory plan.

Source: Wuxi municipal government

But the real challenge is whether the market can accept the cost of eco-city development. In Wuxi, the new town has a firm development plan and will be developed anyway regardless of the eco-city component. It might be difficult to apply the eco-city index to the whole city of Wuxi, but it is possible for the pilot area of the new town. Factories and villages in this area have been demolished to allow the creation of a brand new town. Through inserting the control index, the Wuxi government requires new development to adopt development standards that follow eco-city objectives. Some indexes might be difficult to implement, as it is difficult to apply directly the indexes used in Sweden to a Chinese city. Besides different development stages, weather conditions are very different. Wuxi has subtropical weather, with four clearly divided seasons and quite cold winters and hot summers. The Deputy Director of the Planning Bureau of Wuxi new town admitted that it was difficult to adopt some new technologies in the eco-city, such as extensive solar panels, combined power and heating systems, regional energy supply, and a pneumatic waste collection system, because these are quite expensive infrastructure items and the running costs would be a challenge and require extensive subsidies from the government. Water filtering treatment is not viable, because currently the water and sewage charges to residents are quite low in China.[46] However, the development of Wuxi Eco-city is possible from the perspective of the real estate market. It is estimated that the introduction of green building technology

Plate 6.15 The film studio base in Wuxi new town. The new town has mixed-use development. The base is also a major tourist area.

into new town development would add 10 to 20 percent to building costs. This would be detrimental to locations such as Dongtan, because whether Dongtan itself could be a viable real estate project is questionable. But in the convenient location of Wuxi, the new town itself is a viable real estate development project. In addition to residential development, the new town has managed to attract the development of new industries such as a large base of film studios (Plate 6.15), and hence the new town can provide jobs for residents living there.

Conclusion

The Chinese city generally has a higher density than its Western counterpart. For a long time, until the development of a land market in the 1990s, urban dispersal was difficult. Planning for satellite towns in the era of Republican China was utopian, given weak financial capacity and warfare. In the socialist period, the development of new towns was dependent on large state-owned enterprises. These are in fact 'factory towns'—scaled-up working-class communities.[47] The difficulty of building new towns lies in the fact that infrastructure development was regarded as 'non-productive' unless it was directly used for industrial growth. In a sense, new towns in the British style were not built. In the post-reform era, a different type of space was created—the development zone. This is similar to the 'enterprise zone,' because it aimed to 'deregulate state control' to attract inward investment. However, in contrast to the streamlining of planning in the U.K., in China local resistance is weak, and planning permission has never been an obstacle to development. The need to create a development zone is due to the necessity to designate a defined space to apply for preferential treatment for investors. These policies are most effectively implemented if there is a form of planning to support the 'spatialization' of state policies. For example, the Huaqiao Business Park was specifically created to capture the opportunity of being an edge city location in the Shanghai city-region. Planning has thus been strengthened and re-oriented to suit this demand. In this sense, development zones can be regarded as the first generation of new towns in China. They were created initially for the purpose of economic development. For example, Beijing ETDZ at Yizhuang was created for the automobile and electronic industries. Songjiang new town was developed to receive relocated industries and electronic industries, and later tertiary education (university campuses). Huaqiao Business Park aimed to attract back-office data processing and offices. Economic development is at the core of new town development. These new towns are master planned. In short, they are more similar to Canary Wharf than Milton Keynes. But in addition to industrial development, new towns under a land-driven fiscal regime created a new opportunity for real estate development. Again, given the high density in the central and inner urban areas, with rising incomes the demand for improved living conditions has been strong. Higher density makes urban redevelopment more difficult. From this perspective, the development of new towns as new residential space is reasonable. But in order to lure upwardly mobile residents to move to the suburbs, these unknown green fields need to be branded and packaged into attractive lifestyles (Wu, 2010a). Thus, new town planning has had an esthetic parameter added to it. Various new ideas have been imported from the West to achieve this purpose, for example, 'new urbanism.' In reviewing Chinese planning history, it can be seen that the concept of the neighborhood unit was imported in the era of the Republic of China (Lu, 2006), and again extensively implemented as the socialist 'working-unit neighborhood.' Thus the concept is not entirely new. Planning plays an active role in enhancing the attractiveness of housing in new towns. But in order to increase profitability, most housing in new towns has been developed into high-rise apartments. This is again due to weak community resistance or virtually unknown 'nimbyism' towards housing development in the suburbs. Local communities in the suburbs have been rural farmers, who are weak actors in Chinese governance. The newly relocated residents are not powerful enough or able to form a local identity to restrict further densification of the suburbs, although some residents have begun to resist the invasion of planned green space into their estates.[48] Besides master planning at the community level, which creates Chinese 'master-planned communities' or gated communities, citywide planning like the scheme of 'one city and nine towns' in Shanghai actively transforms landscapes as an urban strategy (Shen and Wu, 2012a). In this second generation of new town, the marketing of quality of life (green, garden city) is combined with necessary real estate operations for higher density in China. In a wrong location, this model of development may lead to a ghost town of higher density buildings. Rather than following a neoliberal retreat, planning often initiated the aggressive development of suburban mega projects of new towns through a set of planning techniques from the so-called 'concept plan' (urban non-statutory strategic plan) to urban design.

As can be seen, a new town is not a 'deregulated' space. This is particularly obvious for a special kind of new town, the eco-city, which resulted from the increasing state politics of carbon control, as seen in the capitalist state (While, Jonas, and Gibbs, 2010). This new spatial regulation, however, does not mean that eco-cities are a product of state regulation. In practice, the local government has actively and tactically transformed the eco-city agenda into a new growth pole with some added ecological claims. If new towns have been driven by property development, eco-cities are almost always driven by the local state. The 'failure' of Dongtan is partially because it was not the brainchild of a local political leader (or ceased to be so after the imprisonment of the mayor, because of corruption charges).

Increasingly, new towns and eco-cities are used as mega urban projects to stimulate development. Planning always wishes to be at the center of the development agenda. The discourse of 'planning as a dragonhead' suggests the importance of planning—as the head, it leads the body and tail. Planning would be the key coordination mechanism too, according to this metaphor. However, as was sarcastically remarked by a local chief planning officer on the role of new town planning, the new town is "a dragonhead in the dragon dance. When a leader needs to show some idea, it is picked up in the show. And it's always changing!"[49] This reflects the new characteristics of planning under market transition: the role of planning sounds important, but in the end, it is an instrument for key politicians. As a result, the planning process has to follow commissioning projects as contract work rather than being a political process of negotiation between stakeholders. Planning helps to extract value through large-scale development. The public has not been given much consideration. However, this is exactly the style of contract work. Local government justifies it by claiming that this efficient style of planning is ultimately for the public good, because economic growth will generate a trickledown effect. Here, planning in the public domain[50] for the public good is replaced by planning for GDP growth. This GDP-centrism often benefits the 'real' chief planner—the political leader or mayor—and even directly contributes to their personal wealth, as shown in the recent imprisonment of the mayor of Nanjing, Ji Jianye, who was famous as 'Mr. Dig,' because he started digging up the whole city of Nanjing overnight to create a rain and sewage diversion system. In the process of new town planning, overseas consultancy firms are more willing to pursue and follow the requirements of the 'client'; and it is right for them to define 'planning' as contract work. This indeed puts them into a comfortable and realistic position: they do not need to explore the complex dynamic of the planning process, because they are not familiar with the local context. They only need to limit themselves to being technical advisors to win and complete a contract. They are even proud of 'helping to shape a proper business environment,'[51] because the local government (the client) often delays payment to design institutes. But for foreign firms, the government must pay according to the agreed schedule. The planning of new towns, and more recently eco-cities, more than any other type of planning, reveals the new style of planning in post-reform China.

Notes

1 For a summary of the suburbanization process, see Zhou and Ma (2000) and Feng et al. (2008) for an update on Beijing; see also Zhao (2010) for peri-urban land management.
2 See more about this policy in Shen and Wu (2012b, p. 190).

3   Wu and Phelps (2008) discuss the cases of both Beijing and Shanghai. Phelps and Wu (2011) provide an international comparative perspective on suburban development.

4   There are attempts to create regional and national governance through planning approaches, which is discussed in Chapter 5.

5   This figure is from Deng Zhituan's estimation published in *Dongfang Morning Post* (April 8, 2014).

6   Wang (2002), also in Shen and Wu (2012b, p. 191).

7   See Wu (2010a) for a discussion of packaged landscape in the suburban development. See also Pow (2009) and Zhang, L. (2010).

8   Interview in Songjiang, May 2010.

9   The word 'enchanting' is used by Knox (2008) to describe the role of urban design in making the suburban area more attractive.

10 This was initially revealed to me in 2002 in a discussion with a key informant in Nanjing planning bureau, and was confirmed by a provincial officer, personal communication, April 2014.

11 Another is Huaqiao in Kunshan near Shanghai.

12 This is similar to so-called Section 106 planning gain in the U.K., where developers are asked to contribute to the development of affordable housing facilities such as community centers, and other social services.

13 The other three special economic zones are Shenzhen, Zhuhai, and Xiamen. Hainan was the fifth at the provincial scale.

14 T. McGee initially defined the term; McGee and his co-authors applied the concept to Chinese cities, see McGee et al. (2007).

15 See Yang (2007, 2009) for Taiwanese investment in Dongguan and relocation to the Yangtze River Delta.

16 Professor Hongyang Wang at Nanjing University, a PhD graduate from Liverpool University, led the project.

17 A member of the jury, Ma Xiangming, a chief planner at Guangdong Institute of Urban Planning and Design, described in detail the experience in his blog.

18 It was produced by KuiperCompagnons and Paul Andreu Architecte Paris.

19 This is explained by Gijs van den Boomen of Kuiper, the chief designer, in the multimedia presentation as the part of the design package submitted to the Shantou government, October 2013.

20 For the development of British new towns, see Alexander (2009).

21 A typical new town is Almere near Amsterdam. The International New Town Institute is based in this new town. The institute recently launched a program, 'New New Towns', to compare six new towns in the world.

22 Xiangming Ma explained the nature of nine new towns in his Chinese blog, see http://blog.sina.com.cn/s/blog_750193d30101emuz.html, accessed February 20, 2014.

23 Mai and Zhang (2013) describe the development of investment platforms in the city of Wujin.

24 The 'business model' is discussed by Yanjing Zhao, the director of Xiamen Planning Bureau; see Zhao (2013), which argues that such a model is operated but is not fully recognized by planners.

25 Personal communication, June 2008.

26 From Li and Liu (2011).

27 China Society for Urban Studies (2013).

28 This was revealed by an informant during the filed visit, October 2013; before that, a senior planner of CAUPD posted the image and layout in a Chinese *weibo* without giving the name of the city.

29 See also Chang and Sheppard (2013), Wu (2012d), and Shen and Wu (2012a).
30 This was confirmed in an interview with a local business manager at SCII.
31 See Shen and Wu (2012a, 2012b).
32 However, the Sino-Singapore eco-city project is located quite a long way from the center of Tianjin and even at a distance from the district center of Binhai.
33 China Society for Urban Studies (2010, p 382); Li and Li (2012) discussed the problem too.
34 China Society for Urban Studies (2010, p. 385).
35 See legacies of socialist planning, the examples of Caoyang new village in Shanghai in 1950s to 1970s, and Fangzhuang in Beijing in the 1980s in Chapter 2.
36 In contrast to the Zhengdong new district, which lavishly featured a water landscape and thus was criticized.
37 De Jong et al. (2013, p. 108) confirmed this; this was also revealed by an informant in July 2012.
38 See De Jong et al. (2013) about the latter case.
39 He (2013) describes the difficulties experienced in Caofeidian.
40 Beijing is the first of three national 'demonstration zones of indigenous innovation' (*zizhu chuangxin shifanqu*). The other two are Wuhan's Donghu and Shanghai's Zhangjiang. For more information about high-tech park and innovation policies, see Zhang and Wu (2012).
41 This is discussed in China Society for Urban Studies (2010). The senior planner responsible for this project at Beijing Institute of Urban Planning and Design, Ju Pengyan, visited London for four months. The visit was organized by myself.
42 Wu (2014) provides a detailed account on property cycles in China. The tightening policy was relaxed after the global financial crisis. To cope with the decline in exports and the slowing down in economic growth, the central government injected 4 trillion yuan stimulus capital into the economy, which revived the real estate market.
43 However, in 2009, the Beijing municipal government began to require the government to play a greater role in the primary land market, that is, the market to release agricultural land to urban uses. The developer and district investment corporation each own 45 percent of shares, and the town government has 10 percent of shares. *Chinese Real Estate*, January 5, 2010.
44 This is referred to by property advertisements.
45 The planning process was described by an informant during a field visit in November 2013.
46 This information is from Feng and Yi (2012).
47 Stenning (2005) describes the large industrial communities in (post-)socialist Central and Eastern Europe.
48 See Boland and Zhu (2012) for community participation and mobilization for environmental preservation.
49 Personal communication, October 2013.
50 This idea is used by John Friedmann (1987), indicating public planning is not for profit, which is in sharp contrast to the Chinese reality.
51 A view expressed by a chief executive officer of a major global planning firm in the Chinese annual planning meeting, November 2013.

7
Planning During Market Transition

The dismantling of the centrally planned economy in Central and Eastern Europe had a detrimental impact on its planning system (Nedovic-Budic, 2001; Hirt, 2005). The planning profession became disoriented during market transition. In Western market economies, planning has been streamlined since the 'neoliberal' turn.[1] In the U.S., economic restructuring and the discourse of 'postmodernism' made the practice of modernist planning more precarious (Beauregard, 1989). In the U.K., city planning came 'under attack' in the Thatcher era because planning was regarded as a bureaucratic constraint on economic growth (Allmendinger and Tewdwr-Jones, 1997; Lord and Tewdwr-Jones, 2014). In some respects, planning has become more passive,[2] while spatial planning has been created to promote economic competitiveness (Boland, 2014). After a short period of rolling out spatial planning under New Labour, the Coalition government initiated a radical 'rollback' planning reform (Allmendinger and Haughton, 2012; Gallent, Hamiduddin, and Madeddu, 2013). In China, market transition has reduced the state's role in direct resource allocation. After more than 30 years of economic reform, many of the directives and controls of central planning have been abandoned and replaced by the market mechanism. However, urban planning has survived market-oriented reform and become the 'phoenix rising from the ashes.' The planning system was restored after the Cultural Revolution, and the statutory planning system now enables local planning authorities to enforce development control. Since the late 1990s, non-statutory plans have proliferated, and design competitions and planning consultancies have made planning a well-paid profession. In the 2000s, planning entered the 'third spring'[3] (Leaf and Hou, 2006). With increasing demand for urban planning, institutes of urban planning and design are overwhelmed by requests to draw up plans. This phenomenon cannot be simply attributed to fast growing economies which require more construction plans. This concluding chapter offers three explanations for this growing planning profession. First, planning survived during market transition because it managed to adapt itself to a market environment and became an instrument for place marketing.[4] This point will be elaborated later in this chapter.

Second, the introduction of the market mechanism has triggered social and environmental challenges and crises. The state has had to respond to these challenges, which required new regulatory controls. For example, rampant land encroachment raised an imperative to manage urban growth and protect 'basic agricultural land.' Fierce inter-city competition led to redundant construction and environmental problems, requiring collaboration between cities. This need eventually initiated the 'urban cluster plan' and the 'regional coordination plan.' In other words, the development of the market requires greater coordination and regulatory control. It has been argued in the context of U.K. planning that the market itself requires some certainty, and therefore so-called 'project-led planning' in the initial stage of deregulation has since shifted to 'plan-led planning.'[5] That is, the emergence of national and regional planning is seen as a regulatory response to rampant local market development. This perspective has been applied in earlier studies of emerging regional plans in China[6] and is discussed in Chapter 5. In China, leading planning practitioners have attempted to use these arguments to defend their profession. For example, Baojun Yang, chief planner at CAUPD, has always highlighted the reckless way local governments encroached on agricultural land, while Yanjing Zhao at CAUPD in the mid-2000s argued that in the new environment planning should adapt to serve the 'client' (see later in this chapter). Both of them strived to justify the existence of Chinese planners, though in different ways. However, what has not been fully understood in the Chinese planning literature is the new 'imperative' of planning in the context of changing state and market relations—asking the question, planning for whom? Intriguingly, this leads to the third explanation for booming planning activities since the late 2000s, especially after the global economic crisis in 2008.

The third explanation is that the market mechanism was introduced into China so as to expand the scope of capital accumulation rather than to reduce state dominance. This fundamentally requires a more historical understanding of market transition in so-called transitional economies.[7] As described in earlier chapters, the rationale of planning in post-reform China is for growth. Since the mid-2000s, when the regulatory control of the central government was strengthened under the ethos of scientific development, planning has been involved in complex central and local dynamics. The plan-making for urban planning is funded by ambitious local governments to justify their expansionist approach to the central government, to circumvent the regulatory constraints imposed by the central government, and even to capture opportunities such as special entitlements when up-scaling governance. For example, in response to the designation of various 'national strategic and experimental zones,' local governments utilized planning consultancy services to compete for these entitlements. So far this point has not been discussed in the literature of Chinese planning, or more broadly in the literature of neoliberal planning (Sager, 2011). As shown in this book, the notion of 'planning for growth' in China is not equivalent to 'planning for the market'; planning has been transformed and utilized to defend the dominance of the state during market transition. The argument is reminiscent of the 'post-political' perspective in the advanced market economy (Swyngedouw, 2009), which argues that the essence of neoliberal governance is a departure from a democratic process of politics.[8] In China, although there was no liberal democratic process of decision-making in the socialist period, central planning was a political process through which resources were distributed. It was believed that this approach was inefficient and needed to be changed. The reform introduced a complementary market approach and used technocratic rationalities to defend the interests of powerful elites. In short, the functionality of planning in today's China cannot be sufficiently understood with the reference to 'neoliberalism,' but has to be seen in the context of transformation of governance. Planning is a commoditized instrument that uses the discourse of planning for growth to justify the legitimacy and interests of the state during market transition. In the remainder of this chapter, these three explanations will be elaborated.

'Phoenix rising from the ashes': planning adaptation during market transition

As described in earlier chapters, planning in China has a tortuous history and was not the central concern in decision-making in the socialist period. Economic planning provided necessary conditions for industrial development. In the post-reform period, planning became a central issue in local development. In the spring of 2014, the new Chinese leader, Xi Jinping, started his field inspection of the city of Beijing at the Beijing Planning Exhibition Hall. He then visited an old *hutong* (alleyway) neighborhood and expressed his concern about old Beijing. His visit led to a vision of a capital city-region that incorporates Beijing, Tianjin, and Hebei province to improve collaboration and coordination. The overconcentration of economic activities in the capital Beijing was believed to be a threat to the city, as evidenced by the frequent appearance of smog. The visit highlighted the importance of city planning in China's development. The promulgation of a new urbanization strategy by the Chinese government suggests that city planning was considered an important method to achieve national strategies. The subject of planning is now raised to the same primary level as architecture and engineering (previously planning was a sub-discipline under architecture). At the local level, planning has now become the top priority of the local party leader and mayor. The rising status of planning is firstly attributable to the adaptation of planning to the new environment.

The introduction of the market mechanism has had a significant impact on the planning profession.[9] The major challenge for planning is overall institutional change, for example, the establishment of a new land use system, housing commodification, and the shift of governance from an interventionist to a more entrepreneurial approach. At the initial stage, planning became less effective in regulating land use,[10] as it could not deal with spontaneous land conversions in the central areas or contain urban sprawl at the fringes.[11] However, planning has quickly adapted to the new environment and instigated a series of changes. The changes from pre-reform to post-reform are summarized in Table 7.1.[12] In terms of planning rationale, planning used to be treated as a technical feasibility study and physical design. Now, it has become a medium to formulate and declare development targets. In terms of aims, the planning objective used to be to 'serve production and facilitate the living of the working class.' Now, enhancing economic competitiveness, branding the place, and attracting investment are major objectives. Consequently, the style of planning has shifted from blueprint physical design to policy statement. Increasingly since the introduction of the concept plan or the urban strategic plan, planning also includes policy recommendations. For functionality, the purpose of planning was to produce an internal document for the government, which was often kept confidential, and guidelines were produced to coordinate different industrial sectors. Now, planning also produces statements, slogans, and policy suggestions. One purpose of making these statements is to encourage the governments at lower levels to coordinate their developments. Another purpose is to provide justification to the government at the upper level for exceeding planning standards, or to compete for entitlements and preferential policies from the central government. This transformation is accompanied by changing the input to and the output of planning. In the planned economy, economic planning gave some certainty to physical planning, and thus the inputs were usually government commands and national economic plans. In the post-reform era, the local party leader or mayor increasingly influences plan-making, taking advice from external consultants, to such an extent that planning vision is heavily dominated by key politicians. The output of planning is no longer confined to a master plan and a detailed construction plan. The strategic plan has been introduced, and at a lower level, the detailed development control plan[13] has been invented. Regarding the approach to plan-making, planning work is no longer a design task assigned to local planning and design institutes. Instead, planning consultancy and design competitions are widely used to increase publicity, and external consultants are brought in through tender and contract. Through these changes, the local government uses planning as its instrument for growth promotion.

Table 7.1 The change in the Chinese planning system: contrasting planning during and after the socialist period.

	Pre-reform period	*Post-reform period*
Planning rationality	Technical/physical design	Economic/development declaration
Aims	'Serving the production and facilitate the living'	Branding the place, enhancing economic competitiveness, and serving investment
Style	Blue-print design	Strategy and policy recommendation
Input of the planning system	Commands from the supervisory government departments and national planning standards	Vision of political elites and the professionals, purchased consultant services
Output of the planning system	Master plans and detailed plans	Concept plan (strategic plan) and project-based urban design
Approach of plan-making	Internal tasks assigned to planning and design institutes	External consultation and planning contests
Functionality of planning	Production of internal government documents, development guidelines, coordination of different economic sectors	Production of external statement, slogans, policy recommendations, convincing investors, coordinating lower governments such as districts and suburban counties, justification for exceeding national standards

Source: Adapted from Wu, 2007

The plan-making method has also experienced some changes. Chinese planning emphasizes actions rather than analyzing the current situation and identifying problems. For example, Fuhai Wang, chairman of a private planning firm, proposes an action plan approach. This emphasizes setting up practical planning targets (rather than a grand utopian vision) and finding the pathway to achieve these targets. This is in contrast to the land use plan. For example, the plan for green space is a traditional land use planning approach. But proposing to build a greenway is an active action (see the image of greenway in Guangdong later in this chapter). The action plan approach thus aims to find actions to achieve planning targets. Another example of changing working methods is a holistic approach to planning. Hongyang Wang, professor at Nanjing University, argues for an holistic approach of 'multiple scenario selection,' because linear reasoning is not appropriate for complex institutional changes. Moreover, current land use and population data are usually non-existent. However, because planning is for the future and aims to make a change, it should not interpolate present conditions into the future. It should instead raise some possible alternatives for the local government to consider. Under this approach, the planning task should heavily involve visioning and normative persuasion about how to become 'a better city by doing the right thing at the right time.'[14]

One important change to the urban planning profession is the promulgation of the rate of the service charge, which transformed the planning profession from a government activity to a consultancy service. Seeing planning as investment in land development, the local government is willing to fund planning through public finance in the hope of greater returns from land revenue and tax. For example, the city of Kunshan spent about 20 million yuan in the revision of its master plan. However, the government felt it was worthwhile, because compared with massive investment, "This was little money, and in fact we did not expect that the master plan could make an instant change. Nevertheless, it did bring some certainty of development, at least it did not become a constraint for our growth."[15] As a result, the planning market is booming. From 2009 to 2011, the city of Qingdao was given funding of 89 million yuan for planning services. In Nanchang, planning fees reached 35 million yuan in 2011 and increased to 50 million yuan in 2012. Hangzhou invested 54 million yuan in 2011, and Chengdu's budget for project planning was 31 million yuan in 2014.[16] Once the plans have been made, local government is keen to display them, for example through gigantic models of future cities in magnificent planning exhibition halls equipped with multimedia technologies. Through planning consultancies, the government may receive the sensational endorsement of a 'world planning guru' to justify its ambition.

In response to the commodification of planning services, Yanjing Zhao, former senior planner of CAUPD and now director of Xiamen Planning Bureau, bluntly posed the question, 'Who is the client of the planning profession?' (Zhao, 2013). He argues,

> Surely this could not be the public, because the planner is not directly commissioned by the public; [and as long as this is true,] the planner cannot circumvent its client—the government—to serve the public. . . . The [local] government is the client of planning, and the government is 'an enterprise of space production,' the core technique of urban planning is to design the best 'business model' for the government . . . to maximize the interest of the client should be the major objective of professional planners. The role of the planner is to lobby the government and sell professional knowledge to those cities that wish to adopt its advice; the purpose is to help the client 'defeat' other city competitors. This is now the new professional ethics of planners. (*Ibid.*, pp. 1, 3, 5)

He argued that China is different from the West, because

> the public did not 'pay' the government. The government provides
> better services, not for the maximization of public welfare but rather
> maximizing its own interest. Just like a public radio station, the government
> strives to improve its programs so as to attract the audience, for the purpose
> of getting more income from advertisement, and winning in competition.
> (*Ibid*, p. 8)

According to Zhao, his advice is also for planners' own benefit:

> In today's world, planning also faces competition from other disciplines.
> If you were not prepared to do what the real world asks you to do, others
> would replace you for the profession. To realize its real role in the
> competitive world will help the planning profession back to the center of
> academia. Only in this way can planners invent more professional
> techniques to gain more power of discourse in professional competition.
> (*Ibid*, p. 5)

The warning is not a false alarm. The risk of not heeding it is that urban
planners will be marginalized, according to Zhao. Faced with competition from
the NDRC sector, a provincial official[17] deplored that the oversea consultant
commissioned by a "local government did not come from the planning
profession. The consultant might not even bother employing someone who
has proper drawing skill." But to his/her dismay, the senior governor of the
province actually liked the bold idea and publicly said the planning department
should learn from it. It was said that the plan was used to persuade NDRC to
approve yet another pilot zone. This made her/him feel pressurized and he/she
advised the urban planning and design institute, "You should learn from them
how to sell the idea to the government."[18] This example shows that professional
urban planners are facing competition from various kinds of consultants, not
necessarily in the field of physical design and planning.

Neoliberal or post-political?

Retreat or rescaling?

Decentralization in the post-reform era has caused local governments to behave
in an entrepreneur-like manner. In some aspects of urban planning, the state
has retreated from direct service provision, for example, the abolition of in-
kind occupation-based public housing. There is some debate about whether

Plate 7.1 The building of Yuhua district government of Nanjing. Built in the style of the United States Capitol in the U.S., the district government building symbolizes the dominance of state power during market transition. This makes an interesting comparison with socialist monumentalism and socialist splendor. Building styles changed during market transition but there is a continuation of grandeur and dominance.

Chinese urban development in the post-reform period resembles neoliberalism or, more precisely, a variegated form of neoliberalism.[19] But from the planning perspective studied in this book, it seems that the post-reform planning landscape is characterized by rescaling rather than retreat. In aspects other than social provision, the role of the state has been strengthened, for example, facilitating land clearance and the strategic designation of development zones. As shown earlier in Chapter 6, the development of eco-cities has been largely driven by the local state under central government initiatives. The state plays an active role in the development of science parks such as Zhangjiang High-tech Park in Shanghai. The policy of focusing on Zhangjiang has been noted as a factor contributing to biotech clustering (Zhang and Wu, 2012). Seen from the 'restless urban landscape,'[20] despite dramatic transformation, the dominance of the state has left an imprint on the built environment, revealing continuation rather than transition (Plate 7.1).

Shortly after the introduction of 'scientific development' in the mid-2000s, social policy researchers speculated that China might depart from neoliberal-

ism resulting from the 'double movement'—the Polanyi argument of social
self-protection movement, evidenced by increasing expenditure on education,
the implementation of minimum livelihood support, and greater inter-
government transfer to poor areas.[21] In the planning sphere, Chinese planners
believed there had been a shift of planning towards public policy.[22] But seen
from the perspective of this book, this shift has not been made, despite greater
attention to social problems and policies. Rather, marketization has been
maneuvered by a self-regulating party-state, to such an extent that 'a self-
regulating state can deactivate society, closing down opportunities for its
citizens to participate in policy making and counter-movements' (Zhang, 2013,
p. 1621). There have been parallel processes of down-scaling and up-scaling.
For example, two types of regional plans co-exist at the same time. The bottom-
up urban cluster plans aim to strengthen the central city and its competitiveness in inter-city competition, while top-down regional plans initiated by
central government departments, sometimes with local governments at various
levels, strive to foster inter-city collaboration and restore spatial order. These
two processes may be intertwined in some cases. For example, for the eastern
Guangdong region, three cities took the opportunity initiated by the province
to build up their own strength, which defeated the intention of the upper
government. Similarly, in the Pearl River Delta region, Guangzhou, Shenzhen,
and Zhuhai proposed their strategic zones of producer services and managed
to gain national entitlements at various stages. For example, Nanshan of
Guangzhou managed to up-scale its status from an Economic and Technological
Development Zone to a national new district in 2012. Following the designation of the Shanghai Free Trade Zone, these three zones of Guangdong
(Nansha, Qianhai, and Henqin) wished to make a coalition to apply to become
a national free trade zone in 2014. These attempts are intertwined with local
entrepreneurial initiatives and the central endorsement of the 'zone of
exception.'[23] At a regional and national scale, as can be seen in Chapter 5, a
new spatial order has been created through the up-scaling of governance and
reinsertion of state control through top-down planning and land management
(Li and Wu, 2012b; Xu and Wang, 2012).

The global financial crisis which started in 2008 provided an historical
moment for reinstating the visible hand of government, which further
strengthened state power. Through the creation of a 4 trillion yuan stimulus
package, responsibility for capital resource distribution returned to the central
government. This change consolidated NDRC as a powerful department, as a
'small cabinet within the cabinet' (the State Council), and at the same time
the post-crisis change drove the formation of large state-owned enterprises as
interest groups. For large projects, the state required planning justification and
support, which in turn raised the status of planning as a growth tool.

The role of the state is also reflected in the development of environmental management. Planning nowadays incorporates greater environmental awareness. China now faces international pressure to cut carbon emission, which has led to the formulation of a low-carbon strategy. MOHURD consequently supported the initiative of eco-cities. But this initiative was very much built upon locally initiated entrepreneurial growth projects. For example, the much criticized Chenggong new town of Kunmin was listed among eight green eco-cities and received initial funding of 50 million yuan from MOHURD for eco-city planning and green building design.[24] Outside the central government initiative, there have been various local experiments. For example, in Jiangsu, the village improvement program of 2012 tried to upgrade the rural environment without large-scale demolition.[25] In Gaochun, a county near Nanjing, the selling point of rural tourism is branded as the 'first slow-town in China,' through an initiative of the town government.[26] In a rural county of Zhejiang province, the county government promotes the development of a local economy based on re-use of local agricultural resources and eco-tourism.[27] In Guangdong, the development of a greenway network connects parks and green spaces, provides amenity for its residents, and enhances the quality of the environment (Plate 7.2). These programs are initiatives of the provincial government, under the Department of Construction.

Plate 7.2 The 'greenway' of Guangzhou. The greenway system has been developed in Guangdong province to improve the ecological quality as well as provide an amenity. The objective is to achieve sustainable development.

Source: Xiangming Ma

Market-technocratic rationality, inter-referencing, and policy mobility

Related to market-technocratic rationality is the use of inter-referencing and policy mobility in China. Inter-referencing is an important technique in market development and governance (Roy and Ong, 2011). Concepts such as 'new urbanism' and TOD are borrowed and referenced in Chinese planning and design. They are actively used in the real estate market, for example, for the development of villa compounds (gated communities). Sometimes, the authenticity of such linkage cannot be verified. For example, it was claimed that the design of a luxury housing project in a northern suburb of Beijing, McAllen (*maikalundi*), involved Elizabeth Plater-Zyberk, the founder of the new urbanism school, who gave an endorsement:

> All these excite me, and bring me back suddenly to the small town of McAllen in Texas in the States: tall palm trees, never-ending green fields, streets with luxury sports cars, layers of Chateau houses; this piece of land in front of me represents the future, and here it will be glorified because of the future. I name this project as McAllen Courtyard Villas, and hope she would, like her counterpart across the Pacific Ocean, bring the enjoyment of life dreamed by the people.[28]

As seen in Chapter 4, foreign consultants actively participated in the Chinese planning market, due to their ability to inter-reference with exemplars from across the world. Thames Town at Songjiang new town of Shanghai was designed by Atkins, a U.K.-based planning firm, with inter-reference to a generic English market town. In Jiangsu province, a village called Yaxi at Gaochun county near Nanjing built the 'first slow-town' in China (Plate 7.3). The international slow-city movement (*cittaslow*) officially endorsed Yaxi village as a member in 2010. The official webpage of Gaochun government quotes the endorsement of a former vice-president of *cittaslow*, Angelo Vassallo, that "all perfectly fitted the requirement for a slow city."[29]

But recently, the Chinese media have begun to question the introduction of foreign concepts and argue that the 'foreign species might not suit the Chinese soil.'[30] It has been said that the new town of Chenggong at Kunming is such an example. The project started in 2003, following the concept of TOD. After ten years of construction, the place is becoming a ghost town. The concept of the new town plan was to develop a new town with a population of 1.5 million by 2020, but in 2013 the population was less than 350,000 and even so, rows of newly built housing remained empty.[31] Calthorp Associates was involved in the preparation of the concept of the new town plan. According to the advocate of TOD, Peter Calthorp, the design was to achieve a more

Plate 7.3 The statue of a snail at the Yaxi village of Gaochun, symbolizing the first slow-city in China. The snail is the logo of the international *cittaslow*, originating in Italy. Using eco-tourism and organizing villagers to lead happy rural lives, the small town of Yaxi strives to show visitors a scene of sustainable development.

human scale city.[32] Now, the media have declared the concepts of new urbanism and TOD were not suitable for the local condition. However, it is not clear whether the concept plan set the population target or whether this may have been pre-set by contract outside the scope of the design. Indeed, in many other projects, international consultants brought in planning and design techniques. For example, in eco-cities and green buildings, the use of codes represents an engineering-dominated ethos for green urbanism.

Planning has become a conduit for policy transfer and mobility (Healey, 2012). As described in Chapter 4, local government is keen to involve foreign consultants to learn the exemplars from the global North.[33] The award of 'best practice' by international organizations such as Habitat and ISOCARP is of special appeal. The campaign for gaining such recognition may become part of an overall strategy to put the city on the map. International recognition is implicitly important for major urban projects, like the credit rating given by agencies for the securitization of (subprime) mortgages, because it could boost the confidence of the development. Planning by international consultants therefore represents a package, not necessarily just for development of the built environment but also paving the way to going beyond being 'ordinary cities' and becoming a global city on the map.[34] Awards from international organizations or the national recognition of 'strategic experimental zones' represents a strategy of 'jumping scales.'[35]

Under the market-technocratic rationality, planning attempts to use neutral terms such as sustainable cities, scientific development, and eco-cities to depict a planning scenario that cannot be rejected. As seen in Chapter 4, the development of vast rural areas between two separate cities is justified by ecological and sustainable development, with detailed green development codes. This to some extent resembles so-called 'post-political' planning in advanced market economies. For example, experts are brought into planning processes in an apolitical manner (Allmendinger and Haughton, 2012). As argued by Swyngedouw (2009, p. 608), the governance modes are 'autocratic governance-beyond-the-state.' As shown by MacLeod (2013), the U.S. 'new urbanism' model was introduced to Scotland through post-political planning that forged a technocratic consensus. However, the exact term 'post-political' needs to be interrogated in China, not just because China has not experienced the liberal democratic politics embedded in the capitalist state but also because the state has been visible throughout the prioritization of market-technocratic rationality, to which the next section will turn.

'Planning for growth' is not equivalent to 'planning for the market'

'Planning for growth' means the local government, as the client of the planning product, is more interested in future possibilities and actions. However, these actions are broad and not necessarily triggered by the market. The planning of mega urban projects in China is keen to find international partners, because the involvement of a foreign government, however limited, would up-scale the development project. It is not the foreign official but rather the official from powerful departments such as NDRC of the central government that are particularly important to the local government. Professor Zhigang Li from Sun Yat-sen University gave an interesting explanation:

> If a project involves a Singapore partner, senior government officials might attend some events; they could be a minister or even deputy prime-minister. Thus, Beijing has to send an official at the equivalent rank. It would be easier for the local government to show achievement on these occasions to the top leader, which may be helpful for career prospects. The Sino-Singapore Suzhou Industrial Park and Sino-Singapore Eco-cities at Tianjin Binhai New District are good examples of collaborative projects.[36]

For other cities that rely more on bottom-up initiatives, the motivation may not aim at a national entitlement but rather just at defending themselves from disturbance from the central or upper government. The city of Kunshan has received little support from the state in the past as a lower rank county-level city. It is less interested in getting a title from the state. When he was asked about the possible impact of the Yangtze River Delta Regional Plan, a mayoral-level official said, "We should and can do things by ourselves"[37]; indeed, as can be seen in this case, the purpose of plan-making is not to chase the market but rather to protect growth through minimizing potential constraints from the upper government. In the last five years (2009–2014), the newly revised master plan "has achieved this purpose. It did not become an obstacle for growth, which is good enough for us."[38] This reveals a complex message. Even though the city does not hope to gain preferential treatment from the state, in order to plan for growth, the purpose of plan-making is still *for* the state, or more precisely, not to be constrained from growth. Interestingly, the making of the plan is through a market service-provision approach. In Henan province, the capital city of Zhengzhou failed to defend its expansionist approach in Zhengdong new district (see Chapter 4), but after several attempts, Henan province managed to get central government approval for its concept of a 'central China economic region' centered on the city of Zhengzhou.

The finding makes an interesting contrast to the liberal market context where 'planning for the market' is thought of as the means to achieve 'planning for growth,' and the demand for planning may originate from the market. As shown in planning policy changes in the U.K., the real estate market requires certainty. The streamlining of land use planning using a 'project-led' approach in the early 1990s had to shift into a 'plan-led' approach in the late 1990s (Allmendinger, 2011). We may be tempted to explain the rise of planning in China in the same way. For example, the geographical coverage of planning has been extended from urban to rural areas. The development of the market itself began to put pressure on planning for proper control and coordination. This might be a plausible explanation, as planning increasingly uses the discourse of environmental quality and sustainable development to defend its position. However, rampant land development is not just a result of the unregulated market. Land encroachment originated from a unique land use system that gave monopolistic power to local government. The expansion of urban areas is promoted by the local state.[39] Planning contributes to the operation of the local growth machine. Under the discourse of scientific development and a harmonious society, planning has strengthened state power and its dominance over society. The state uses planning for growth as a governance technique to restore the structural coherence that had been temporarily disrupted by opening China to the world and the shift in capital accumulation (from industrial-based internal circulation in the socialist period to a globally connected urban-based development in post-reform China).

Now, when planning for growth, it is particularly interesting to ask, 'planning for whom?' In the Chinese case, planning for growth created complex central and local dynamics. The local government tries to use planning to unshackle regulatory constraints from the central government, while the central government aims to use planning to restore a spatial order. In addition to personnel appointments, the central government uses planning approval to strengthen the authority of the state. Planning is a new governance technique. This dynamic has been strengthened under Hu-Wen's leadership since the mid-2000s. In a sense, increasing government expenditure is not just a result of a double movement through which society reacts to the marketization process and increases its self-protection,[40] but rather represents the rising interest and capacity of the state during market transition. Planning for growth is not the same as planning for the market. Planning, as an instrument of market operation, extends the state apparatus into the market. In this sense, it is planning for the state. The unspoken 'side effect' of planning for growth as seen in housing demolition and urban redevelopment is the strengthening of state dominance (Plate 7.4). The purpose of planning is to maximize the land income of the growth machine or open up a new space for growth to generate taxes. Planning tries to remove informality (Roy, 2011b) and impose a new order of formality—but this kind of informality is created by the the peculiar governance that endorses the state's monopolistic right to convert rural land into urban land without adequate housing provision (Wu et al., 2013). In China, planning lacks the experience of dealing with informality and informal settlements; urbanization takes a formal form of industrial zones and planned new towns (see Chapter 6). Planning plays hardly any role in coordinating stakeholders. Because of the lack of a participation mechanism, planning cannot explicitly represent the 'public interest' (as argued by Yanjing Zhao in an earlier discussion in this chapter) to regulate the built environment.

Planning for social justice: re-politicizing Chinese planning

The logic of planning for growth is justified by the 'trickle-down effect' of growth. The growth of GDP is important, according to this ethos, because it provides necessary employment, which is critical for fast urbanization in China. However, the trickle-down effect is not guaranteed. In the U.K., the institutional design of 'planning gain'[41] is to negotiate for a share of the development profit and social benefits for the local community, but this approach has led to growth-dependent planning and unsustainable development (Rydin, 2013). In China, 'planning gain' is transferred to the profit of the initial land sale by the local state. Such a growth-dependent approach prioritizes exchange value over use value, which is determined by the imperative of the local

Plate 7.4 The demolition of an informal settlement that accommodated rural migrants in Shanghai. The neighborhood has been demolished, and the space is becoming part of the Caohejin High-tech Park. The redevelopment, however, is not for instant land profit. The new space is used for office buildings, which generate long-term business taxes for the local government.

growth machine (Logan and Molotch, 1987). As discussed earlier, the market-technocratic approach has been utilized to ensure the efficient operation of growth-dependent planning. Because social benefit is believed to be dependent upon the operation of entrepreneurial land development, the question of social justice has not been explicitly raised in the planning process in China.[42]

Recently, social justice and the right to the city have become subjects of concern in the Global North (Brenner, Marcuse, and Mayer, 2012) as well as in the Global South (Samara, He, and Chen, 2013). The concept of 'the just city' was developed by Fainstein (2010) to apply social justice to the city and formulate the principles of policy formation. It has been argued that among the probably conflicting values of equity, diversity, and democracy, planning has to prioritize the principle of equity (*ibid*). In Chinese planning policy, growth was prioritized, as it was believed that from growth, equity could be achieved later through the trickle-down effect. The issue of equity is not explicitly raised in decision-making. Alternative development has not been fully debated. There has been a call for a more participatory approach (through communicative rationality (Healey, 2006)). In the context of the Global South, the participatory approach has been difficult to implement or less relevant (Watson, 2009; Parnell and Robinson, 2012). In Chinese planning, the commodification of planning and state dominance mean that public participation is more at the stage of policy dissemination rather than policy formulation. The 'stakeholders' are not able to achieve alternative outcomes through negotiation.[43] Their right to the city can still be argued, as, derived from their lived experience and as the 'producers' of the city; the people have the right to affect the city as well as claiming the benefits of its economic growth. However, in reality, this is difficult, even for technocrats. Following the orders of a 'client' does not enhance the status of planners, especially when this is a commissioned project, as a professor from Sun Yat-sen University observed: "Increasingly, they [the local government in the Pearl River Delta] are not respecting us!"[44] The demand from the 'client' is overwhelming and difficult to negotiate.

In the operational modality of market-technocratic planning, Chinese professional planners feel frustrated by politicians' intervention. Professor Yuan Qifeng at Sun Yat-sen University claimed, "Once I had an argument with a section director of planning bureau, and at the end of day I have been completely dismissed [from the planning market of the city]".[45] Another planner from CAUPD lamented his experience, "Several of us had dinner last night. During the dinner, the client—director of the planning bureau—frankly said, 'planning is politics! You should not just follow the technocratic rationality'".[46] This comment triggered a series of debates on the Chinese *weibo*. Wang Fuhai, the chairman of a private planning institute, argued, "Planners should openly uphold upright politics." Another planner pointed out the political nature of planning:

> Master plan is politics, it is interest negotiation and a political game, and cannot be dealt simply [with technical knowledge]. We are facing more groups with vested interest and their demands. Each plan is a special case, with different objectives and actors. [We have to] find out the conflict and manage the way out. The major problem is that planners are unwilling to face political reality.[47]

Fulong Wu then commented:

> The director's verdict is incisive. The planning community knew it but just didn't speak out. In the time of the planned economy, planning was confined to technical rationality (blueprint) and outside politics. This apolitical nature actually gave Chinese planners a survival tactic. Planners now even had a chance to go to the banquet with politicians, and formed a close client–supplier relationship.[48]

These debates suggest that Chinese planning has not seen a shift from technical design to public policies.

What do we learn from Chinese planning?

Planning theories have so far largely been derived from the Global North. There has been an appeal to see planning from the South (Watson, 2009) and 'technologies of crossing' and 'slow learning' in contrast to 'fast' policy transfer (Roy, 2011a). However, in reality this is very difficult (Yiftachel, 2006; Watson, 2012) because the study of a particular planning system can hardly 'travel' from the South to academia in the North. Comparison between different economies in the South is inadequate; and often comparing planning in the South with its counterpart in the West focuses on its pragmatic and rational aspects (Wang and Hoch, 2013) rather than their substantial contrasts. This book is an attempt to interpret planning practice in China as a 'comparative gesture' (Robinson, 2011). First and foremost, without indulging too much in fascinating empirical details, it is a surprise to note that the concept of 'planning' can be paradigmatically different. In the recent history of planning policy in the U.K., "Planning has suffered a decades-long character assassination in the popular imagination of being procedural" but still provided "the last line of defence to space itself being neoliberalized" (Lord and Tewdwr-Jones, 2014, p. 357). In other words, planning has long been regarded as an obstacle to growth. The Coalition government of the U.K. stated in its growth review: "The reforms will ensure that the planning system incentivises growth with development driven from the bottom up, understands and is more responsive to changing demands of business, and is less bureaucratic."[49] In a paper with the same title as this book, David Cameron, Prime Minister of the U.K., is quoted as saying, "We are taking on the enemies of enterprise," including "the town hall officials who take forever with those planning decisions that can be make or break for a business—and the investment and jobs that go with it."[50] It is quite difficult to explain to Chinese professional planners that in the U.K., planning has been rolled back in order to promote growth (Lord and Tewdwr-Jones, 2014). In a quite different Chinese context, the first thing a newly appointed party leader or mayor would do is to fund a grand plan that is different from what was prepared by the previous leader. Chinese planning has experienced dramatic transformation and is booming. Its desire for modernization remains (Plate 7.5). In a different context, planning can be 'pro-growth' in its own way and be utilized by the state to unshackle institutional and spatial growth constraints.

Despite planning being a prosperous profession, Chinese professional planners still feel frustrated by pragmatism and conflicts of fragmented government departmental interests. There is still a lack of a unified planning system in China today. A professional planner commented on the strange deviation of planning practices in China:

Plate 7.5 **(a)** The Shanghai Stadium (now Shanghai Jiangwan stadium) at the new civic
center proposed by the Great Shanghai Plan (1929) during the era of the
Republic of China. The development of a new civic center has not materialized.
Now, a sunken square and a cluster of office buildings for R&D have been built
near the entrance to the stadium. **(b)** The project Chuangzhi Tiandi, or
'knowledge and innovation community,' is a mega urban project developed by
Shui On Group originating in Hong Kong. The same developer built Xintiandi,
a trendy entertainment district.[51] Like Canary Wharf in London, behind the
seemingly ordinary urban scene is corporate ownership.[52] The desire for
modernization cherished by the Chinese planning profession has been achieved
in a way that has not been possible previously, but the vision of a *civic* center
remains to be realized in Chinese planning.

Among three types of plan, although urban planners mostly cherish utopianism, the plan becomes an accomplice of home demolition, agricultural land encroachment, and artificial lake digging. The land use plan controls the quota for land leasing and captures the huge value from the gap between agricultural and urban built-up land rents, while claiming to safeguard the 1.8 billion *mu* agricultural land. Economic planning approves projects but is actually the approver of highly energy intensive and highly polluted projects; it pretends to be the promoter of sustainable development. (Wang Xinzhe, April 2014, Chinese *weibo*)

Confronted with a series of economic, social, and environmental challenges, Chinese planners have begun to realize that the current model of administratively dominated, race-to-the-bottom, land-driven development is unsustainable.[53] Although China has not totally abandoned growth targets, some Chinese planners believe that in the future, planning will have to confront the possibility of slow growth, de-industrialization, and even urban shrinkage in some early-industrialized areas. Planning has to adopt multiple objectives other than growth targets and shift from actively proposing new developments to regulating development and managing planning applications. Instead of following an expansionist approach, planning may have to fix existing urban and industrial areas.[54] These speculations are mind blowing. The question is, without a change in the political economic system, how can the transformation of the planning system occur?[55] Will Chinese planning that has been captured by the local growth machine[56] be able to overcome its limitations to address major problems during fast urbanization? How can planning go beyond pursuing its own power and the vested interests of government departments? The future of Chinese planning will be determined by its ability to deal with the fundamental challenges faced by the nation during fast urbanization and economic transformation. Chinese urbanization may be part of the process of 'planetary urbanization' described by Brenner (2013). We see in China the expansion of the 'urban' model of accumulation, namely, the deprivation of labor and monopolistic land (spatial) development for the maximization of exchange value based on the indicator of GDP growth rate, which exacerbates the trend of growth without development. Chinese planning has been instrumental in assisting the formation of this urban-accumulation model and consolidating monopolistic power in spatial development. Can Chinese planning help rebalance the consideration of use value and exchange value in its development and respond to the appeal to the 'right to the city'?[57] This requires planning to go beyond the market-technocratic rationality that has been fostered in the post-reform era. The Chinese exception—planning is not necessarily 'an enemy of growth'—would not be sufficient to justify its existence.

Notes

1　Yiftachel and Alexander (1995) summarize the five major changes in the 1980s and early 1990s: a shift from managerialism to entrepreneurialism; a retreat from managerialism to 'passive instrumentalism'; further fragmentation of the planning process; a focus on localities; and a continuing gap between aspiration and implementation. See also Allmendinger (2009) for the theoretical background of these changes.

2　See Rydin (1998); Allmendinger (2011).

3　From earlier chapters of this book, it can be seen that the 'first spring' occurred in the 1950s, when large-scale economic construction raised the status of city planning. The 'second spring' occurred after 1978, when planning was restored after having been abandoned in the Cultural Revolution.

4　This argument was developed in earlier studies in: Yeh and Wu (1999); Wu (2007); and Wu and Zhang (2007).

5　See Allmendinger (2011, p. 163) for periodization of the U.K. planning system; the original argument was elaborated in Allmendinger and Tewdwr-Jones (1997).

6　Wu and Zhang (2010) applied this to the conceptualization of emerging regional governance, which was further elaborated in Li and Wu (2012b). Li and Wu (2013) examine this argument in the context of the Yangtze River Delta Regional Plan.

7　He and Wu (2009) describe how the market mechanism is applied in China's inner city redevelopment to open up a frontier of neoliberalization; Wu, F. (2008) provides a further overview of China's market oriented reform and its implication for governance. See Wu (2010b) for an elaboration which argues that market development was introduced to strengthen state control rather than to replace or threaten its status. This is not a result of the 'authoritarian' regime (Harvey, 2005) but of a requirement to provide new growth areas, for example, through real estate development. The new development requires a strong state role, for example, support for the demolition of old urban areas and the building of new towns.

8　See also MacLeod (2011); Raco (2014).

9　Chapter 4 describes the practices of planning under entrepreneurialism. For the impact of economic reform on planning, see: Leaf (1998); Ng and Tang (1999); Yeh and Wu (1999); Xu (2001); Abramson et al. (2002); Ng and Tang (2004); Abramson (2006); Liang (2013).

10　The same was found in the post-socialist economies; see Hirt (2012).

11　See Ng and Tang (1999); Yeh and Wu (1999); Smart and Tang (2005).

12　The periodization of pre- and post-reform, however, is a conceptual one. In reality, the transformation is more gradual.

13　Also translated as 'regulatory detailed plan'; see Chapter 3.

14　The discussion is in Chinese and can be seen in Wang (2013). See Wang and Dubbeling (2013) about the strategic plan of Shantou led by Wang.

15　Personal communication during a field visit, April 2014.

16　These figures were mentioned in a presentation in April 2014 by Professor Cui Gonghao, a renowned planning professor in China; the figures are indicative and not verified.

17　For anonymity, the name of the provice was omitted.

18　From field observation and personal communication; for anonymity, the location is omitted here, April 2014.

19　Walker and Buck (2007); He and Wu (2009); Wu (2010b); Peck and Zhang (2013).

20 The notion of 'restless' was initially raised by David Harvey; see Knox (1991), and for Chinese examples of heritage preservation and modification, Western-style gated communities, and eco-cities and eco-modernization, see Shen and Wu (2012a).

21 See Wang (2008), in Chinese.

22 Zhang and Luo (2013), in Chinese, described how this shift happened.

23 See Roy and Ong (2011) for the concept.

24 See later the criticism in an article in *China Business* (February 15, 2014) which argues 'foreign planning idea cannot suit Chinese situation.'

25 This program is described in Wu and Zhou (2013).

26 The slow movement, also known as 'cittaslow', originated in Italy.

27 See Marsden et al. (2011) for detailed examples.

28 See Wu (2010a) for a description of gated and packaged landscapes in China. The original quote was accessed in 2008; since the completion of the project, the developer's website is no longer available. However, the quote can still be found on multiple websites of real estate agents; the website, bj.house.sina.com.cn/scan/2006–05–18/1513128512.html, provides a detailed story of an involved Chinese planner, Dr. Chengren Sun, accessed May 2014.

29 www.njgc.gov.cn/rdzt/gjmc (accessed May 2014). There is also a newspaper report in English, by *China Daily*, www.chinadaily.com.cn/cndy/2010–12/05/content_11653523.htm (accessed April 14, 2014). Mr. Angelo Vassallo was killed by the Camorra two months after his visit to China in his native town of Acciaroli.

30 The newspaper report in *Chinese Business* (February 15, 2014), online at finance.sina.com.cn/china/dfjj/20140215/005218219188.shtml, accessed February and May 2014).

31 A photo essay is available at *The Foreign Policy*, www.foreignpolicy.com/articles/2013/06/21/photos_ghost_city_chenggong_china, accessed May 2014.

32 See www.calthorpe.com/chenggong.

33 Sometimes there is a preference for Western-looking consultants for the authenticity of Western experiences.

34 See Robinson (2006) for a critique of global cities and the argument for the study of global processes in ordinary cities.

35 For 'jumping scales,' see Brenner (1999).

36 Personal communication, May 2014.

37 Personal communication during a field visit, June 2008.

38 Personal communication during a field visit, April 2014.

39 See Zhang (2000, 2002b), Zhu (2004), and Wu et al. (2007) for earlier discussions.

40 This concept of 'double movement', originally discussed by Polanyi (1944), was applied by Wang (2008) to China to explain the new era of implementing social policies.

41 Through Section 106, which requires a contribution to the community through negotiation, see Hall and Tewdwr-Jones (2011).

42 Ma (2007) discusses the source of social and environmental injustices in China and how urban geography should promote more just development.

43 However, public resistance has recently begun to affect decision-making, as shown by the abandonment of the PX plant in Xiamen.

44 Personal conversation, March 2014, London.

45 Yuan Qifeng, Chinese *weibo*, November 20, 2012.

46 Zhang Yunfeng@CAUPD, Chinese *weibo*, November 19, 2014.

47 From Chinese *weibo*, 'one head N bigger', November 19, 2012.

48 *weibo*, November 21, 2014.

49 From HM Treasury/BIS, quoted in Valler et al. (2012, p. 457).

50   This is from his speech at the Conservative Party Conference 2011; see Valler et al. (2012, p. 459).
51   See He and Wu (2005).
52   The author was entirely unaware of this when he took the photo of the stadium for this book at the square until a security guard approached him and reminded him that this is private property and photography was banned. Permission has to be obtained from the property management company to take photos, April 2014.
53   Wu (2012c) provides an overview of this urbanization model and challenges. Some Chinese planners have started thinking about the end of the growth-oriented development approach; see Zhang and Luo (2013).
54   These are discussed in the Chinese literature (Zhang and Luo, 2013).
55   Yu, Wang, and Li (2011) argued that planning should play a more active role in control – which they called 'anti-planning'.
56   In the U.K., the promotion of localism by the Coalition government clashes with a strong local NIMBY (Not in My Back Yard) tendency (Tewdwr-Jones, 2013).
57   See Brenner et al. (2012); Harvey (2008).

References

Aalbers, M. B. ed. 2012. *Subprime cities: The political economy of mortgage markets*. Oxford: Wiley-Blackwell.

Abramson, D. B. 2006. Urban planning in China – continuity and change. *Journal of the American Planning Association* 72 (2):197–215.

Abramson, D. B., M. Leaf, and Y. Tan. 2002. Social research and the localization of Chinese urban planning practice: Some ideas from Quanzhou, Fujian. In *The new Chinese city: Globalization and market reform*, ed. J. R. Logan, 167–180. Oxford: Blackwell Publishers.

Alexander, A. 2009. *Britain's new towns: Garden cities to sustainable communities*. London: Routledge.

Allmendinger, P. 2009. *Planning theory (2nd edition)*. Basingstoke, UK: Palgrave Macmillan.

——— . 2011. *New Labour and planning: From New Right to New Left*. London: Routledge.

Allmendinger, P., and G. Haughton. 2012. Post-political spatial planning in England: A crisis of consensus? *Transactions of the Institute of British Geographers* 37 (1):89–103.

Allmendinger, P., and M. Tewdwr-Jones. 1997. Post-Thatcherite urban planning and politics: A major change? *International Journal of Urban and Regional Research* 21:100–116.

——— . 2000. New Labour, new planning? The trajectory of planning in Blair's Britain. *Urban Studies* 37 (8):1379–1402.

Beauregard, B. A. 1989. Between modernity and postmodernity: The ambiguous position of US planning. *Environment and Planning D: Society and Space* 7:381–395.

Berg, P. O., and E. Björner eds. 2014. *Branding Chinese mega-cities: Policies, practices and positioning*. Cheltenham, UK: Edward Elgar.

Boland, A., and J. Zhu. 2012. Public participation in China's green communities: Mobilizing memories and structuring incentives. *Geoforum* 43 (1):147–157.

Boland, P. 2014. The relationship between spatial planning and economic competitiveness: The 'path to economic nirvana' or a 'dangerous obsession'? *Environment and Planning A* 46:770–787.

Brenner, N. 1999. Beyond state-centrism? Space, territoriality, and geographical scale in globalization studies. *Theory and Society* 28:39–78.

Brenner, N. ed. 2013. *Implosions/Explosions: Towards a study of planetary urbanization*. Berlin: Jovis.

Brenner, N., P. Marcuse, and M. Mayer eds. 2012. *Cities for people, not for profit: Critical urban theory and the right to the city*. New York: Routledge.

Castells, M. 1977. *The urban question*. London: Edward Arnold.

Chan, K. W. 1994. *Cities with invisible walls*. Hong Kong: Oxford University Press.

Chang, I. C. C., and E. Sheppard. 2013. China's eco-cities as variegated Urban Sustainability: Dongtan Eco-city and Chongming Eco-island. *Journal of Urban Technology* 20 (1):57–75.

Cheung, P. T. Y. 2012. The politics of regional cooperation in the Greater Pearl River Delta. *Asia Pacific Viewpoint* 53 (1):21–37.

Chien, S.-S. 2007. Institutional innovations, asymmetric decentralization, and local economic development: A case study of Kunshan, in post-Mao China. *Environment and Planning C* 25 (2):269–290.

——. 2008. The isomorphism of local development policy: A case study of the formation and transformation of national development zones in post-Mao Jiangsu, China. *Urban Studies* 45 (2):273–294.

——. 2013. New local state power through administrative restructuring – a case study of post-Mao China county-level urban entrepreneurialism in Kunshan. *Geoforum* 46:103–112.

China Society for Urban Studies ed. 2010. *China low-carbon eco-city development report*. Beijing: Chinese Architecture and Building Industries Press (in Chinese).

——. 2013. *China urban planning and development report, 2012–2013*. Beijing: China Architecture and Building Industries Press (in Chinese).

Cochrane, A. 2007. *Understanding urban policy: A critical approach*. Oxford: Blackwell Publishing.

Cody, J. W. 1996. American planning in Republican China, 1911–1937. *Planning Perspectives* 11 (4):339–377.

——. 2001. *Building in China: Henry K. Murphy's 'adaptive architecture', 1914–1935*. Hong Kong: Chinese University Press.

de Jong, M., D. Wang, and C. Yu. 2013. Exploring the relevance of the eco-city concept in China: The case of Shenzhen Sino-Dutch low carbon city. *Journal of Urban Technology* 20 (1):95–113.

Deng, F. 2009. Housing of limited property rights: A paradox inside and outside Chinese cities. *Housing Studies* 24 (6):825–841.

Deng, Z. 2014. The virtualization of new town management committee: The institutional issue to be solved. *Dongfang Morning Post* April 8, 2014 (dfdaily.com) (in Chinese).

Dong, J. 2004. *History of city building in China*. Beijing: Chinese Architecture and Building Press (in Chinese).

Dühr, S., C. Colomb, and V. Nadin. 2010. *European spatial planning and territorial cooperation*. London: Routledge.

Fainstein, S. S. 2010. *The just city*. Ithaca, NY.: Cornell University Press.

Fan, C. C. 1997. Uneven development and beyond: Regional development theory in post-Mao China. *International Journal of Urban and Regional Research* 21 (4):620–641.

Fan, J., W. Sun, Z. Yang, P. Fan, and D. Chen. 2012. Focusing on the major function-oriented zone: A new spatial planning approach and practice in China and its 12th Five-Year Plan. *Asia Pacific Viewpoint* 53 (1):86–96.

Fei, X. 1992. *From the soil: The foundations of Chinese society (a translation of Fei Xiaotong's Xiangtu Zhongguo, by Gary G Hamilton and Wang Zhen)*. Berkeley, CA: California University Press.

Feng, J., Y. X. Zhou, and F. L. Wu. 2008. New trends of suburbanization in Beijing since 1990: From government-led to market-oriented. *Regional Studies* 42 (1):83–99.

Feng, X., and Y. Yi. 2012. A comparison of urban planning and management between Hammarby Sjostad and Sino-Sweden low-carbon eco-city in Wuxi. *Urban Planning Forum* 200 (2):82–90 (in Chinese).

Fisher, J. C. 1962. Planning the city of socialist man. *Journal of the American Institute of Planners* 28 (4):251–265.

Forest, B., and J. Johnson. 2002. Unraveling the threads of history: Soviet-era monuments and post-Soviet national identity in Moscow. *Annals of the Association of American Geographers* 92 (3):524–547.

French, R. A., and F. E. I. Hamilton eds. 1979. *The socialist city.* Chichester: John Wiley and Sons.

Friedmann, J. 1987. *Planning in the public domain: From knowledge to action.* Princeton, NJ: Princeton University Press.

———. 2005. *China's urban transition.* Minneapolis: University of Minnesota Press.

Gallent, N., I. Hamiduddin, and M. Madeddu. 2013. Localism, down-scaling and the strategic dilemmas confronting planning in England. *Town Planning Review* 84 (5):563–582.

Gao, H., J. Zhang, and Z. Luo. 2014. Regeneration or alienation? Spatial transformation of rural space driven by consumer culture: An empirical observation on Dashan village in Gaochun International Slow City. *Urban Planning International* 29 (1):68–73 (in Chinese).

Gaubatz, P. R. 1996. *Beyond the Great Wall: Urban form and transformation on the Chinese frontiers.* Stanford, CT: Stanford University Press.

Grava, S. 1993. The urban heritage of the Soviet Regime: The case of Riga, Latvia. *Journal of the American Planning Association* 59:9–30.

Gunder, M. 2010. Planning as the ideology of (neoliberal) space. *Planning Theory* 9 (4):298–314.

Hall, P., and M. Tewdwr-Jones. 2011. *Urban and regional planning* (5th edition). London: Routledge.

Harvey, D. 1989. From managerialism to entrepreneurialism: The transformation in urban governance in late capitalism. *Geografiska Annaler* 71B (1):3–18.

———. 2003. *Paris, capital of modernity.* New York: Routledge.

———. 2005. *A brief history of neoliberalism.* Oxford: Oxford University Press.

———. 2008. The right to the city. *New Left Review* 53:23–39.

He, J. 2013. Caofeidian: The last episode of government-led development zone. *Chaixin Net* May 27, 2013 (on business.sohu.com).

He, S., and F. Wu. 2005. Property-led redevelopment in post-reform China: A case study of Xintiandi redevelopment project in Shanghai. *Journal of Urban Affairs* 27 (1):1–23.

———. 2009. China's emerging neoliberal urbanism: perspectives from urban redevelopment. *Antipode* 41 (2):282–304.

Healey, P. 2004. The treatment of space and place in the new strategic spatial planning in Europe. *International Journal of Urban and Regional Research* 28 (1):45–67.

———. 2006. *Collaborative planning (2nd edition).* New York: Palgrave Macmillan.

———. 2012. The universal and the contigent: Some reflections on the transnational flow of planning ideas and practices. *Planning Theory* 11 (2):188–207.

Hirt, S. A. 2005. Planning the post-communist city: Experience from Sofia. *International Planning Studies* 10 (3–4):219–240.

———. 2012. *Iron curtains: Gates, suburbs and privatization of space in the post-socialist city.* Oxford: Wiley-Blackwell.

Hou, L. 2010. New understandings on Chinese history of urbanization in the planned economy. *Urban Planning Forum* 187 (2):70–78 (in Chinese).

Hou, L., and Y. Zhang. 2013. 1958 Qingdao Conference: Retrospect, verification, and reflection. In *Urban age, collaborative planning: Proceedings of Urban Planning Society of*

China Annual Conference 2013, ed. Urban Planning Society of China. Qingdao: China: UPSC.

Hsing, Y.-T. 2010. *The great urban transformation: Politics of land and property in China.* Oxford: Oxford University Press.

Jessop, B., and N. L. Sum. 2000. An entrepreneurial city in action: Hong Kong's emerging strategies in and for (inter)urban competition. *Urban Studies* 37 (12):2287–2313.

Joss, S., and A. P. Molella. 2013. The eco-city as urban technology: Perspectives on Caofeidian International Eco-city (China). *Journal of Urban Technology* 20 (1):115–137.

Knox, P. L. 1991. The restless urban landscape: Economic and sociocultural change and the transformation of Metropolitan Washington, DC. *Annals of the Association of American Geographers* 87 (2):181–209.

——. 2008. *Metroburbia, USA.* New Brunswick, NJ: Rutgers University Press.

Kunshan Planning Bureau. 2010. *From pioneering in well-off to leading modernisation: Kunshan Urban Master Plan (2009–2030).* Beijing: China Architecture and Building Industries Press (in Chinese).

Leaf, M. 1998. Urban planning and urban reality under Chinese economic reforms. *Journal of Planning Education and Research* 18 (2):145–153.

Leaf, M., and L. Hou. 2006. The 'third spring' of urban planning in China: The ressurrection of professional planning in the post-Mao China. *China Information* 20 (3):553–585.

Li, H. 2012. Retrospect and rethinking: 50 years after the suspension of urban planning. *City Planning Review* 36 (1):73–79 (in Chinese).

Li, H., and J. Li. 2012. The effectiveness of eco urban planning: A study of the contradiction and complexity of eco-city planning and development. *Urban Development Research* 19 (3):53–57 (in Chinese).

Li, X., and Y. Liu. 2011. Low-carbon eco-cities development in China: Current development, problems and policy recommendations. *Urban Planning Forum* 196 (4):23–28 (in Chinese).

Li, Y., and F. L. Wu. 2012a. Towards new regionalism? Case study of changing regional governance in the Yangtze River Delta. *Asia Pacific Viewpoint* 53 (2):178–195.

——. 2012b. The transformation of regional governance in China: The rescaling of statehood. *Progress in Planning* 78:55–99.

——. 2013. The emergence of centrally initiated regional plan in China: A case study of Yangtze River Delta Regional Plan. *Habitat International* 39:137–147.

Li, Z., and C. Gu. 2011. *Chinese urban social spatial structure and its transformation.* Nanjing: Southeast University Press (in Chinese).

Li, Z., and F. Wu. 2006. Socioeconomic transformations in Shanghai (1990–2000): Policy impacts in global–national–local contexts. *Cities* 23 (4):250–268.

——. 2008. Tenure-based residential segregation in post-reform Chinese cities: A case study of Shanghai. *Transactions of the Institute of British Geographers* 33 (3):404–419.

Liang, S. Y. 2013. Planning and its discontents: Contradictions and continuities in remaking China's great cities, 1950–2010. *Urban History* 40:530–553.

Lin, G. C. S. 2009. *Developing China: Land, politics and social conditions.* London: Routledge.

Lin, G. C. S., and S. Ho. 2005. The state, land system, and land development processes in contemporary China. *Annals of Association of American Geographers* 95 (2):411–436.

Lin, S. 2013. *Guangzhou Chengji.* Guangzhou: Guangdong People's Publisher (in Chinese).

Liu, Y., and F. Wu. 2006. Urban poverty neighbourhoods: Typology and spatial concentration under China's market transition, a case study of Nanjing. *Geoforum* 37 (4):610–626.

Logan, J. R., and H. L. Molotch. 1987. *Urban fortunes: The political economy of place.* Berkeley: University of California Press.

Lord, A., and M. Tewdwr-Jones. 2014. Is planning 'under attack'? Chronicling the deregulation of urban and environmental planning in England. *European Planning Studies* 22 (2):345–361.

Lu, D. 2006. *Remaking Chinese urban form: Modernity, scarcity and space, 1949–2005*. London: Routledge.

Lu, H. 1999. *Beyond the neon lights: Everyday Shanghai in the early twentieth century*. Berkeley: University of California Press.

Lu, H. C. 1995. Creating urban outcasts: Shantytowns in Shanghai, 1920–1950. *Journal of Urban History* 21 (5):563–596.

Luo, X. L., and J. Shen. 2007. Models of inter-city cooperation and its theoretical implications: An empirical study of the Yangtze River Delta. *Acta Geographica Sinica* 62 (2):156–126 (in Chinese).

––––––. 2008. Why city-region planning does not work well in China: The case of Suzhou-Wuxi-Changzhou. *Cities* 25 (4):207–217.

––––––. 2009. A study on inter-city cooperation in the Yangtze River Delta region, China. *Habitat International* 33 (1):52–62.

Ma, L. J. C. 1979. The Chinese approach to city planning: Policy, administration, and action. *Asian Survey* 19 (9):838–855.

––––––. 2005. Urban administrative restructuring, changing scale relations and local economic development in China. *Political Geography* 24 (4):477–497.

––––––. 2007. From China's urban social space to social and environmental justice. *Eurasian Geography and Economics* 48 (5):555–566.

––––––. 2009. Chinese urbanism. In *Interenational Encyclopedia of Human Geography*, eds. R. Kitchin and N. Thrift, 69–71. Oxford: Elsevier.

Ma, L. J. C., and M. Fan. 1994. Urbanisation from below: The growth of towns in Jiangsu, China. *Urban Studies* 31 (10):1625–1645.

Ma, L. J. C., and E. W. Hanten. 1981. *Urban development in modern China*. Boulder, CO: Westview.

McCann, E., and K. Ward eds. 2011. *Mobile urbanism: Cities and policy making in the global age*. Minneapolis: Minnesota University Press.

McGee, T. G., G. C. S. Lin, A. M. Marton, M. Y. L. Wang, and J. Wu. 2007. *China's urban space: Development under market socialism*. London: Routledge.

MacLeod, G. 2011. Urban politics reconsidered: Growth machine to post-democratic city? *Urban Studies* 48 (12):2629–2660.

––––––. 2013. New urbanism/Smart growth in the Scottish highlands: Mobile policies and post-politics in local development planning. *Urban Studies* 50 (11):2196–2221.

MacPherson, K. L. 1990. Design China's urban future: The Greater Shanghai Plan, 1927–1937. *Planning Perspectives* 5 (1):39–62.

Mai, J., and J. Zhang. 2013. New urban spatial development led by the local urban entrepreneurialism: A case study of Wujin new urban district. *Urban Planning Forum* 208 (3):54–60 (in Chinese).

Marsden, T., L. Yu, and A. Flynn. 2011. Exploring ecological modernisation and urban-rural eco-developments in China: The case of Anji county. *Town Planning Review* 82 (2):195–224.

May, S. 2011. Ecological urbanization: Calculating value in an age of global climate change. In *Worlding cities: Asian experiments and the art of being global*, eds. A. Roy and A. Ong, 98–126. Oxford: Wiley-Blackwell.

MOHURD, and CAUPD. 2010. *National Urban System Plan (2006–2020)*. Beijing: Commercial Press (in Chinese).

Nedovic-Budic, Z. 2001. Adjustment of planning practice to the new eastern European context. *Journal of American Planning Association* 67 (1):38–52.

Newton, J., and A. Franklin. 2011. Delivering sustainable communities in China: Using a sustainable livelihoods framework for reviewing the promotion of 'ecotourism' in Anji. *Local Environment* 16 (8):789–806.

Ng, M. K., and W. S. Tang. 1999. Land-use planning in 'One County, Two Systems': Hong Kong, Guangzhou and Shenzhen. *International Planning Studies* 4 (1):7–27.

———. 2004. Theorising urban planning in a transitional economy: The case of Shenzhen, People's Republic of China. *Town Planning Review* 75 (2):173–201.

Ng, M. K., and J. Xu. 2000. Development control in post-reform China: The case of Liuhua Lake Park, Guangzhou. *Cities* 17 (6):409–418.

Oi, J. C. 1992. Fiscal reform and the economic foundations of local state corporatism. *World Politics* 45:99–126.

———. 1995. The role of the local state in China's transitional economy. *China Quarterly* 144:1132–1149.

Olds, K. 2001. *Globalization and urban change: Capital, culture, and Pacific Rim mega-projects.* Oxford: Oxford University Press.

Olds, K., and H. W. C. Yeung. 2004. Pathways to global city formation: A view from the developmental city-state of Singapore. *Review of International Political Economy* 11 (3):489–521.

Parnell, S., and J. Robinson. 2012. (Re)theorizing cities from the Global South: Looking beyond neoliberalism. *Urban Geography* 33 (4):593–617.

Peck, J., and J. Zhang. 2013. A variety of capitalism . . . with Chinese characteristics. *Journal of Economic Geography* 13:357–396.

Phelps, N., and F. Wu eds. 2011. *International perspectives on suburbanization: A post-suburban world?* Basingstoke: Palgrave Macmillan.

Po, L. 2008. Redefining rural collectives in China: Land conversion and the emergence of rural shareholding co-operatives. *Urban Studies* 45 (8):1603–1623.

Polanyi, K. 1944. *The Great Transformation.* New York: Rinehart.

Pow, C. P. 2009. *Gated communities in China: Class, privilege and the moral politics of the good life.* Abingdon: Routledge.

Pow, C. P., and H. Neo. 2013. Seeing red over green: Contesting urban sustainabilities in China. *Urban Studies* 50 (11):2256–2274.

Qian, H., and C. Wong. 2012. Master planning under urban-rural integration: The case of Nanjing, China. *Urban Policy and Research* 30 (4):403–421.

Qian, Y., and B. R. Weingast. 1997. Federalism as a commitment to preserving market incentives. *Journal of Economic Perspectives* 11 (4):83–92.

Qian, Z. 2011. Building Hangzhou's new city center: Mega project development and entrepreneurial urban governance in China. *Asian Geographer* 28 (1):3–19.

———. 2013. Master plan, plan adjustment and urban development reality under China's market transition: A case study of Nanjing. *Cities* 30:77–88.

Raco, M. 2014. Delivering flagship projects in an era of regulatory capitalism: State-led privatization and the London Olympics 2012. *International Journal of Urban and Regional Research* 38 (1):176–197.

Raco, M., and K. Gilliam. 2012. Geographies of abstraction, urban entrepreneurialism, and the production of new cultural spaces: The West Kowloon Cultural District, Hong Kong. *Environment and Planning A* 44 (6):1425–1442.

Raco, M., G. Parker, and J. Doak. 2006. Reshaping spaces of local governance? Community strategies and the modernisation of local government in England. *Environment and Planning C* 24:475–496.

Rithmire, M. 2013. Land politics and local state capacities: The political economy of urban change in China. *The China Quarterly* 216:872–895.

Robinson, J. 2006. *Ordinary cities: Between modernity and development*. London: Routledge.

———. 2011. Cities in a world of cities: The comparative gesture. *International Journal of Urban and Regional Research* 35 (1):1–23.

Roy, A. 2011a. Commentary: Placing planning in the world—transnationalism as practice and critique. *Journal of Planning Education and Research* 31 (4):406–415.

———. 2011b. Slumdog cities: Rethinking subaltern urbanism. *International Journal of Urban and Regional Research* 35 (2):223–238.

Roy, A., and A. Ong eds. 2011. *Worlding cities: Asian experiments and the art of being global*. Oxford: Wiley-Blackwell.

Rydin, Y. 1998. The enabling local state and urban development: Resources, rhetoric and planning in East London. *Urban Studies* 35:175–192.

———. 2013. *The future of planning: Beyond growth dependence*. Bristol: Policy Press.

Sager, T. 2011. Neo-liberal urban planning policies: A literature survey 1990–2010. *Progress in Planning* 76:147–199.

Samara, T. R., S. He, and G. Chen eds. 2013. *Locating right to the city in the Global South*. Abingdon: Routledge.

Shanghai Planning History Office (SPHO) ed. 1999. *Shanghai planning history*. Shanghai: Shanghai Social Science Academy Press (in Chinese).

Shao, Q. 2013. *Shanghai gone: Domicide and defiance in a Chinese megacity*. Lanham, MD: Rowman & Littlefield Publishers.

Shen, J. 2005. Space, scale and the state: Re-organizing urban space in China. In *Restructuring the Chinese city: Changing society, economy and space*, eds. L. J. C. Ma and F. Wu, 39–58. London: Routledge.

Shen, J., Z. Feng, and K.-Y. Wong. 2006. Dual-track urbanization in a transitional economy: The case of Pearl River Delta in South China. *Habitat International* 30:690–705.

Shen, J., and F. Wu. 2012a. Restless urban landscapes in China: A case study of three projects in Shanghai. *Journal of Urban Affairs* 34 (3):255–277.

———. 2012b. The development of master-planned communities in Chinese suburbs: A case study of Shanghai's Thames Town. *Urban Geography* 33 (2):183–203.

———. 2013. Moving to the suburbs: Demand-side driving forces of suburban growth in China. *Environment and Planning A* 45 (8):1823–1844.

Shen, X., and L. J. C. Ma. 2005. Privatization of rural industry and de facto urbanization from below in southern Jiangsu, China. *Geoforum* 36:761–777.

Short, J. R., L. M. Benton, W. B. Luce, and J. Walton. 1993. Reconstructing the image of an industrial city. *Annals of the Association of American Geographers* 83 (2):207–224.

Sit, V. F. S. 1995. *Beijing: The nature and planning of a Chinese capital city*. New York: John Wiley.

Sit, V. F. S., and C. Yang. 1997. Foreign-investment-induced exo-urbanisation in the Pearl River Delta, China. *Urban Studies* 34:647–677.

Skinner, G. W. ed. 1977. *The city in late imperial China*. Stanford, CA: Stanford University Press.

Smart, A., and W. S. Tang. 2005. Irregular trajectories: Illegal building in mainland China and Hong Kong. In *Restructuring the Chinese city: Changing society, economy and space*, eds. L. J. C. Ma and F. Wu, 80–97. London: Routledge.

Smith, C., J. 2008. Monumentality in urban design: The case of China. *Eurasian Geography and Economics* 49 (3):263–279.

Song, Y. 2012. Planning institutions: China. In *International encyclopedia of housing and home*, Vol. 5., eds. S. J. Smith, M. Elsinga, L. F. O'Mahony, O. S. Eng, S. Wachter and S. Tsenkova, 196–201. Oxford: Elsevier.

Stenning, A. 2005. Post-socialism and the changing geographies of the everyday in Poland. *Transactions of the Institute of British Geographers* 30:113–127.

Strand, D. 2000. 'A high place is no better than a low place': The city in the making of modern China. In *Becoming Chinese: Passages to modernity and beyond*, ed. W.-H. Yeh, 98–136. Berkeley, CA: University of California Press.

Su, X. 2014. Urban entrepreneurialism and the commodification of heritage in China. *Urban Studies* on-line first, DOI: 10.1177/0042098014528998.

Sun, S. 2006. Unbearable pressure on urban planning: The debate on the value of planning. *Urban Planning Forum* 161 (1):11–17 (in Chinese).

Swyngedouw, E. 2009. The antinomies of the postpolitical city: In search of a democratic politics of environmental production. *International Journal of Urban and Regional Research* 33 (3):601–620.

Szelenyi, I. 1996. Cities under socialism – and after. In *Cities after socialism: Urban and regional change and conflict in post-socialist societies*, eds. G. M. Andrusz, M. Harloe, and I. Szelenyi, 286–317. Oxford: Blackwell.

Tang, M. 2013. Enhancing multiple dialogues for the innovation of urban and rural planning system. In *Proceedings of Annual UPSC Conference 2013*, ed. Urban Planning Society of China. Beijing: UPSC (in Chinese).

Tang, W.-S. 1994. Urban land development under socialism: China between 1949 and 1977. *International Journal of Urban and Regional Research* 18 (3):392–415.

——— . 2000. Chinese urban planning at fifty: An assessment of the planning theory literature. *Journal of Planning Literature* 14:347–366.

Tao, R., F. B. Su, M. X. Liu, and G. Z. Cao. 2010. Land leasing and local public finance in China's regional development: Evidence from prefecture-level cities. *Urban Studies* 47 (10):2217–2236.

Tewdwr-Jones, M. 2013. New urban movements? Resistance and altruism in territorial planning and localism. *Presentation at Regional Studies Association Winter Conference* (November 22, 2013, London).

Tian, L., and T. Y. Shen. 2011. Evaluation of plan implementation in the transitional China: A case of Guangzhou city master plan. *Cities* 28 (1):11–27.

Tsui, C. 2012. State capacity in city planning: The reconstruction of Nanjing, 1927–1937. *Cross-currents: East Asian History and Culture Review* 1 (1):12–46.

Valler, D., N. A. Phelps, and A. M. Wood. 2012. Planning for growth? The implications of localism for 'Science Vale', Oxfordshire, UK. *Town Planning Review* 83 (4):457–487.

Wade, R. 1990. *Governing the market: Economic theory and the role of government in East Asian industrialization*. Princeton, NJ: Princeton University Press.

Walder, A. G. 1995. Local governments as industrial firms: An organizational analysis of China's transitional economy. *American Journal of Sociology* 101 (2):263–301.

Walder, A. G. 1986. *Communist neo-traditionalism: Work and authority in Chinese industry*. Berkeley, CA: University of California Press.

Walker, A., and D. Buck. 2007. The Chinese road: Cities in the transition to capitalism. *New Left Review* 46:39–46.

Wang, H. 2012. Building a scientific theory on urban-rural integration and the Chinese model of urbanization. *Urban Planning International* 27 (4):77–88 (in Chinese).

——— . 2013. The third prosperous period of Chinese regional planning. *Urban and Regional Planning Review* 1 (1):20–36 (in Chinese).

Wang, H., and M. Dubbeling. 2013. The big jump forwards: An example of China's pursuit towards a new pattern of growth. In *Frontiers of planning: Visionary futures for human settlements*, eds. J. Bolman and C. Gossop, 188–199. The Hague: ISOCARP.

Wang, J. 2011a. *Beijing record: A physical and political history of planning modern Beijing*. Singapore: World Scientific Publishing.

———. 2011b. City-eyes. *Wang Jun's blog at Caixin* wangjun.blog.caixin.com (accessed February 2014).

———. 2011c. Transformation of urbanization. *Liaowang* 11 (in Chinese): on-line at http://wangjun.blog.caixin.com/archives/date/2011/03 (accessed February 2014).

Wang, L., and C. Hoch. 2013. Pragmatic rational planning: Comparing Shanghai and Chicago. *Planning Theory* 12 (4):369–390.

Wang, L., C. Potter, and Z. Li. 2014. Crisis-induced reform, state-market relations, and entrepreneurial urban growth in China. *Habitat International* 41:50–57.

Wang, S. 2008. Great transformation: The double movement in China since the 1980s. *Chinese Social Sciences* 1 (1):129–207 (in Chinese).

Wang, Y. P., and C. Hague. 1993. Territory planning in China: A new regional approach. *Regional Studies* 27 (6):561–573.

Wang, Z. 2002. System innovation in the rapid development process of Songjiang: New town in Shanghai *Urban Planning Forum* 142 (6):51–54 (in Chinese).

Watson, V. 2009. Seeing from the south: Refocusing urban planning on the globe's central urban issues. *Urban Studies* 46 (11):2259–2275.

———. 2012. Planning and the 'stubborn realities' of global south-east cities: Some emerging ideas. *Planning Theory* 12 (1):81–100.

Wei, Y. D. 2000. *Regional development in China: States, globalization, and inequality*. London: Routledge.

———. 2002. Beyond the Sunan model: Trajectory and underlying factors of development in Kunshan, China. *Environment and Planning A* 34 (10):1725–1748.

While, A., A. E. G. Jonas, and D. Gibbs. 2010. From sustainable development to carbon control: Eco-state restructuring and the politics of urban and regional development. *Transactions of the Institute of British Geographers* NS35:76–93.

Whitehand, J. W. R., and K. Gu. 2006. Research on Chinese urban form: Retrospect and prospect. *Progress in Human Geography* 30 (3):337–355.

Whyte, M. K., and W. L. Parish. 1984. *Urban life in contemporary China*. Chicago, IL: University of Chicago Press.

Wong, C., H. Qian, and K. Zhou. 2008. In search of regional planning in China: The case of Jiangsu and the Yangtze Delta. *Town Planning Review* 79 (2–3):295–329.

Wong, S. 2013. The planning connection between Clarence Stein and Liang Sicheng in Republican China. *Planning Perspectives* 28 (3):421–439.

Woo-Cumings, M. ed. 1999. *The developmental state*. Ithaca, NY: Cornell University Press.

Wu, F. 1996. Changes in the structure of public housing provision in urban China. *Urban Studies* 33 (9):1601–1627.

———. 1997. Urban restructuring in China's emerging market economy: Towards a framework for analysis. *International Journal of Urban and Regional Research* 21:640–663.

———. 2000. Place promotion in Shanghai, PRC. *Cities* 17:349–361.

———. 2002. China's changing urban governance in the transition towards a more market-oriented economy. *Urban Studies* 39 (7):1071–1093.

———. 2003a. The (post-)socialist entrepreneurial city as a state project: Shanghai's reglobalisation in question. *Urban Studies* 40 (9):1673–1698.

———. 2003b. Transitional cities. *Environment and Planning A* 35:1331–1338.

———. 2005. Rediscovering the 'gate' under market transition: From work-unit compounds to commodity housing enclaves. *Housing Studies* 20 (2):235–254.

———. 2007. Re-orientation of the city plan: Strategic planning and design competition in China. *Geoforum* 38 (2):379–392.

———. 2008. China's great transformation: Neoliberalization as establishing a market society. *Geoforum* 39 (3):1093–1096.

———. 2010a. Gated and packaged suburbia: Packaging and branding Chinese suburban residential development. *Cities* 27 (5):385–396.

———. 2010b. How neoliberal is China's reform? The origins of change during transition. *Eurasian Geography and Economics* 51 (5):619–631.

———. 2011. Retreat from a totalitarian society: China's urbanism in the making. In *The new Blackwell companion to the city*, eds. G. Bridge and S. Watson, 701–712. Oxford: Blackwell Publishing Ltd.

———. 2012a. Globalisation. In *International encyclopedia of housing and home*, eds. M. E. Susan, J. Smith, L. F. O'Mahony, O. S. Eng, S. Wachter, K. Gibb, 292–297. Oxford: Elsevier.

———. 2012b. Housing and the state in China. In *International encyclopedia of housing and home*, eds. S. J. Smith, M. Elsinga, L. F. O'Mahony, O. S. Eng, S. Wachter and C. Hamnett, 323–329. Oxford: Elsevier.

———. 2012c. Urbanization. In *Handbook of contemporary China*, eds. A. So and W. Tay, 237–262. Singapore: World Scientific Publishing.

———. 2012d. China's eco-cities. *Geoforum* 43 (2):169–171.

———. 2014. Commodification and housing market cycles in Chinese cities. *International Journal of Housing Policy* (on-line dx.doi.org/10.1080/14616718.2014.925255).

Wu, F., and N. A. Phelps. 2008. From suburbia to post-suburbia in China? Aspects of the transformation of the Beijing and Shanghai global city regions. *Built Environment* 34 (4):464–481.

———. 2011. (Post-)suburban development and state entrepreneurialism in Beijing's outer suburbs. *Environment and Planning A* 43 (2):410–430.

Wu, F., J. Xu, and A. G.-O. Yeh. 2007. *Urban development in post-reform China: State, market and space* London: Routledge.

Wu, F., and F. Z. Zhang. 2010. China's emerging city region governance: Towards a research framework. *Progress in Planning* 73 (1):60–63.

Wu, F., and J. Zhang. 2007. Planning the competitive city-region: The emergence of strategic development plan in China. *Urban Affairs Review* 42 (5):714–740.

Wu, F. L., F. Z. Zhang, and C. Webster. 2013. Informality and the development and demolition of urban villages in the Chinese peri-urban area. *Urban Studies* 50 (10):1919–1934.

Wu, F., and L. Zhou. 2013. Beautiful China: The experience of Jiangsu's rural village improvement program. In *Frontiers of planning: Visionary futures for human settlements*, eds. J. Colman and C. Gossop, 156–169. The Hague: ISOCARP.

Wu, S. 2008a. New residential development: The 'six unification' of housing construction. In *The historical echo: 60 years of urban planning in the capital*, eds. Beijing Planning Commission and Beijing Urban Planning Society, 0914–0919. Beijing: Beijing Planning Commission.

———. 2008b. The planning and management of Fangzhuang residential area. In *The historical echo: 60 years of urban planning in the capital*, eds. Beijing Planning Commission and Beijing Urban Planning Society, 0940. Beijing: Beijing Planning Commission.

Wu, W., and P. Gaubatz. 2013. *The Chinese city*. New York: Routledge.

Xie, Y., and F. J. Costa. 1993. Urban planning in socialist China. *Cities*:103–114.

Xu, J. 2001. The changing role of land-use planning in the land-development process in Chinese cities: The case of Guangzhou. *Third World Planning Review* 23 (3):229–248.

———. 2008. Governing city-regions in China: Theoretical issues and perspectives for regional strategic planning. *Town Planning Review* 70 (2–3):157–185.

Xu, J., and J. J. Wang. 2012. Reassembling the state in urban China. *Asia Pacific Viewpoint* 53 (1):7–20.

Xu, J., and A. G.-O. Yeh. 2005. City repositioning and competitiveness building in regional development: new development strategies in Guangzhou, China. *International Journal of Urban and Regional Research* 29 (2):283–308.

Xu, J., and A. G.-O. Yeh eds. 2011. *Governance and planning of mega-city regions: An international comparative perspective.* London: Routledge.

Xu, J., A. G.-O. Yeh, and F. Wu. 2009. Land commodification: New land development and politics in China since the late 1990s. *International Journal of Urban and Regional Research* 33 (4):890–913.

Xue, C. Q. L., Y. Wang, and L. Tsai. 2013. Building new towns in China – a case study of Zhengdong New District. *Cities* 30 (1):223–232.

Yan, Y. 2010. The Chinese path to individualization. *The British Journal of Sociology* 61 (3):489–512.

Yang, B., and K. Dong. 2008. The theory and practice of eco-city planning: A case study of Sino-Singapore Tianjin Eco-city Master Plan. *City Planning Review* 32 (8):10–14 (in Chinese).

Yang, C. 2007. Hong Kong and Taiwan investment in Dongguan: Divergent trajectories and impacts. In *China's emerging cities: The making of new urbanism*, ed. F. Wu, 89–108. London: Routledge.

———. 2009. Strategic coupling of regional development in global production networks: Redistribution of Taiwanese personal computer investment from the Pearl River Delta to the Yangtze River Delta. *Regional Studies* 43 (3):385–407.

Yang, D. Y. R., and H. K. Wang. 2008. Dilemmas of local governance under the development zone fever in China: A case study of the Suzhou region. *Urban Studies* 45 (5–6): 1037–1054.

Yang, J., and G. Li. 2014. Fiscal and spatial characteristics of metropolitan government and planning in China: Understanding centralization trends in a decentralization context. *Habitat International* 41:77–84.

Ye, B., and L. Zhao. 2013. The development of urban planning and research centers under reform: A case study of Nanjng. *City Planning Review* 37 (9):76–80 (in Chinese).

Yeh, A. G. O., and F. Wu. 1996. The new land development process and urban development in Chinese cities. *International Journal of Urban and Regional Research* 20 (2):330–353.

———. 1999. The transformation of the urban planning system from a centrally-planned to transitional economy. *Progress in Planning* 51:167–252.

Yeh, W.-H. 2008. *Shanghai splendor: Economic sentiments and the making of modern China, 1843–1949.* Berkeley, CA: University of California Press.

Yiftachel, O. 2006. Re-engaging planning theory? Towards 'south-eastern' perspectives. *Planning Theory* 5 (3):211–222.

Yiftachel, O., and I. Alexander. 1995. The state of metropolitan planning: Decline or restructuring? *Environment and Planning C* 13:273–296.

Yu, K., S. Wang, and D. Li. 2011. The negative approach to urban growth planning of Beijing, China. *Journal of Environmental Planning and Management* 54 (9):1209–1236.

Zacharias, J., and Y. Z. Tang. 2010. Restructuring and repositioning Shenzhen, China's new mega city. *Progress in Planning* 73:209–249.

Zhang, F. Z., and F. L. Wu. 2012. Fostering 'indigenous innovation capacities': The development of biotechnology in Shanghai's Zhangjiang High-tech Park. *Urban Geography* 33 (5):728–755.

Zhang, J. 2013. Marketization beyond neoliberalization: A neo-Polanyian perspective on China's transition to a market economy. *Environment and Planning A* 45:1605–1624.

Zhang, J., and Z. Luo. 2013. *Urban and rural planning thoughts in contemporary China.* Nanjing: Southeast University Press (in Chinese).

Zhang, J., and F. Wu. 2006. China's changing economic governance: Administrative annexation and the reorganization of local governments in the Yangtze River Delta. *Regional Studies* 40 (1):3–21.

——. 2008. Mega-event marketing and urban growth coalition: A case study of Nanjing Olympic New Town. *Town Planning Review* 79 (2–3):209–226.

Zhang, L. 2010. *In search of paradise: Middle-class living in a Chinese metropolis.* Ithaca, NY: Cornell University Press.

Zhang, Q. 2010. Low carbon Kunshan: Towards a sustainable future. In *Sustainable city/developing world,* ed. C. Gossop, 142–164. The Hague: ISOCARP.

Zhang, T. 2000. Land market forces and government's role in sprawl. *Cities* 17 (2):123–135.

——. 2002a. Decentralization, localization, and the emergence of a quasi-participatory decision-making structure in urban development in Shanghai. *International Planning Studies* 7 (4):303–323.

——. 2002b. Urban development and a socialist pro-growth coalition in Shanghai. *Urban Affairs Review* 37 (4):475–499.

——. 2006. From intercity competition to collaborative planning: The case of the Yangtze River Delta region of China. *Urban Affairs Review* 42 (1):26–56.

——. 2015. Urban planning in China. In *International encyclopedia of social and behavioral sciences (2nd edition),* ed. J. D. Wright. Oxford: Elsevier.

Zhao, P. 2010. Implementation of the metropolitan growth management in the transition era: Evidence from Beijing. *Planning Practice and Research* 25 (1):77–93.

Zhao, Y. 2013. Thinking on the profession of city planning from economics. *Urban Development Research* 20 (2):1–11 (in Chinese).

Zhou, L. 2002. The approach of preparation of new-round urban master plan: A case study of the adjustment of Nanjing Urban Master Plan. *City Planning Review* 26 (1):46–49 (in Chinese).

Zhou, M., and J. R. Logan. 1996. Market transition and the commodification of housing in urban China. *International Journal of Urban and Regional Research* 20:400–421.

Zhou, Y. 2013. *Exploring the road of urban planning.* Beijing: The Commercial Press (in Chinese).

Zhou, Y., and L. J. C. Ma. 2000. Economic restructuring and suburbanization in China. *Urban Geography* 21 (3):205–236.

Zhu, J. 2004. Local development state and order in China's urban development during transition. *International Journal of Urban and Regional Research* 28:424–447.

Index

Printed by PGSTL